Verse by Verse Commentary on

LEVITICUS

Enduring Word Commentary Series
By David Guzik

The grass withers, the flower fades,
but the word of our God stands forever.
Isaiah 40:8

Commentary on Leviticus

Copyright ©2021 by David Guzik

Printed in the United States of America
or in the United Kingdom

Print Edition ISBN: 978-1-939466-71-6

Enduring Word

5662 Calle Real #184

Goleta, CA 93117

Electronic Mail: ewm@enduringword.com

Internet Home Page: www.enduringword.com

Contents

Leviticus 1 – The Burnt Offering

A. Introduction: the idea of sacrifice in ancient Israel.

1. (1) God speaks to Moses from the tabernacle.

Now the LORD called to Moses, and spoke to him from the tabernacle of meeting, saying,

> a. **Now the LORD called to Moses**: The story of Leviticus picks up where Exodus left off. The people of Israel, the covenant descendants of Abraham, Isaac, and Jacob, were still camped at the foot of Mount Sinai. They remained at Sinai throughout the time period covered by the book of Leviticus.

> b. **From the tabernacle of meeting**: This indicates that the tabernacle was now completed. The last several chapters of Exodus described the construction of the tabernacle (Exodus 35-40). With the **tabernacle of meeting** complete, the sacrificial system could now be put into operation.

>> i. In John 1:14 there is a deliberate link between this **tabernacle of meeting** and the incarnate Jesus Christ (*the Word became flesh and dwelt* [tabernacled] *among us*. As the **tabernacle of meeting** was a symbol of God's presence among His people, Jesus Christ was God present on earth.

2. (2) What to do when you bring an offering to LORD.

"Speak to the children of Israel, and say to them: 'When any one of you brings an offering to the LORD, you shall bring your offering of the livestock—of the herd and of the flock.

> a. **When any one of you brings an offering**: In the covenant God made with Israel at Mount Sinai, there were three major parts. The covenant included the *law* Israel had to obey, *sacrifice* to provide for breaking the

7

law, and the *choice* of blessing or curse that would become Israel's destiny throughout history.

i. The sacrificial system was an essential element of the Mosaic covenant because it was impossible to live up to the requirements of the law. No one could perfectly obey the law, and sin had to be dealt with through sacrifice. Each commanded sacrifice was significant, and they all pointed toward the perfect sacrifice Jesus would offer by His crucifixion (Hebrews 7:27, 9:11-28).

ii. This was not the beginning of God's sacrificial system. Adam knew of sacrifice (Genesis 3:21), as did Cain and Abel (Genesis 4:3-4), and Noah (Genesis 8:20-21). Israel offered sacrifice at the Passover (Exodus 12). Job 1:5 and Exodus 10:25 also mention burnt sacrifices before the book of Leviticus.

iii. The idea of sacrifice to the gods was not unique to Israel. Other nations and cultures practiced sacrifice, often ultimately involving human sacrifice. The universality of sacrifice is evidence that this concept was known to man before the flood and was carried to different cultures from the survivors of the flood in Noah's day.

b. **Brings an offering to the LORD:** Because sacrifice was already known to Israel, these instructions to the priests were not particularly new – they were mostly a clarification of a foundation that was already known to Israel through the traditions of their fathers.

i. God planned wisely in bringing the law of the sacrifices at this time. Before the tabernacle of meeting was built, there was no one place of sacrifice, and the procedures for sacrifice couldn't really be settled and regulated. But now with the completion of the tabernacle, Israel could bring their sacrifice to one place and follow the same procedures for each sacrifice.

ii. The first seven chapters of Leviticus deal with personal, voluntary offerings. Chapters one through five are mostly instructions to the people who bring the offering, and chapters six and seven are mostly instructions to the priests concerning offerings.

iii. Matthew Poole explained why there were so many different kinds of sacrifices: "To represent as well the several perfections of Christ, be true sacrifice, and the various benefits of his death, as the several duties which men owe to their Creator and Redeemer, all which could not be so well expressed by one sort of sacrifices."

iv. The fact that God gave so much instruction on how to specifically offer sacrifices shows that this was not a matter God left up to the creativity of the individual Israelite. They were not free to offer sacrifices any way they pleased, even if they did it with sincerity. God demanded the humility and obedience of His people in the sacrificial system. It had to be carried out in a way that was God-centered, not man-centered.

c. **You shall bring an offering of the livestock—of the herd and of the flock**: This meant that an Israelite worshipper could not offer a "wild" or non-domesticated animal. They could only bring domesticated livestock from **the herd** or from **the flock**. Each animal was part of the Israelite's inventory of animals for fabric, milk and all its products, and meat. Giving to God **of the herd and of the flock** meant that sacrifice *cost* something.

i. "In Numbers and Ezekiel as well as Leviticus, the Hebrew word for offering is a very general term used to designate anything given as a sacrifice to God. In Nehemiah 10:35 and 13:31 it is even used of non-sacrificial offerings made to God." (Peter-Contesse)

B. The procedure for the burnt offering.

1. (3) Bringing the animal for the burnt offering.

'If his offering *is* a burnt sacrifice of the herd, let him offer a male without blemish; he shall offer it of his own free will at the door of the tabernacle of meeting before the LORD.

a. **If his offering is a burnt sacrifice**: The **burnt** offering, as its name implies, was completely burnt before the LORD. It was a total sacrifice. The **burnt sacrifice** was a general offering intended to make one right with God through the atonement of sin (propitiation) or to demonstrate special devotion to God (consecration).

i. "Its name literally means 'that which ascends,' and refers, no doubt, to the ascent of the transformed substance of the sacrifice in fire and smoke, as to God. The central idea of this sacrifice, then, as gathered from its name and confirmed by its manner, is that of the yielding of the whole being in self-surrender, and borne up by the flame of intense consecration to God." (Maclaren)

b. **Let him offer a male**: The animal offered had to be a **male** because male animals were thought to be stronger and usually considered to be more valuable.

c. **Without blemish**: The animal must not have any obvious defect. God would not accept a defective sacrifice. A priest of Israel would examine each animal brought for sacrifice and affirm that it had no obvious **blemish** or defect.

i. This demonstrates the principle that to atone for the sin of another, the sacrifice must be perfect. An imperfect sacrifice could neither atone for its own sin nor for the sins of another.

ii. This wonderfully points toward the perfect, ultimate sacrifice and atonement of Jesus Christ. Jesus fulfilled this standard perfectly, being a sinless and pure sacrifice **without blemish** (John 8:29, 8:46, 14:30, and 15:10).

iii. "The LXX [Septuagint] translated the adjective *tamim* [**without blemish**] with the word *amomos*. Peter employed this Greek adjective to refer to the death of Christ as the offering of a lamb 'unblemished' (1 Pet 1:19)." (Rooker)

iv. This demonstrates the principle that God wants and deserves our best. A farmer in ancient Israel might be happy to give God a diseased and useless animal because it would cost him little. There are many anecdotes and funny stories illustrating this tendency to give God lesser things. These include the story of the farmer whose cow gave birth to twins, and he swore he would give one of the calves to God. He didn't decide which one to give to God until one day one of the calves died. He said to his wife: "Guess what? God's calf died today." In contrast, "Our best is but poor, but that which we do give, must be our best." (Morgan)

v. "The first, dealt with in this chapter, was the burnt offering, suggesting the need of personal dedication to God. Those who are admitted to the place of worship are such as have utterly failed to render their life to God thus perfectly. Therefore the offering they bring must be slain and burned." (Morgan)

vi. Israel did not always live up to this standard, and much later the prophet Malachi rebuked Israel for offering God sub-standard sacrifices: *And when you offer the blind as a sacrifice, is it not evil? And when you offer the lame and sick, is it not evil? Offer it then to your governor! Would he be pleased with you? Would he accept you favorably?* (Malachi 1:8)

d. **He shall offer it of his own free will**: God did not want the offering of the **burnt sacrifice** to be forced. Each animal had to be freely offered. This illustrates the principle that God wants our hearts, freely given to Him.

e. **At the door of the tabernacle of meeting**: The sacrifices were not to be made at the home of each individual Israelite, or at the places they later called the high places. God had an appointed place and order for sacrifice.

i. Some think that the **burnt sacrifice** was the most commonly offered in ancient Israel, therefore it is listed first.

2. (4) The transference of guilt.

'Then he shall put his hand on the head of the burnt offering, and it will be accepted on his behalf to make atonement for him.

a. **Then he shall put his hand on the head of the burnt offering**: This was a clear picture of identification with the animal to be the sacrificial victim. Through this symbol, the guilty person transferred his guilt to the sacrificial victim that would die and be completely consumed for the sin of the one bringing the offering.

i. It was not enough that the victim merely died. The one receiving atonement had to actively identify himself with the sacrifice. In the same way, it is not enough to know that Jesus died for the sins of the world. The one who would receive His atonement must "reach out" and identify himself with Jesus.

ii. Maclaren on the laying of the hands on the head: "Did not the offerer say in effect, by that act, 'This is I? This animal life shall die, as I ought to die. It shall go up as a sweet savour to Jehovah, as my being should.'"

iii. "By means of this gesture the person offering the sacrifice identifies himself as the one who is offering the animal, and in a sense he offers himself to God through the sacrificial animal." (Peter-Contesse)

iv. "Usage of the verb *samak* [**shall put**] suggests that the act of laying on hands implied the exertion of some pressure and should perhaps be rendered 'lean upon.'" (Rooker)

v. "In Leviticus 16:21 in the Day of Atonement ritual laying hands on an offering is associated with the confession of sins, and we should assume that confession accompanied the laying on of hands as the worshiper identified his purpose in bringing an offering." (Rooker)

vi. "His hand, i.e. both his hands, Leviticus 8:14,18 16:21; a common enallage [grammatic form using the singular for the plural]." (Poole)

b. **To make atonement for him**: The idea behind the Hebrew word for atonement (*kophar*) is to cover. The idea was that an individual's sin and guilt were covered over by the blood of the sacrificial victim.

i. Leviticus is a book all about **atonement**. "The word *kipper* ("to make atonement") is used almost fifty times in Leviticus.... It is used about fifty times more in the rest of the OT." (Harris)

ii. But there is a difference between the Old Testament idea of atonement and the New Testament idea. In the Old Testament, sin is "covered over" until redemption was completed by Jesus on the cross. In the New Testament, sin is done away with – and a true "at-one-ment" was accomplished by Jesus' sacrifice. The believer is therefore right with God on the basis of what Jesus has done at the cross, not on the basis of what the believer does. "There are two ruling religions around us at this day, and they mainly differ in tense. The general religion of mankind is '*Do*,' but the religion of a true Christian is '*Done*.'" (Spurgeon)

iii. Significantly, the burnt offering was more about total surrender to God than about sin. Yet this shows that when we come to God with the greatest surrender possible for us, we are still marked by sin and in great need of atonement. Efforts of greater devotion and surrender to God should, if done properly, drive us to greater dependence on God's perfect sacrifice of atonement in and through Jesus Christ.

iv. "Our only right to offer anything to God, in any form, is created by the one Offering through which we must be sanctified. Every offering is a symbol still of the One." (Morgan)

3. (5-9) The procedure for offering a bull as a burnt offering.

'He shall kill the bull before the LORD; and the priests, Aaron's sons, shall bring the blood and sprinkle the blood all around on the altar that *is by* the door of the tabernacle of meeting. And he shall skin the burnt offering and cut it into its pieces. The sons of Aaron the priest shall put fire on the altar, and lay the wood in order on the fire. Then the priests, Aaron's sons, shall lay the parts, the head, and the fat in order on the wood that *is* on the fire upon the altar; but he shall wash its entrails and its legs with water. And the priest shall burn all on the altar as a burnt sacrifice, an offering made by fire, a sweet aroma to the LORD.

a. **He shall kill the bull**: It seems as though the one who brought the offering – who laid his hands on the head of the bull – was the same one expected to actually **kill** the animal.

i. In each place the laying of hands on the sacrificial victim is mentioned (Leviticus 1:4-5, 3:2, 3:8, 4:4, 4:15, and 4:24), the killing of the sacrifice – by the one who put his *hand on the head* – is mentioned also.

ii. **He shall kill the bull**: The sacrifice had to die. The animal was without blemish, but that in itself did not atone for sin. It wasn't enough that it was dedicated to God. It may have been a hard-working or kind or wise animal (as animals go); none of that mattered. It had to *die* to atone for sin.

iii. Of course, the priest would assist as necessary, and the priests would do the heavy work of skinning and cutting the animal up. But the one who brought the offering delivered the deathblow. The individual Israelite cut the jugular vein of the bull, in the presence of the priests at the tabernacle of meeting. This was a solemn testimony to the need for sacrifice, a confession of the fact, *I need atonement for my sin.*

b. **He shall kill the bull before the LORD**: This is the second occurrence of the phrase **before the LORD** in Leviticus; it occurs more than 60 times – more than any other book in the Bible. What happens in Leviticus happens **before the LORD**, and every sacrifice that was made was to be made **before the LORD**.

i. For the Christian, it is appropriate to live our entire life in the conscious presence of God (Colossians 3:17). Yet this is especially true of our spiritual exercises, our acts of worship, prayer, and receiving God's word. It would transform those acts to consciously do them **before the LORD**. *For who is this who pledged his heart to approach Me?' says the LORD.* (Jeremiah 30:21)

c. **Bring the blood and sprinkle the blood all around**: The blood of the animal – representing the life of the animal (Leviticus 17:11) – was sprinkled on the altar of sacrifice.

i. **The altar**: "The Hebrew word for altar comes from the verb 'to slaughter.' Eventually, however, it took on a more general meaning that included any place where any kind of sacrifice was offered to God." (Peter-Contesse)

ii. "The *head* is mentioned separately because it would have been detached from the body in the process of skinning." (Harrison)

iii. **And the fat**: "All the fat, which was to be separated from the flesh, and to be put together, to increase the flame, and to consume the other parts of the sacrifice more quickly." (Poole)

iv. **In order on the wood**: "It seems to indicate that the priests could not be satisfied with simply piling wood or pieces of meat in bulk on the altar; they had to be arranged in the proper manner, although we do not know precisely how this was done." (Peter-Contesse)

d. **And the priest shall burn all on the altar as a burnt sacrifice, an offering made by fire**: The rest of the animal, having been washed from excrement or impurity, was burnt on the altar. The complete offering (**shall**

burn all on the altar), burnt before God, was **a sweet aroma** before God's throne.

i. This reflects the heart behind the burnt offering. It was a desire to give everything to God, an "I surrender all" attitude. When everything was burnt before the LORD on the altar, there was nothing held back.

ii. "What a scene it must have been when, as on some great occasions, hundreds of burnt offerings were offered in succession! The place and the attendants would look to us liker shambles and butchers than God's house and worshippers." (Maclaren)

e. **A sweet aroma to the LORD**: This is stated for all aspects of the burnt sacrifice. The atoning for sin and the giving of all, in obedience to God's instruction, pleased God as a **sweet aroma** pleases the senses. The Bible specifically tells us that Jesus Christ fulfilled this sacrifice with His own offering, perfectly pleasing God in laying down His life at the cross: *As Christ also has loved us and given Himself for us, an offering and a sacrifice to God for a sweet-smelling aroma.* (Ephesians 5:2)

i. The burning carcass of a dead animal may not, in itself, smell good. This was noted by Matthew Poole ("it rather caused a stink") and by John Trapp: "The burning and broiling of the beasts could yield no sweet savour; but thereto was added wine, oil, and incense, by God's appointment, and then there was a savour of rest in it."

4. (10-13) The procedure for offering a sheep or a goat as a burnt offering.

'If his offering *is* of the flocks—of the sheep or of the goats—as a burnt sacrifice, he shall bring a male without blemish. He shall kill it on the north side of the altar before the LORD; and the priests, Aaron's sons, shall sprinkle its blood all around on the altar. And he shall cut it into its pieces, with its head and its fat; and the priest shall lay them in order on the wood that *is* on the fire upon the altar; but he shall wash the entrails and the legs with water. Then the priest shall bring *it* all and burn *it* on the altar; it *is* a burnt sacrifice, an offering made by fire, a sweet aroma to the LORD.

a. **If his offering is of the flocks; of the sheep or of the goats**: The procedure here was essentially the same as that for offering a bull, except that a sheep or a goat was not skinned. A bull presented as a burnt offering had to be skinned (Leviticus 1:6), but not a sheep or a goat.

i. Peter-Contesse on the lack of mention of placing the hands on the head of the sheep: "The absence of any mention of the gesture does not necessarily indicate that it was omitted in the sacrifice of sheep or goats. It is possible that the author simply decided not to repeat all the mechanical details of the ritual."

b. **He shall wash the entrails and the legs with water**: Since the entire animal was to be burned, only the impurities of the **entrails** had to be washed before the sacrifice was burnt.

c. **A sweet aroma to the LORD**: This sacrifice, done the way God commanded, was pleasing to Him. It demonstrated the awareness of sin, the need for a substitute, the need for total dedication to God, and was a look forward to the perfect sacrifice of Jesus Christ to come. That ultimate sacrifice would be perfectly **sweet** and pleasing to God, and therefore be offered once-for-all (Hebrews 7:27, 9:12, 10:10).

> i. "The burnt-offering was an imperfect type of His entire devotion to His Father's will. When Jesus saw the inability of man to keep the holy law, and volunteered to magnify it, and make it honourable; when He laid aside His glory, and stepped down from His throne, saying, 'I delight to do Thy will, O my God'; when He became obedient even to the death of the cross—it was as sweet to God as the fragrance of a garden of flowers to us." (Meyer)

> ii. Spurgeon said this about the perfect sacrifice of Jesus: "There must be an infinite merit about his death: a desert unutterable, immeasurable. Methinks if there had been a million worlds to redeem, their redemption could not have needed more than this 'sacrifice of himself.' If the whole universe, teeming with worlds as many as the sands on the seashore, had required to be ransomed, that one giving up of the ghost might have sufficed as a full price for them all."

5. (14-17) The procedure for offering a bird as a burnt offering.

'**And if the burnt sacrifice of his offering to the LORD *is* of birds, then he shall bring his offering of turtledoves or young pigeons. The priest shall bring it to the altar, wring off its head, and burn *it* on the altar; its blood shall be drained out at the side of the altar. And he shall remove its crop with its feathers and cast it beside the altar on the east side, into the place for ashes. Then he shall split it at its wings, *but* shall not divide *it* completely; and the priest shall burn it on the altar, on the wood that *is* on the fire. It *is* a burnt sacrifice, an offering made by fire, a sweet aroma to the LORD.**

a. **If the burnt sacrifice of his offering to the LORD is of birds**: This procedure followed the same principles, adapted to the sacrifice of birds instead of bulls, sheep, or goats. The animal was killed, its blood was offered, the carcass was first prepared and then burnt before the LORD.

i. Trapp on **wring off its head**: "Or, Pinch it with his nail, that the blood might go out, without separating it from the rest of the body. This prefigured the death of Christ without either breaking a bone or dividing the Godhead from the manhood; as also the skill that should be in ministers, to cut or divide aright the word of truth."

ii. **Drained out at the side of the altar**: "The body of the bird was squeezed against the side of the altar, since there would not have been enough blood to perform the complete ritual described earlier." (Peter-Contesse)

iii. **On the east side**: "To wit, of the tabernacle. Here the filth was cast, because this was the remotest place from the holy of holies, which was in the west end; to teach us, that impure things and persons should not presume to approach to God, and that they should be banished from his presence." (Poole)

b. **He shall bring his offering of turtledoves or young pigeons**: God would not accept *any* kind of bird, but He would accept **turtledoves or young pigeons** as sacrifices. The fact that God would accept a bull, a goat, a sheep, or a bird shows that God was more interested in the heart behind the sacrifice than in the actual animal being offered. If the sacrifice was made with the right heart, God accepted the poor man's bird as much as the rich man's bull; the simple sacrifice of a poor man could still be **a sweet aroma to the LORD**.

i. At the same time, the sacrifice had to correspond with what one could afford. It was wrong for a rich man to only offer a bird as a burnt offering. The greatness of the sacrifice had to correspond with the greatness of the one who brought the offering. Therefore, when God made His offering for sin, He gave the richest, most costly thing He could – Himself.

ii. "These birds were appointed for the relief of the poor who could not bring better. And these birds are preferred before others, partly because they were easily gotten, and partly because they are fit representations of Christ's chastity, and meekness, and gentleness, for which these birds are remarkable." (Poole)

Leviticus 2 – The Grain Offering

A. The procedure for the grain offering.

1. (1-3) The presentation of the grain offering.

'When anyone offers a grain offering to the LORD, his offering shall be *of* fine flour. And he shall pour oil on it, and put frankincense on it. He shall bring it to Aaron's sons, the priests, one of whom shall take from it his handful of fine flour and oil with all the frankincense. And the priest shall burn *it as* a memorial on the altar, an offering made by fire, a sweet aroma to the LORD. The rest of the grain offering *shall be* Aaron's and his sons'. *It is* most holy of the offerings to the LORD made by fire.

   a. **When anyone offers a grain offering to the LORD:** The **grain offering** was typically **fine flour**, mixed with a bit of **oil** and **frankincense**. A portion of the flour was burnt before the LORD on the altar. The remainder was given to the priests for their own use in making bread for the priest and his family (**the rest of the grain offering shall be Aaron's and his sons'**).

     i. G. Campbell Morgan rightly saw the **grain offering** as suggestive of our service to God. "This meal offering was the work of men's hands, of the fruits of the ground, the result of cultivation, manufacture, and preparation; and it was the symbol of service offered."

     ii. Matthew Poole considered three reasons for the **grain offering**.

       • Grains and things that grow are of great necessity and benefit to man, and it is appropriate to honor God with such things.

       • Even the poorest could offer a **grain offering**, and God wanted to open the door for the poor to bring offerings to Him.

       • This brought necessary and helpful grain and other produce to the priests.

iii. Poole described **fine flour**: "Searched, or sifted, and purged from all bran, it being fit that the best things should be offered to the best Being."

iv. **All with frankincense**: "This substance was often used in rituals of antiquity, because it produces a pleasant odor when burned. It was a very expensive product because it was usually imported from the southeastern coast of the Arabian peninsula, through the intermediary of Arabia. Normally it was used only in ritual ceremonies." (Peter-Contesse)

v. "Because the priests represent God, they have a right to those sacrifices offered to God. The grain offering apparently provided the main source of income for the priesthood." (Rooker)

vi. Nehemiah 13:12 tells us that the tithes of wine, grain, and oil were stored in special rooms at the temple.

b. **A memorial on the altar, an offering made by fire, a sweet aroma to the LORD**: God allowed and received this bloodless sacrifice as an expression of thanksgiving, not as atonement for sin. In a society where most people were farmers, this was a fitting symbol of thanks for God's faithful provision.

c. **It is most holy of the offerings to the LORD made by fire**: The emphasis of the **grain offering** was gratitude. That it was called **most holy of the offerings** shows the high regard God has of our thankfulness.

2. (4-10) Different types of grain offering.

'And if you bring as an offering a grain offering baked in the oven, *it shall be* unleavened cakes of fine flour mixed with oil, or unleavened wafers anointed with oil. But if your offering *is* a grain offering *baked* in a pan, *it shall be of* fine flour, unleavened, mixed with oil. You shall break it in pieces and pour oil on it; it *is* a grain offering. 'If your offering *is* a grain offering *baked* in a covered pan, it shall be made *of* fine flour with oil. You shall bring the grain offering that is made of these things to the LORD. And when it is presented to the priest, he shall bring it to the altar. Then the priest shall take from the grain offering a memorial portion, and burn *it* on the altar. *It is* an offering made by fire, a sweet aroma to the LORD. And what is left of the grain offering *shall be* Aaron's and his sons'. *It is* most holy of the offerings to the LORD made by fire.

a. **If you bring as an offering a grain offering baked in the oven**: A grain offering could also be brought in the form of **fine flour** already **baked**. It could be baked in an oven, cooked on a flat griddle, or prepared in a covered pan.

i. No matter what form it was in, the grain offering had to be prepared at home. We can imagine an ancient Jewish woman carefully preparing the best her kitchen could make and presenting it to God as a sacrifice. This expression of devotion to God began *at home* and if offered with the right heart, was **a sweet aroma to the LORD**.

ii. The **covered pan** worked like a modern deep fat fryer. "Authorities suggest that the cereal offering cooked in the [covered pan] would look rather like a modern deep-fried doughnut" (Harrison). "These cakes may have been deep fried or even boiled, dumpling style." (Harris)

b. **Unleavened cakes...unleavened wafers**: As will be specifically commanded later in Leviticus 2:11, God did not want leaven (yeast) in the **grain offering**. In the picture of the grain offering, we can say that God did not want His service to be corrupted by sin, by leaven.

- Jesus spoke of the *leaven of the Pharisees and Sadducees* (Matthew 16:6-12) and *the leaven of Herod* (Mark 8:15), by which He meant their doctrines, their philosophy.

- Paul spoke of the *old leaven* of corruption and sin (1 Corinthians 5:6-9).

    i. "The leaven of the Pharisees was hypocrisy; that is, of ritualism without spiritual and moral content. The leaven of the Sadducees was rationalism; that is, Herodianism or worldliness; the elimination of the supernatural. Paul speaks of the leaven of 'malice and wickedness,' as the opposite of 'sincerity and truth.'" (Morgan)

    ii. "These then are the corrupting influences which are not to be mixed with our service. In all the work we do for God, there is to be an absence of hypocrisy, of materialism, of the spirit which is contrary to love and truth." (Morgan)

    iii. If the grain offering is a picture of proper service to God, it is also a reminder that we fall short in serving God as we should. We are grateful that Jesus fulfilled the heart and meaning of the grain offering for us, as the One who perfectly served God, whose service was never touched with leaven in any way.

    iv. "The New Testament believer is also reminded that as the believer in Old Testament times offered this grain to God, so Jesus Christ as the Bread of life offered his life to God (John 6:32–35)." (Rooker)

c. **Fine flour mixed with oil**: The grain offerings needed **oil** with them. This was practical, helping with the binding together of the flour of the offering, and helping it to burn properly. It was also symbolic of the fact that our service, our offering, should be always in the presence and under the influence of the Holy Spirit.

> i. "Jacob was the first we read of that consecrated his offerings with oil. [Genesis 28:18] Probably he had it from his predecessors." (Trapp)

d. **What is left of the grain offering shall be Aaron's and his sons'**: If the grain offering was brought as fine flour or as prepared bread, a portion went to the priests for their provision.

B. Special instructions regarding the grain offering.

1. (11) The addition of leaven or honey was prohibited.

'No grain offering which you bring to the LORD shall be made with leaven, for you shall burn no leaven nor any honey in any offering to the LORD made by fire.

a. **No grain offering which you bring to the LORD shall be made with leaven**: Yeast (**leaven**) was not allowed because it was a picture or representation of sin and the effects of sin. Ancient Israelites brought **leaven** into their dough by a pinch of dough left over from the previous batch, as in the making of sourdough bread.

> i. A little pinch of dough from the old batch made a whole new lump of dough rise and puff up, spreading through the entire new batch. Therefore, the work of leaven was considered an illustration of the work of sin and pride. The presence of a little can corrupt everything.

> ii. "As the burnt offering was to be 'without blemish' so the meal offering was to be without leaven." (Morgan)

> iii. However, bread with leaven was a part of the peace offering, but *not* offered on the altar (**you shall burn no leaven**). In the peace offering, the bread with leaven was part of a heave offering (Leviticus 7:11-14) or a wave offering (Leviticus 23:17).

b. **Nor any honey in any offering to the LORD made by fire**: Honey was not allowed because it was a favorite thing to sacrifice to pagan deities. God did not want to be worshipped in the same way that false, pagan gods were worshipped.

> i. "*Honey*: this word is used both of honey from bees and a kind of concentrated fruit syrup made from raisins or dates." (Peter-Contesse)

> ii. One reason God did not want **honey** in the sacrifice was "To teach us that God's worship is not to be governed by men's fancies and appetites, to which honey might have been grateful, but by God's will." (Poole)

iii. Leaven can make things artificially sour and honey can make things artificially sweet. God did not want either of these in sacrifice. When we offer ourselves as a living sacrifice (Romans 12:1-2) He wants us to come just as we are, without artificially making ourselves more sour or sweet.

iv. F.B. Meyer considered it like this:

- "*No leaven* – the symbol of the rising pride and self."
- "*No honey* – that which is merely attractive and sensuous."

2. (12) The offering of firstfruits.

As for the offering of the firstfruits, you shall offer them to the LORD, but they shall not be burned on the altar for a sweet aroma.

a. **As for the offering of the firstfruits**: The best of the first of the harvest (**firstfruits**) were to be offered **to the LORD**, but not as other grain offerings. They were never to be **burned on the altar** but offered with a different procedure.

b. **They shall not be burned on the altar**: God had a different procedure for the **offering of the firstfruits** than for the grain offering in general. This is described in Leviticus 2:14-16.

3. (13) Each grain offering must include salt.

And every offering of your grain offering you shall season with salt; you shall not allow the salt of the covenant of your God to be lacking from your grain offering. With all your offerings you shall offer salt.

a. **Every offering of your grain offering you shall season with salt**: Salt was an important part of the offering because it spoke of *purity*, of *preservation*, and of *expense*. Every sacrifice offered to God should be *pure*, should be *enduring*, and should *cost* something. In this one verse, God repeated the command three times.

i. As a preservative salt will slow or virtually stop the normal process of rot in meat. It is the nature of flesh to spoil, but salt-cured meats stay good.

ii. Salt also spoke of friendship. According to ancient custom, a bond of friendship was established through the eating of salt. It was said that once you had eaten a man's salt, you were his friend for life. God wanted every sacrifice to be a reminder of *relationship*.

iii. Previously, God commanded that sacrifices *should not* contain honey (Leviticus 2:11). The command to include **salt** and exclude honey means God wants the sincerity of our service, not things made artificially sweet. "There is a kind of molasses godliness which I can never stomach." (Spurgeon)

iv. The fact that God commanded that every **grain offering** should include a pinch of salt shows that small things matter in our service to God. Our faithfulness in small things honors God. "My brethren, nothing in the service of God is trifling. A pinch of salt may seem to us exceedingly unimportant, but before the Lord it may not be so." (Spurgeon)

v. "A special chamber in the temple was designated for the storage of salt (m. Mid. 5:3)." (Rooker)

b. **The salt of the covenant of your God**: Therefore, a covenant of salt had specific characteristics. It was:

- A *pure* covenant (salt stays pure as a chemical compound).

- An *enduring* covenant (salt makes things preserve and endure).

- A *valuable* covenant (salt was expensive).

    i. "Salt is a preservative, so it symbolizes the notion that the covenant cannot be destroyed by fire or decay. The phrase 'covenant of salt' emphasizes the durability or eternality of the covenant." (Rooker)

    ii. The idea of the covenant of salt is repeated in Numbers 18:19 and 2 Chronicles 13:5.

c. **With all your offerings you shall offer salt**: Jesus spoke of the idea of salt and sacrifice in Mark 9:49-50. There He said that people, as living sacrifices to God, must be seasoned with fire and salt.

    i. Because salt spoke of so many things – the covenant, fellowship, sincerity, purity – the inclusion of salt with **all your offerings** speaks to the way we should serve God. In all our service, we must:

- Remember the covenant.

- Remember fellowship.

- Remember sincerity.

- Remember purity.

4. (14-16) Procedure for a grain offering of firstfruits.

'If you offer a grain offering of your firstfruits to the LORD, you shall offer for the grain offering of your firstfruits green heads of grain roasted on the fire, grain beaten from full heads. And you shall put oil on it, and lay frankincense on it. It *is* a grain offering. Then the priest shall burn the memorial portion: *part* **of its beaten grain and** *part* **of its oil, with all the frankincense, as an offering made by fire to the LORD.**

a. **If you offer a grain offering of your firstfruits to the LORD**: In Leviticus 2:12 God told Israel to *not* bring firstfruits offerings in the same manner as grain offerings. Here God told them *how* to bring a **firstfruits** offering.

i. The *idea* of **firstfruits** was important. The first of the harvest and the firstborn of livestock belonged to the LORD. This could be considered risky giving because the land might not yield much more produce, and the cow or ewe might not give birth again – yet the first still belonged to God.

ii. The LORD promised to bless this giving of the firstfruits and firstborn in faith: *Honor the LORD with your possessions, and with the firstfruits of all your increase; so your barns will be filled with plenty, and your vats will overflow with new wine.* (Proverbs 3:9-10)

iii. God was delighted with the **green heads of grain**: "To signify that God should be served with the firstfruits of our age, the primrose of our childhood." (Trapp)

b. **The priest shall burn the memorial portion**: It seems that none of the **firstfruits** offering were kept by the priests, but all of it was burnt to thank God, to honor God, and to declare their trust in God's provision of a full harvest.

c. **You shall put oil on it, and lay frankincense on it**: These were thought to sweeten the sacrifice and make it costlier.

d. **An offering made by fire to the LORD**: We see that Jesus, in His life and work, fulfilled the grain and the firstfruits offering. 1 Corinthians 15:20 presents Jesus as the firstfruits of the resurrection, the first of God's new order of resurrection life: *But now Christ is risen from the dead, and has become the firstfruits of those who have fallen asleep.*

Leviticus 3 – The Peace Offering

A. Offering cattle for the peace offering.

1. (1-2) The presentation and killing of cattle for the peace offering.

'When his offering *is* a sacrifice of a peace offering, if he offers *it* of the herd, whether male or female, he shall offer it without blemish before the LORD. And he shall lay his hand on the head of his offering, and kill it *at* the door of the tabernacle of meeting; and Aaron's sons, the priests, shall sprinkle the blood all around on the altar.

a. **When his offering is a sacrifice of a peace offering**: In contrast to the burnt offering (Leviticus 1:3), the sacrifice of a **peace offering** could be either a **male or female** animal. However, the animal still had to be **without blemish**.

- **Without blemish** means we give God the best.
- **Without blemish** means we need a sinless substitute.
- **Without blemish** points to Jesus, the perfect sacrifice (1 Peter 1:19).

i. The **peace offering** was not an offering to *make* peace with God (this was the purpose of the sin offering of Leviticus 4), but an offering to *enjoy* peace with God. The whole reason Jesus made peace between the Father and the believer is so that the peace could be enjoyed.

ii. The greatest *animal* peace offering ever made happened when Solomon dedicated the temple, offering 22,000 cattle and 120,000 sheep (1 Kings 8:63). That must have been history's greatest barbecue. Later, Hezekiah gave a festival where 2,000 bulls and 17,000 sheep were given for peace offerings (2 Chronicles 30:24).

iii. The greatest peace offering ever made happened when Jesus gave Himself as a sacrifice on the cross. His sacrifice not only paid the penalty of our sin, but He also made peace between the believer and God that can now be enjoyed: *Therefore, having been justified by faith,*

24

we have peace with God through our Lord, Jesus Christ (Romans 5:1). Ephesians 2:14-16 notes that Jesus Christ Himself has become our peace and has broken down the wall of separation.

iv. Notably, either a **male or female** animal could be used. When it comes to peace with God and fellowship with God, there is no male or female (Galatians 3:28), all are welcome before God. Leviticus 7:11-14 further explains that the peace offering made for thanksgiving was to be presented with an offering of unleavened cakes or wafers *and* leavened bread. These two were presented as a wave offering and may be considered a prophetic announcement of God bringing Jew and Gentile together in the peace of Jesus the Messiah (Ephesians 2:11-18).

b. **He shall lay his hand on the head of the offering**: As with the burnt offering (Leviticus 1:4), the one bringing the offer identified with the substitute sacrifice and symbolically transferred their sin to the sacrifice by laying **his hand on the head of the offering**.

c. **Kill it at the door of the tabernacle**: As with the burnt offering (Leviticus 1:5), the sense is *probably* (though not certainly) that the Israelite bringing the offering actually made the cut to the animal's neck that bled the animal to death. Afterwards, it was the job of **the priests** to **sprinkle the blood all around on the altar**.

i. This happened **at the door of the tabernacle**, at the very entrance. This was where the Israelites brought their sacrifice to the priests. The non-priestly Israelite did not go into the tabernacle court, except here at the very entrance, **at the door of the tabernacle**.

2. (3-5) The presentation of the parts of the animal sacrifice.

Then he shall offer from the sacrifice of the peace offering an offering made by fire to the LORD. The fat that covers the entrails and all the fat that *is* on the entrails, the two kidneys and the fat that *is* on them by the flanks, and the fatty lobe *attached* to the liver above the kidneys, he shall remove; and Aaron's sons shall burn it on the altar upon the burnt sacrifice, which *is* on the wood that *is* on the fire, *as* an offering made by fire, a sweet aroma to the LORD.

a. **The fat that covers the entrails and all the fat that is on the entrails**: In the peace offering, the blood of the animal was offered to God (Leviticus 3:2) along with the **fat**, which was burned **on the altar** of sacrifice.

i. The *heleb*, 'the fat' that covers the organs and entrails, was not to be eaten but was to be burned. The fat represented the choicest part of the offering. The fat belonged to God and had to be offered to him in sacrifice." (Rooker)

b. **On the altar upon the burnt sacrifice**: The altar that received God's portion of the peace offering was the same **altar** that received **the burnt sacrifice** – which comes first. Peace and fellowship with God come on the same basis as God's sacrifice for sin.

i. In Christian terminology, we would say that the cross of Jesus Christ is not only the place where our sin was paid for by the sacrifice of Jesus, it is also the place where we enjoy peace and fellowship with God.

c. **An offering made by fire, a sweet aroma to the LORD**: The offering of the animal's **fat** from the different parts of the cut-up sacrifice pleased God; it was a pleasant, **sweet aroma to the LORD**.

- **Fat** was considered to be the prime portion, giving flavor and moisture to the meat of the animal.

- **Fat** is the stored energy of the animal; it is a way of offering one's energy and work to God.

i. There is no mention made of what to do with meat portions of the animal. This is because the meat portion was to be shared, with a part given to the priests and a part given to the one who brought the offering. That one ate his portion of meat as part of a fellowship meal with God, normally with a gathering of immediate and extended family.

ii. "Think of this blessed feast with God. We who were once far off in the wicked and hostile imaginings, are now made nigh; we sit at God's table as His children and hear Him say. Let us make merry and be glad; this My son was dead and is alive again." (Meyer)

- We can feast because we have peace *with* God.

- We can feast because we have the *peace* of God.

- We can feast because we have *the God of peace*.

d. **A sweet aroma to the LORD**: Morgan points out that this phrase is used of the first three offerings (the burnt offering, the grain offering, and the peace offering). It is *not* used of the sin offering or the trespass offering. The idea is that in the first three the fire brings out the aroma; in the last two, the fire destroys.

i. Morgan drew this spiritual principle from this: "If a man be in rebellion, a sinner persisting in his sin, the fire destroys him. If he be yielded, the fire brings out the beauty of character. Christ knew the fire bringing out sweet savour in His absolute perfections; He knew it as consuming, as He represented the sinner, and was made sin."

B. Offering sheep or goats for the peace offering.

1. (6-8) Offering a lamb as a peace offering.

'If his offering as a sacrifice of a peace offering to the LORD *is* of the flock, *whether* male or female, he shall offer it without blemish. If he offers a lamb as his offering, then he shall offer it before the LORD. And he shall lay his hand on the head of his offering, and kill it before the tabernacle of meeting; and Aaron's sons shall sprinkle its blood all around on the altar.

a. **Is of the flock**: The **peace offering** could also be an animal from the flock, a sheep or a goat. If it was from the flock, it had to be **without blemish**, and the one bringing the sacrifice had to **lay his hand on the head of the offering** and **kill it**, as in the offering of cattle from the herd in the peace offering (Leviticus 3:2).

b. **Aaron's sons shall sprinkle its blood all around on the altar**: The presentation of the **blood** to God was the duty of the priests.

2. (9-11) Offering the fat of a lamb presented as the peace offering.

'Then he shall offer from the sacrifice of the peace offering, as an offering made by fire to the LORD, its fat *and* the whole fat tail which he shall remove close to the backbone. And the fat that covers the entrails and all the fat that *is* on the entrails, the two kidneys and the fat that *is* on them by the flanks, and the fatty lobe *attached* to the liver above the kidneys, he shall remove; and the priest shall burn *them* on the altar *as* food, an offering made by fire to the LORD.

a. **He shall offer**: The procedure was generally the same as the offering of a bull or cow (Leviticus 3:3-5). The blood and the fat were given to the LORD, while the unmentioned meat portions were for the one who brought the offering and for the priest.

b. **Its fat and the whole fat tail which he shall remove close to the backbone**: The offering of the **whole fat tail** was significant. That portion of the animal was considered a delicacy and could weigh as much as 60 pounds (27 kilograms). This part of the animal, though valued for eating, was not eaten by the priests or by the one bringing the offering in the fellowship meal that accompanied the peace offering. It was burned **on the altar as food**, to God.

i. Commentators such as John Trapp and Matthew Poole say that the **fat tail** of this ancient breed of sheep was "larger and better" than what they saw among sheep of their own day. Adam Clarke also has an extended comment on this.

ii. "The tail of the kind of sheep raised in Palestine may have contained as much as seven or more kilograms of fat and was considered a delicacy." (Peter-Contesse)

iii. **The fatty lobe attached to the liver**: "among certain neighboring tribes of the Israelites, the liver was used in divination rites. Possibly this is why Jewish legislation required that it be burned. But it is also true that, like the fat, this particular part of the liver referred to as the *appendage* was considered a delicacy and was therefore appropriate to be set aside for God." (Peter-Contesse)

c. **The priest shall burn them on the altar as food**: The idea was that this was "God's **food**," His portion of the sacrifice. The family that brought the peace offering would eat their portion, and this portion belonged to God, in a meal that they shared together.

i. "The worshiper in this sense shared a meal with the Lord, which means that he had fellowship with him." (Rooker)

3. (12-16) Offering a goat as a peace offering.

'And if his offering *is* a goat, then he shall offer it before the LORD. He shall lay his hand on its head and kill it before the tabernacle of meeting; and the sons of Aaron shall sprinkle its blood all around on the altar. Then he shall offer from it his offering, as an offering made by fire to the LORD. The fat that covers the entrails and all the fat that *is* on the entrails, the two kidneys and the fat that *is* on them by the flanks, and the fatty lobe *attached* to the liver above the kidneys, he shall remove; and the priest shall burn them on the altar *as* food, an offering made by fire for a sweet aroma; all the fat *is* the LORD's.

a. **If his offering is a goat**: God accepted both sheep and goats in the peace offering. When it was offered, the same steps were followed as in the offering of cattle or sheep, as described earlier in Leviticus 3.

b. **All the fat is the LORD's**: This sacrifice demonstrates God's claim upon all that is valued, and upon all our energy. **Fat** is essentially stored energy, and it belongs to the LORD.

4. (17) Conclusion: The fat and the blood belong to God.

'*This shall be* a perpetual statute throughout your generations in all your dwellings: you shall eat neither fat nor blood.'"

a. **You shall eat neither fat nor blood**: There was a *spiritual* significance to this command relevant to the peace offering. We enjoy peace with God by giving Him the best and our energy (represented by the **fat**), and by giving Him our lives (represented by the **blood**).

i. Even as it was impossible to remove *all* the blood from an animal, so was it impossible to remove *all* the fat from meat – this speaks of removing as much as one can practically.

ii. "By the fat therefore mentioned here and in the preceding verse, we may understand any fat that exists in a separate or unmixed state, such as the omentum or caul, the fat of the mesentery, the fat on the kidneys, and whatever else of the internal fat was easily separable." (Clarke)

b. **You shall eat neither fat**: There was a *practical* significance to this command. Whatever other benefits there may be in eating less fat and blood, it is true that parasites such as tapeworms were often found in the fatty tissues. By obeying this command, the ancient Israelites avoided great exposure to these dangerous parasites.

i. Matthew Poole described another reason why this normally desired portion of the animal was given to God: "To exercise them in obedience to God, and self-denial, and mortification of their appetites, even in those things which probably many of them would much desire."

c. **You shall eat neither fat nor blood**: The ritual eating of blood was a common practice of pagan peoples, both ancient and modern. God wanted His people separated from these pagan rituals, and to instead recognize that life and blood are strongly connected (Genesis 9:4, Leviticus 17:11-14).

i. "This was forbidden, partly, to maintain reverence to God and his worship; partly, out of opposition to idolaters, who used to drink the blood of their sacrifices; partly, with respect unto Christ's blood, thereby manifestly signified; and partly, for moral admonition about avoiding cruelty." (Poole)

ii. **A perpetual statute throughout your generations**: This phrase is used 17 times throughout Leviticus. "It indicates a rule that is to be observed by all Israelites for all time." (Peter-Contesse) It was also to be observed wherever they lived, in whatever land (**in all your dwellings**).

Leviticus 4 – The Sin Offering

A. The procedure for the Sin Offering.

1. (1-2) The purpose of the Sin Offering.

Now the LORD spoke to Moses, saying, "Speak to the children of Israel, saying: 'If a person sins unintentionally against any of the commandments of the LORD *in anything* which ought not to be done, and does any of them,

> a. **If a person sins unintentionally**: The idea is not so much of an *accidental* sin, but of a sin committed by a person whose life is lived in general obedience and surrender to God. The contrast is between sins of human frailty, and sins of outright rebellion.
>
>> i. The root of the Hebrew word translated **unintentionally** has the idea of "to wander" or "to get lost." No one intends to get lost; but when it happens, you are still lost – and, if truly lost, need to be rescued.
>>
>> ii. Another contrast to an unintentional sin is to sin *presumptuously* (Numbers 15:30). Literally, the presumptuous sin of Numbers 15:30 is "to sin with a high hand." There was no atonement available under the Old Covenant for the one whose heart was so defiantly turned against the LORD in presumptuous sin. We are grateful that under the New Covenant, there is atonement available for *every* sin (1 John 1:9).
>>
>> iii. "No amount of sincerity can turn injustice into righteousness, or transform falsehood into truth." (Spurgeon)
>
> b. **Sins unintentionally**: Leviticus 4:2 is the first time the word *sin* appears in Leviticus, and the Hebrew root of the word essentially means "to miss." The same root is used in Judges 20:16 in describing men who could sling a stone and not *miss*.

i. Peter-Contesse on the word translated **sins**: "At the heart of its meaning is the notion of 'missing the mark,' or 'failure to attain something,' or 'to be out of harmony with someone,' or 'not to be in a normal and right relationship with someone.' In this case, it is God that has been harmed."

ii. **Sins unintentionally**: "These words recognise an aspect of sin which we are at least in danger of thinking of lightly. There is a great tendency to imagine that sin is only in the will. There is a sense in which this is true. Guilt never attaches to sin until it is an act of the will. But imperfection and pollution exclude from God, even though there be no responsibility for them." (Morgan)

iii. Adam Clarke quoted an Anglican litany: "That it may please thee to give us *true repentance;* to forgive us all our *sins, negligences,* and *ignorances;* and to endue us with the grace of thy Holy Spirit, to *amend our lives* according to thy HOLY WORD."

c. **Against any of the commandments of the LORD**: Though God made a distinction between **sins unintentionally** done, and those done presumptuously (as in Numbers 15:30), a sin **against any of the commandments of the LORD** had to be dealt with. This is the principle of James 2:10.

i. As this chapter unfolds, God will direct a sacrifice for unintentional sins for the priests, for Israel as a whole, for the rulers, and for a common person. From the highest to the lowest in the land, God cared about unintentional sins.

2. (3-12) The sin offering for a priest.

If the anointed priest sins, bringing guilt on the people, then let him offer to the LORD for his sin which he has sinned a young bull without blemish as a sin offering. He shall bring the bull to the door of the tabernacle of meeting before the LORD, lay his hand on the bull's head, and kill the bull before the LORD. Then the anointed priest shall take some of the bull's blood and bring it to the tabernacle of meeting. The priest shall dip his finger in the blood and sprinkle some of the blood seven times before the LORD, in front of the veil of the sanctuary. And the priest shall put some of the blood on the horns of the altar of sweet incense before the LORD, which is in the tabernacle of meeting; and he shall pour the remaining blood of the bull at the base of the altar of the burnt offering, which is at the door of the tabernacle of meeting. He shall take from it all the fat of the bull as the sin offering. The fat that covers the entrails and all the fat which *is* on the entrails, the two kidneys and the fat that *is* on them by the flanks, and the fatty lobe

attached to the liver above the kidneys, he shall remove, as it was taken from the bull of the sacrifice of the peace offering; and the priest shall burn them on the altar of the burnt offering. But the bull's hide and all its flesh, with its head and legs, its entrails and offal—the whole bull he shall carry outside the camp to a clean place, where the ashes are poured out, and burn it on wood with fire; where the ashes are poured out it shall be burned.

a. **If the anointed priest sins, bringing guilt on the people**: If a priest needed a sin offering to be made on his behalf, a bull had to be sacrificed on his behalf, with the priest identifying with the victim through the laying on of hands.

i. The presence of a separate ritual of cleansing for the sin of the priest shows that they had a greater accountability before the LORD and were, in a sense, judged according to a stricter measure. James applied the same principle to teachers among God's people (James 3:1).

ii. Most think that **the anointed priest** refers to the high priest. However, it is worth remembering that even the "common" priests were anointed (as commanded in Exodus 29). It may refer to anyone who was an **anointed priest**.

b. **Priest sins...offer to the LORD for his sin...a sin offering**: Paul wrote in 2 Corinthians 5:21: *For He made Him who knew no sin to be sin for us, that we might become the righteousness of God in Him.* According to Adam Clarke, the word for *sin* in 2 Corinthians 5:21 (*hamartian*) is the same ancient Greek word used in the Septuagint (an ancient Greek translation of the Hebrew Scriptures) to translate **sin offering**. In 2 Corinthians 5:21, Paul said that God the Father made Jesus Christ our sin offering.

c. **Lay his hand on the bull's head**: The idea of laying the hand on the head of the sacrifice is repeated five times in the chapter – at 4:4, 4:15, 4:24, 4:29, and 4:33. It is an important part of the idea of the sacrifice of a substitute. Spurgeon considered two important aspects of this symbol.

i. The Meaning of the Symbol.
- It was a confession of sin.
- It was a consent to the plan of substitution.
- It was the acceptance of that victim in the sinner's place.
- It was a belief in the transference of the sin.
- It was a dependence, a leaning on the victim.

ii. The Simplicity of the Symbol.

- There was no preparatory ceremony.
- There was to be nothing in his hand.
- There was nothing to be done with the hand, except to lay it.
- There was nothing to be done to the man's hand.

iii. **A young bull**: "The same sacrifice that should be offered for the sin of the whole people, [Leviticus 4:14] to note the heinousness of the priest's sin above others. The sins of teachers are the teachers of sins." (Trapp)

iv. **A young bull**: "Our Lord Jesus Christ is like the firstling of the bullock, the most precious thing in heaven, strong for service, docile in obedience, one who was willing and able to labour for our sakes; and he was brought as a perfect victim, without spot or blemish, to suffer in our stead." (Spurgeon)

d. **To the tabernacle**: In contrast to the sacrifices for unintentional sins for others, the blood of the sacrifice for the priest was brought into the tabernacle itself for application to various places in the tabernacle. This shows, that in some sense, the sins of the priest were regarded as more serious.

e. **Sprinkle some of the blood seven times before the LORD, in front of the veil of the sanctuary**: The blood of the sacrificed bull was collected, then applied by sprinkling to the veil in the tabernacle of meeting and to the **altar of sweet incense**. The remaining blood was poured out at the **base of the altar of the burnt offering**, outside the tent of the tabernacle.

i. Sin is an offense against the holiness of God, and so the **veil** guarding His holy presence must receive sacrificial blood. This blood had to be sprinkled **seven times before the LORD** – before the veil or curtain that separated the holy place and the Holy of Holies. This showed the seriousness of even unintentional sins for the priest.

- "The sevenfold sprinkling was also part of the Day of Atonement ritual (Lev 16:14, 15, 19), the purification of the leper ritual (14:7), and the dedication of the altar (8:11)." (Rooker)

- "Whether the blood fell on the veil or not we are not certain; but we have good reason to believe that it was cast upon the veil itself. The veil, of costliest tapestry, would thus become by degrees more and more like a vesture dipped in blood." (Spurgeon)

ii. Sin affects our prayer life, and so the **altar of sweet incense** representing the prayers of God's people must receive sacrificial blood.

iii. Sin makes our atonement necessary, so the **altar of the burnt offering** – the place of atonement – must receive sacrificial blood.

f. He shall take from it all the fat of the bull as the sin offering: The fatty portions of the animal were offered to God. In this, the best was dedicated to God (as in the peace offering of Leviticus 3) after the blood covered the sin.

g. The bull's hide and all its flesh...burn it on wood with fire: The valuable hide and the meat of the bull were burnt **outside the camp**, along with the worthless portions of the bull. It could not be offered to God, but it was burned as if it were a worthless thing. This had to be done **outside the camp** to show that the effects and memory of this sin were removed from the people.

i. All selfish motives had to be removed in the sin offering. If a priest brought the offering, the whole offering had to be destroyed. If a non-priest brought the offering, the priest could eat of it, but not the one bringing the sacrifice. You couldn't bring a sin offering because you wanted meat or leather, but only because you wanted to be made right with God. This emphasized the idea that there is no benefit to our sin.

ii. Paul expressed this attitude in Philippians 3:7-8: *But what things were gain to me, these I have counted loss for Christ. Yet indeed I also count all things loss for the excellence of the knowledge of Christ Jesus my Lord, for whom I have suffered the loss of all things, and count them as rubbish, that I may gain Christ.*

3. (13-21) The sin offering for the whole congregation of Israel.

'Now if the whole congregation of Israel sins unintentionally, and the thing is hidden from the eyes of the assembly, and they have done *something against* any of the commandments of the LORD *in anything* which should not be done, and are guilty; when the sin which they have committed becomes known, then the assembly shall offer a young bull for the sin, and bring it before the tabernacle of meeting. And the elders of the congregation shall lay their hands on the head of the bull before the LORD. Then the bull shall be killed before the LORD. The anointed priest shall bring some of the bull's blood to the tabernacle of meeting. Then the priest shall dip his finger in the blood and sprinkle *it* seven times before the LORD, in front of the veil. And he shall put *some* of the blood on the horns of the altar which *is* before the LORD, which *is* in the tabernacle of meeting; and he shall pour the remaining blood at the base of the altar of burnt offering, which is at the door of the tabernacle of meeting. He shall take all the fat from it and burn *it* on the altar. And he shall do with the bull as he did with the bull as a sin offering;

thus he shall do with it. So the priest shall make atonement for them, and it shall be forgiven them. Then he shall carry the bull outside the camp, and burn it as he burned the first bull. It *is* a sin offering for the assembly.

a. **If the whole congregation of Israel sins unintentionally**: The procedure was the same as the sin offering on behalf of a priest as described in the previous verses. The bull was killed, the blood of the bull was distributed by sprinkling to the veil, the altar of incense, and the remainder poured out at the base of the altar of burnt offering. Then the bull and its fat were burned on the altar, while the entrails and the hide were burned **outside the camp**.

b. **The elders of the congregation shall lay their hands on the head of the bull before the LORD**: This was the one significant difference between the sin offering for the **whole congregation of Israel** and the sin offering for the priests (Leviticus 4:3-12). The **elders of the congregation** laid their hands on the head of the bull, representing the nation.

i. "This laying of the hand does not appear to have been a mere touch of contact, but in some other places of Scripture has the meaning of leaning heavily.... Surely this is the very essence and nature of faith, which doth not only bring us into contact with the great Substitute, but teaches us to lean upon Him with all the burden of our guilt; so that if our sins be very weighty, yet we see Him as able to bear them all." (Spurgeon)

c. **It shall be forgiven them**: This is the wonderful assurance. There is forgiveness when we come to God as He commands, and receive atonement as He directs. This promise is even greater under the New Covenant (1 John 1:9).

4. (22-26) The sin offering for a ruler of the people.

'**When a ruler has sinned, and done** *something* **unintentionally** *against* **any of the commandments of the LORD his God** *in anything* **which should not be done, and is guilty, or if his sin which he has committed comes to his knowledge, he shall bring as his offering a kid of the goats, a male without blemish. And he shall lay his hand on the head of the goat, and kill it at the place where they kill the burnt offering before the LORD. It** *is* **a sin offering. The priest shall take some of the blood of the sin offering with his finger, put** *it* **on the horns of the altar of burnt offering, and pour its blood at the base of the altar of burnt offering. And he shall burn all its fat on the altar, like the fat of the sacrifice of the peace offering. So the priest shall make atonement for him concerning his sin, and it shall be forgiven him.**

a. **When a ruler has sinned**: The procedure was similar to, yet distinct from, the offering for a priest or the nation at large.

i. Clarke on **ruler**: "Under the term *nasi*, it is probable that any person is meant who held any kind of political dignity among the people, though the rabbins generally understand it of the *king*."

b. **If his sin which he has committed comes to his knowledge**: We can't specifically deal with our sins until we know we have committed them. When we do become aware of those sins, we are responsible to confess them and deal with them in light of God's sacrifice, ultimately fulfilled in the sacrificial death of Jesus on the cross.

c. **He shall bring as his offering a kid of the goats**: The sin offering for a **ruler** was a *lesser* animal than that for the priest or the nation as a whole. This demonstrates that the **ruler** was not greater than God (represented by the priests) or the people as a whole.

d. **The priest shall take**: After the ruler **lay his hand on the head of the goat**, the animal was killed and its blood drained. The blood never came into the tent of meeting as was the case with the sin offering for a priest (Leviticus 4:3-12) or for the people as a whole (Leviticus 4:13-21). The blood was wiped **on the horns of the altar of burnt offering**, and the remaining blood was poured out **at the base of the altar of burnt offering**.

e. **He shall burn all its fat on the altar**: The fat was burned before the LORD, but according to Leviticus 6:24-30, the rest of the animal was available for the priest.

5. (27-35) The sin offering for a common man or woman.

'If anyone of the common people sins unintentionally by doing *something against* any of the commandments of the LORD *in anything* which ought not to be done, and is guilty, or if his sin which he has committed comes to his knowledge, then he shall bring as his offering a kid of the goats, a female without blemish, for his sin which he has committed. And he shall lay his hand on the head of the sin offering, and kill the sin offering at the place of the burnt offering. Then the priest shall take *some* of its blood with his finger, put *it* on the horns of the altar of burnt offering, and pour all *the remaining* blood at the base of the altar. He shall remove all its fat, as fat is removed from the sacrifice of the peace offering; and the priest shall burn it on the altar for a sweet aroma to the LORD. So the priest shall make atonement for him, and it shall be forgiven him.

'If he brings a lamb as his sin offering, he shall bring a female without blemish. Then he shall lay his hand on the head of the sin offering, and kill it as a sin offering at the place where they kill the burnt offering. The priest shall take *some* of the blood of the sin offering with his finger, put *it* on the horns of the altar of burnt offering, and pour all *the remaining* blood at the base of the altar. He shall remove all its fat, as the fat of the lamb is removed from the sacrifice of the peace offering. Then the priest shall burn it on the altar, according to the offerings made by fire to the LORD. So the priest shall make atonement for his sin that he has committed, and it shall be forgiven him.

a. **If anyone of the common people sins unintentionally**: This was the same procedure for a ruler of the people, except that a female goat or a lamb could be offered instead of a male goat.

i. The point is obvious and must not be overlooked: *God cares about the unintentional sins of common people.* "It is very needful, then, for us to be perpetually cleansed in the precious blood of Christ. We must ask to be forgiven for the many sins which we know not, as well as for those we know. The work of confession and forgiveness must therefore go on to life's end, applied to each heart and conscience by the Holy Spirit." (Meyer)

ii. "It is true the sins of great men cover a larger space, but yet there must be a bloody sacrifice for the smallest offenses. For the sins of a housewife or of a servant, of a peasant, or of a crossing-sweeper, there must be the same sacrifice as for the sins of the greatest and most influential." (Spurgeon)

b. **He shall bring as his offering**: After the common person **lay his hand on the head of the sin offering**, the animal was killed and its blood drained. The blood never came into the tent of meeting as was the case with the sin offering for a priest (Leviticus 4:3-12) or for the people as a whole (Leviticus 4:13-21). The blood was wiped **on the horns of the altar of burnt offering**, and the remaining blood was poured out **at the base of the altar** of burnt offering.

i. "Sometimes, according to the Rabbis, those who brought the victim leaned with all their might, and pressed upon it as if they seemed to say by the act, "I put the whole burden, weight, and force of my sin upon this unblemished victim." O my soul, lean hard on Christ, throw all the weight of thy sin upon him, for he is able to bear it and came on purpose to bear it." (Spurgeon)

ii. The constant reference to **blood** is unmistakable. "There are many ways by which men may die without the shedding of blood; the capital punishment of our own country is free from this accompaniment; but our Saviour was ordained to die by a death in which the shedding of blood was conspicuous, as if to link him forever with those sacrifices

which were made as types and symbols of his great atoning work."
(Spurgeon)

c. **Then the priest shall burn it on the altar, according to the offerings made by fire to the LORD**: Again, presumably, the rest of the animal was available for the priest. This meant that the sin offering for a civil ruler or common man was less costly than the sin offering for a priest or the nation as a whole, and that the only profit a priest could gain from his own sin offering was spiritual, not material.

Leviticus 5 – The Trespass Offering and the Guilt Offering

A. Specific occasions requiring the trespass offering.

1. (1) Failing to be a truthful witness, or being a false witness.

'If a person sins in hearing the utterance of an oath, and *is* a witness, whether he has seen or known *of the matter*—if he does not tell *it*, he bears guilt.

a. **If a person sins in hearing the utterance of an oath, and is a witness, whether he has seen or known of the matter**: It wasn't enough to merely not tell lies. God also required His people to make the truth known, so even if one merely *knew about a lie*, they were responsible to make the truth known.

b. **If he does not tell it, he bears guilt**: Therefore, it was the duty of someone who was a witness to come forward and tell the truth about the matter. To fail in faithfully representing the truth was to bear **guilt**.

i. "In Israel all the people were to be involved in seeing that justice was done. Not to witness was a sin." (Harris)

ii. "He shall suffer for his sinful silence; because he could, but would not, help the truth in necessity, but stand as if he were gagged by Satan." (Trapp)

iii. We can say that the same principle applies to our witness of Jesus Christ. It isn't enough that we refrain from actively denying Jesus or lying about our relationship with Him. We must also take every opportunity to tell the truth about Jesus.

2. (2-3) Ceremonial uncleanness.

'Or if a person touches any unclean thing, whether *it is* the carcass of an unclean beast, or the carcass of unclean livestock, or the carcass of

unclean creeping things, and he is unaware of it, he also shall be unclean and guilty. Or if he touches human uncleanness—whatever uncleanness with which a man may be defiled, and he is unaware of it—when he realizes *it*, then he shall be guilty.

a. **If a person touches any unclean thing**: The cleansing of the sin offering was also necessary when a person became ceremonially unclean through touching **any unclean thing**. This could happen accidentally or purposefully, but if a person touched **any unclean thing**, they had to be ceremonially cleansed. This was *ceremonial* guilt, not moral guilt.

b. **Whether it is the carcass of an unclean beast.... Or if he touches human uncleanness**: There were several things that might make a person ceremonially unclean. These included touching the **carcass of an unclean** animal or a person who was already ceremonially unclean. The sin offering was a remedy for this uncleanness.

i. "Either the *dead* body of a *clean* animal, or the *living* or *dead carcass* of any *unclean* creature. All such persons were to wash their clothes and themselves in clean water, and were considered as unclean till the evening, chap. 11:24-31. But if this had been neglected, they were obliged to bring a *trespass-offering*." (Clarke)

c. **When he realizes it, then he shall be guilty**: In this context, the guilt did not begin when he realized it; he was guilty when he committed the sin. However, **when he realizes it**, then he was responsible for dealing with the sin as God commanded. We must deal with sin as we become aware of it, under the work of the Holy Spirit upon our heart and conscience.

3. (4) Swearing a false oath.

'Or if a person swears, speaking thoughtlessly with *his* lips to do evil or to do good, whatever *it is* that a man may pronounce by an oath, and he is unaware of it—when he realizes *it*, then he shall be guilty in any of these *matters*.

a. **If a person swears, speaking thoughtlessly**: A careless promise was still a promise before the LORD and had to be observed. If the promise was not kept it had to be atoned for by a sin offering.

b. **When he realizes it, then he shall be guilty**: When we are aware of our broken vows, we must repent of them. It is common to make vows and promises in the Christian life that are not kept, and when we see this we must repent and trust in the atoning, covering blood of Jesus to bring forgiveness.

i. Think of these common examples of broken vows:

- To spend more time in prayer.

- To make more intercession for others.

- To do more devotional reading.

- To practice more intense Bible study.

- To be more of a personal witness.

- To be more faithful in tithing.

- To live as a better example to others.

- To have more patience with the children.

- To be pure in sexual matters.

ii. It may not be wrong to make such vows. They may be the legitimate, decisive expression of a move of the Holy Spirit in a person's life. Yet if the vow is not kept, it must be confessed as sin and repented of.

B. The Trespass Offering.

1. (5) Preparation for the trespass offering.

'And it shall be, when he is guilty in any of these *matters,* that he shall confess that he has sinned in that *thing*;

a. **When he is guilty**: This more has the sense of "when he realizes his guilt." Though a person is guilty of sin the moment he commits the sin, he has no idea he needs to make atonement for the sin until he *realizes* his sin (5:3-4).

b. **He shall confess**: This was an important preparation for the trespass offering. To **confess** meant one would agree with God that the sin was wrong. If there was not confession of sin before the sacrifice, then the sacrifice would do no good. Confession of crossing God's boundary is still an important principle for clearing away sin that hinders our fellowship with God.

i. "Confession is taking God's side against ourselves. It is the act of judging evil in the light of the Throne. It is like the unpacking of a box, in which one begins with the lighter things at the top, and works steadily down to the heavy articles underneath." (Meyer)

ii. According to Rooker, the Hebrew word translated **confess** is from the root word with the meaning "expose or reveal" and can be rendered "confess" or "praise." "The connection between these two concepts is determined by whether the focus of the action is upon God or man. If man is the object, the idea of confession of sin is paramount; but if God is the object, the notion of praise is called for."

iii. The proper confession of sin is a neglected practice among modern believers. There is a lack of serious recognition and confession of sin, both to God (1 John 1:9) and to others (James 5:16). We don't need to confess to a priest, but for the sake of honesty, humility, accountability, and cleansing more confession of sin should be made "one to another" (as in James 5:16).

iv. Real, deep, genuine confession of sin has been a feature of every genuine awakening or revival in the past 250 years. But it isn't anything new, as demonstrated by the revival in Ephesus recorded in Acts 19:17-20. It says, *many who believed came confessing and telling their deeds.* This was *Christians* getting right with God, and open confession was part of it.

2. (6-7) Presenting the trespass offering.

And he shall bring his trespass offering to the LORD for his sin which he has committed, a female from the flock, a lamb or a kid of the goats as a sin offering. So the priest shall make atonement for him concerning his sin. 'If he is not able to bring a lamb, then he shall bring to the LORD, for his trespass which he has committed, two turtledoves or two young pigeons: one as a sin offering and the other as a burnt offering.

a. **His trespass offering to the LORD**: A **trespass** is a particular kind of sin (**for his sin which he has committed**). *Trespassing* is the unlawful crossing of a boundary. God has certain boundaries for humanity in general and for His people specifically, and when they cross those boundaries it is a sin of **trespass**.

i. It's important to remember that according to verse 5, this had to be preceded by confession of sin. "The necessity of confession indicated that forgiveness for the Israelite could not be attained simply by following the prescribed procedure given for a sacrifice. This would be tantamount to magic, which the Old Testament condemns." (Rooker)

b. **Two turtledoves or two young pigeons; one as a sin offering and the other as a burnt offering**: The trespass offering of a poor Israelite shows how it was really two offerings in one. It was a **sin offering**, to make atonement for the sin of trespass. It was also a **burnt offering**, to express renewed, complete commitment to walking within God's boundaries.

3. (8-10) The priest presents the trespass offering of the poor man.

And he shall bring them to the priest, who shall offer *that* which *is* for the sin offering first, and wring off its head from its neck, but shall not divide *it* completely. Then he shall sprinkle *some* of the blood of the sin offering on the side of the altar, and the rest of the blood shall be

drained out at the base of the altar. It *is* a sin offering. And he shall offer the second *as* a burnt offering according to the prescribed manner. So the priest shall make atonement on his behalf for his sin which he has committed, and it shall be forgiven him.

a. **For the sin offering first**: The offering for atonement always came **first**. Sin had to be dealt with before the **burnt offering** could be made (which was a picture of renewed commitment and consecration).

b. **It shall be forgiven him**: God assured the one who brought the trespass offering that sin would be **forgiven** if the sacrifice was made according to God's **prescribed manner**.

4. (11-13) The priest presents the trespass offering of the poorest man.

'**But if he is not able to bring two turtledoves or two young pigeons, then he who sinned shall bring for his offering one-tenth of an ephah of fine flour as a sin offering. He shall put no oil on it, nor shall he put frankincense on it, for it *is* a sin offering. Then he shall bring it to the priest, and the priest shall take his handful of it as a memorial portion, and burn *it* on the altar according to the offerings made by fire to the LORD. It *is* a sin offering. The priest shall make atonement for him, for his sin that he has committed in any of these matters; and it shall be forgiven him. *The rest* shall be the priest's as a grain offering.'**

a. **If he is not able to bring two turtledoves or two young pigeons**: Cleansing from trespass was available to everyone, even if they couldn't offer a sheep or a goat, or even if they could not afford to bring birds as an offering. If a man was too poor to offer two birds, even **fine flour** could be offered as a sin offering.

i. The other side of this principle was also true. If a person *could* offer a greater sacrifice, it would be a sin to offer a lesser one. "If a man's means sufficed for the appointed lamb or a goat, and he brought two turtle doves or pigeons, or a tenth part of an ephah of fine flour, such action would show that he had no adequate sense, either of his own sin, or of the Divine grace." (Morgan)

b. **He who sinned shall bring for his offering one-tenth of an ephah of fine flour as a sin offering**: We see in this that it was not so much the *substance* of the sacrifice that was important, but the heart of the one who brought the offering. In some sacrifices, the shedding of blood was essential for the forgiveness of sins (Hebrews 9:22). But when it came to the walk of a humble, poor Israelite believer, God looked to the heart and not the nature of the sacrifice itself. It could be said of the one who properly brought a flour offering, **it shall be forgiven him**.

i. **Put no oil on it, nor shall he put frankincense on it**: In the grain offering of the poorest Israelite, they could not add oil or frankincense. "In the normal presentation of the grain offering these elements would accompany the sacrifice and would accentuate the joy of the occasion. Because in this exceptional case the grain offering was being substituted for the sin offering; those elements that would be associated with joy are omitted." (Rooker)

ii. When we see how strongly the principle of atonement by sacrifice is emphasized in the Old Testament, many people wonder why the Jewish people today no longer make sacrifices. The most common answer is that they believe their good works will substitute for animal sacrifice.

iii. "Indeed, when the second temple fell, the rabbis, denied an altar in Jerusalem, came to the conclusion that gifts and prayers were as acceptable as animal sacrifice." (Harris)

C. The Guilt Offering.

1. (14-16) The procedure for the guilt offering.

Then the LORD spoke to Moses, saying: "If a person commits a trespass, and sins unintentionally in regard to the holy things of the LORD, then he shall bring to the LORD as his trespass offering a ram without blemish from the flocks, with your valuation in shekels of silver according to the shekel of the sanctuary, as a trespass offering. And he shall make restitution for the harm that he has done in regard to the holy thing, and shall add one-fifth to it and give it to the priest. So the priest shall make atonement for him with the ram of the trespass offering, and it shall be forgiven him.

a. **If a person commits a trespass**: The guilt offering was essentially the same procedure used in the sin offering, except that the guilt offering was used when someone had sinned **in regard to the holy things**. This spoke of some type of desecration of the tabernacle or its associated items.

i. According to Peter-Contesse, the literal sense is more, *if a person trespasses a trespass* – that is, that the "noun and the verb have the same root. This is a rather emphatic addition."

b. **In regard to the holy things of the LORD**: These included the firstfruits (Leviticus 2:14, 23:9-14), the firstborn (Leviticus 27:26-27), the tithe (Leviticus 27:30-33, Deuteronomy 14:22-29), and vowed offerings (Leviticus 27:1-25, Numbers 30:1-16). When an Israelite failed to fulfill these, they had to make this atonement. This was something of a "repayment offering."

c. **He shall make restitution for the harm that he has done in regard to the holy thing**: When holy things had been desecrated in some way, a mere sin offering was not enough. Restitution was also required, paying back what was lost plus twenty percent (he **shall add one-fifth to it**).

> i. "If one has been unfaithful in the holy things of Jehovah it is not enough that one should confess and bring a sin-offering. Restitution must be made for the wrong done; it must be put right. There was something due to God that was not rendered in its season, and things will not be right until it is rendered." (Coates)

> ii. With the guilt offering, the priest was allowed to keep the hide of a bull that was sacrificed (Leviticus 7:8).

2. (17-19) The necessity of the guilt offering even when a person did not know they had sinned in regard to the holy things.

"If a person sins, and commits any of these things which are forbidden to be done by the commandments of the Lord, though he does not know *it*, yet he is guilty and shall bear his iniquity. And he shall bring to the priest a ram without blemish from the flock, with your valuation, as a trespass offering. So the priest shall make atonement for him regarding his ignorance in which he erred and did not know *it*, and it shall be forgiven him. It is a trespass offering; he has certainly trespassed against the Lord."

a. **Though he does not know it, yet he is guilty and shall bear his iniquity**: If someone desecrated the holy things of the tabernacle, "I didn't know" was not an acceptable excuse. They had to still make a sacrifice to atone for their sin.

> i. Sins of ignorance do differ from sins done with knowledge in the degree of guilt. Jesus said so in Luke 12:47-48: *And that servant who knew his master's will, and did not prepare himself or do according to his will, shall be beaten with many stripes. But he who did not know, yet committed things deserving of stripes, shall be beaten with few.*

> ii. Yet, it is important and necessary to remember that one may be guilty of sin without feeling it or thinking it so. "If, again, the guilt of an action depended entirely upon a man's knowledge, we should have no fixed standard at all by which to judge right and wrong: it would be variable according to the enlightenment of each man, and there would be no ultimate and infallible court of appeal.... The art of forgetting

would be diligently studied, and ignorance would become an enviable inheritance." (Spurgeon)

b. **So the priest shall make atonement for him regarding his ignorance in which he erred and did not know it**: Atonement had to be made, even for sins done in **ignorance**. It is no excuse; the one who sins in ignorance has still **certainly trespassed against the LORD**.

i. "Ignorance of the law of God is itself a breach of law, since we are bidden to know and remember it." (Spurgeon)

Leviticus 6 – Instructions for the Priests

A. More instances for performing the guilt offering.

1. (1-3) Stealing from one's neighbor made a guilt offering necessary.

And the LORD spoke to Moses, saying: "If a person sins and commits a trespass against the LORD by lying to his neighbor about what was delivered to him for safekeeping, or about a pledge, or about a robbery, or if he has extorted from his neighbor, or if he has found what was lost and lies concerning it, and swears falsely—in any one of these things that a man may do in which he sins:

a. **If a person sins and commits a trespass against the LORD**: This continues the section starting at Leviticus 5:14 regarding the guilt offering. Here we see that the guilt offering was required in cases of theft. Sins of lying and deception are also mentioned but these are in connection with lying in order to steal from someone else.

i. We note that it says, **against the LORD**. These were obviously sins against other people but they were also sins against God and had to be dealt with as such.

b. **In any one of these things that a man may do in which he sins**: People may steal through simple **robbery**, or use deception to take what does not belong to them (**lying to his neighbor about what was delivered to him for safekeeping, or about a pledge**). There are many ways to steal but all of them are **sins**.

i. **Extorted from his neighbor**: "The idea here is of one gaining something that belongs to another person by means other than outright theft. It usually involves trickery of some kind." (Peter-Contesse)

ii. All this is founded on a basic idea clearly stated in Exodus 20:15: *You shall not steal.* Every command against stealing in the Bible is a recognition of the right to personal property; that God trusts people

47

to manage property as delegated "owners" of that property. Since ultimately all things belong to God (Psalm 24:1), men only "own" things that are delegated to them by God. Yet, God expects humanity to respect His delegation of property, and other people or states are not permitted to take that property without due process of law.

iii. Therefore, economic or political systems that reject the principle of the private ownership of property – such as communist or socialist systems, which claim that all property belongs to the state or the collective – those systems reject God's wisdom and will and are destined for failure.

2. (4-6) Restitution for the theft had to be made, then the guilt offering.

Then it shall be, because he has sinned and is guilty, that he shall restore what he has stolen, or the thing which he has extorted, or what was delivered to him for safekeeping, or the lost thing which he found, or all that about which he has sworn falsely. He shall restore its full value, add one-fifth more to it, *and* give it to whomever it belongs, on the day of his trespass offering. And he shall bring his trespass offering to the LORD, a ram without blemish from the flock, with your valuation, as a trespass offering, to the priest.

a. **He shall restore what he has stolen**: If a person was guilty of fraud or theft, it wasn't enough to make a sacrifice to cover the guilt of the sin before God. They first had to make restitution to settle the account with the victim of the fraud.

i. **For safekeeping**: Matthew Poole thought that this was a Hebraic way of referring to business or trading. "Which is very usual, when one man puts anything into another's hand, not to keep it…but to use and improve it for the common benefit of them both, in which cases of partnership it is easy for one to deceive the other, and therefore provision is here made against it."

b. **He shall restore its full value, add one-fifth more to it, and give it to whomever it belongs, on the day of his trespass offering**: It wasn't enough to just *return* what was stolen. The thief also had to add 20% (**one-fifth**) to what was stolen as a penalty.

i. In the New Testament, Ephesians 4:28 expresses another aspect of restitution when the thief repents of being a taker and becomes a giver: *Let him who stole steal no longer, but rather let him labor, working with his hands what is good, that he may have something to give him who has need.*

c. **And he shall bring his trespass offering to the** LORD: Restitution and the penalty that went with it had to be made the same **day of his trespass offering**. This powerfully demonstrated that one could *not* get right with God without also making the wrong right with men.

> i. This urgency of making things right with other people before we make things right with God is the same idea Jesus communicated in Matthew 5:23-24.

3. (7) The certainty of forgiveness when the sacrifice is made.

So the priest shall make atonement for him before the LORD, **and he shall be forgiven for any one of these things that he may have done in which he trespasses."**

a. **So the priest shall make atonement for him before the** LORD: This was a marvelous assurance for a guilty conscience. The sinner could depend upon this promise and know his sin was covered before the LORD.

> i. The New Testament makes a similar statement in light of the New Covenant, found in 1 John 1:9: *If we confess our sins, He is faithful and just to forgive us our sins and to cleanse us from all unrighteousness.*

b. **For any one of these things that he may have done**: The emphasis is that *any* sin can be cleansed through an atoning sacrifice. Before the perfect work of Jesus on the cross the cleansing was not perfect, but it could be extended to any sin – in anticipation of the Messiah's perfect sacrifice to come.

B. Specific instructions for the priests regarding the offerings.

1. (8-13) The burnt offering.

Then the LORD **spoke to Moses, saying, "Command Aaron and his sons, saying, 'This** *is* **the law of the burnt offering: The burnt offering** *shall be* **on the hearth upon the altar all night until morning, and the fire of the altar shall be kept burning on it. And the priest shall put on his linen garment, and his linen trousers he shall put on his body, and take up the ashes of the burnt offering which the fire has consumed on the altar, and he shall put them beside the altar. Then he shall take off his garments, put on other garments, and carry the ashes outside the camp to a clean place. And the fire on the altar shall be kept burning on it; it shall not be put out. And the priest shall burn wood on it every morning, and lay the burnt offering in order on it; and he shall burn on it the fat of the peace offerings. A fire shall always be burning on the altar; it shall never go out.**

a. **This is the law of the burnt offering**: This offering was previously described in chapter 1 and spoke of *consecration*. The animal had to remain upon the altar in a slow burn for a long time, tended by the priest (**shall be on the hearth upon the altar all night until morning**).

> i. "We may therefore reasonably conclude that the priests sat up by turns the whole night, and fed the fire with *portions* of this offering till the whole was consumed." (Clarke)

> ii. The description given in chapter 1 did not include the instruction regarding the required garments of the priest (**his linen garment, and his linen trousers he shall put on his body**). It also did not include the direction for the priest to deposit the **ashes** of the burned sacrifice **outside the camp to a clean place**, once he had taken off his priestly **garments**.

> iii. These linen garments for the priests are described in Exodus 28:39-43.

b. **And the fire of the altar shall be kept burning on it**: The long-burning character of the burnt offering is an appropriate illustration of the work of giving ourselves completely to God. Coming to God as a living sacrifice is not a quick work and we may feel that we, like the **burnt offering**, endure the heat of the fire for a long time.

> i. "Does the perpetual fire burn on the altar of *thy* heart? Art *thou* ever looking unto Jesus, and beholding, by faith, the Lamb of God which taketh away the sin of the world?" (Clarke)

c. **The priest shall burn wood on it every morning**: The provision of wood for the altar is later the subject of Nehemiah 10:34 and 13:31. Together with the sacrifices themselves, this **wood** was the fuel for the fire on the altar.

d. **A fire shall always be burning on the altar; it shall never go out**: The phrasing of this is emphatic (according to Peter-Contesse) and shows that keeping the altar fire always **burning** was an important duty of the priests. They had to supply wood to the altar fire through the night. Through the day, the continual offering of sacrifices would keep the fire burning.

> i. As it happened, the altar's fire was ignited by miraculous fire coming from heaven (Leviticus 9:24). This added to the reason why the altar's fire should never be allowed to go out. This was *God's fire*, and it needed to be respected and cared for.

> ii. John Trapp considered that the fire of the altar should not go out and made application of the idea: "No more should our faith, love, zeal (that flame of God, as Solomon calls it, Song of Solomon 8:6-7),

that should never go out; the waters should not quench it, nor the ashes cover it."

iii. F.B. Meyer observed that the perpetual fire was an emblem of:

- *God's love*, because there was never and will never be a time when God does not love.

- *The prayers of Jesus for His people*, because He forever lives to pray for His people (Hebrews 7:25).

- *The ministry of the Holy Spirit*, because the fire first lit on the Day of Pentecost still burns among the people of God.

iv. The perpetual fire was also connected to the idea that these sacrifices must be continually offered. The perfect sacrifice Jesus made on the cross did not need to be a continual sacrifice; it was a once-for-all sacrifice, as described in Hebrews 7:27: *who does not need daily, as those high priests, to offer up sacrifices, first for His own sins and then for the people's, for this He did once for all when He offered up Himself.*

2. (14-18) The ceremony of the grain offering.

'This *is* the law of the grain offering: The sons of Aaron shall offer it on the altar before the Lord. He shall take from it his handful of the fine flour of the grain offering, with its oil, and all the frankincense which *is* on the grain offering, and shall burn *it* on the altar *for* a sweet aroma, as a memorial to the Lord. And the remainder of it Aaron and his sons shall eat; with unleavened bread it shall be eaten in a holy place; in the court of the tabernacle of meeting they shall eat it. It shall not be baked with leaven. I have given it *as* their portion of My offerings made by fire; it *is* most holy, like the sin offering and the trespass offering. All the males among the children of Aaron may eat it. *It shall be* a statute forever in your generations concerning the offerings made by fire to the Lord. Everyone who touches them must be holy.'"

a. **This is the law of the grain offering**: This offering was first mentioned in chapter 2. This portion repeats most of the same details of the **grain offering** given in chapter 2.

b. **Everyone who touches them must be holy**: One aspect of the **grain offering** specifically detailed here, but not included in chapter 2, is that not only was a portion of the offering given to the priests, but only those who were ceremonially clean (**holy**) could eat of it.

3. (19-23) The grain offering at the anointing of the priests.

And the Lord spoke to Moses, saying, "This *is* the offering of Aaron and his sons, which they shall offer to the Lord, *beginning* on the day when he is anointed: one-tenth of an ephah of fine flour as a daily grain offering, half of it in the morning and half of it at night. It shall be made in a pan with oil. *When it is* mixed, you shall bring it in. The baked pieces of the grain offering you shall offer *for* a sweet aroma to the LORD. The priest from among his sons, who is anointed in his place, shall offer it. *It is* a statute forever to the LORD. It shall be wholly burned. For every grain offering for the priest shall be wholly burned. It shall not be eaten."

a. **Beginning on the day when he is anointed**: There was a particular grain offering that was part of the anointing and consecration ceremony for a priest. This general ceremony was first described in Exodus 29 and was carried out in Leviticus 8.

i. **The baked pieces**: "Or *fried*, so that it swells and bubbles up." (Poole)

b. **For every grain offering for the priest shall be wholly burned**: In the normal grain offering, part of the grain went to the priests and they made bread from it for the priest and his family. But the grain offering associated with the anointing ceremony for the priests was not to **be eaten**, it was to be **wholly burned** before the LORD.

4. (24-30) The sin offering.

Also the LORD spoke to Moses, saying, "Speak to Aaron and to his sons, saying, 'This *is* the law of the sin offering: In the place where the burnt offering is killed, the sin offering shall be killed before the LORD. It *is* most holy. The priest who offers it for sin shall eat it. In a holy place it shall be eaten, in the court of the tabernacle of meeting. Everyone who touches its flesh must be holy. And when its blood is sprinkled on any garment, you shall wash that on which it was sprinkled, in a holy place. But the earthen vessel in which it is boiled shall be broken. And if it is boiled in a bronze pot, it shall be both scoured and rinsed in water. All the males among the priests may eat it. It *is* most holy. But no sin offering from which *any* of the blood is brought into the tabernacle of meeting, to make atonement in the holy *place*, shall be eaten. It shall be burned in the fire.

a. **This is the law of the sin offering**: The sin offering was first described in chapter 4. Here, a few additional details are added for the proper sacrifice of the **sin offering**.

b. **The priest who offers it for sin shall eat it**: In some cases, a portion of the meat from the **sin offering** was to be given to the priest who did the work of sacrificing the animal.

c. **In a holy place it shall be eaten…. Everyone who touches its flesh must be holy**: However, the meat from the **sin offering** had to be regarded as **holy**, and everything connected to the eating of it had to be holy (ceremonially clean).

- The place had to be holy (**in the court of the tabernacle of meeting**).

- The person preparing or eating the meat had to be holy (**Everyone who touches its flesh must be holy**).

- The blood from the meat was holy (**you shall wash that on which it was sprinkled**).

- The pot it was cooked in was holy (**the earthen vessel in which it is boiled shall be broken…. in a bronze pot, it shall be both scoured and rinsed in water**).

  i. Anything touched by the meat of the **sin offering** or its blood had to be holy or be cleansed in a special manner because the animal's meat was thought to be infected with the sin of the one who brought the offering.

  ii. When sin "soaks in" to something, there is no way it can be cleansed, and it must be destroyed. Yet a metal, tempered by fire, has already been "judged" – and can therefore simply be cleansed. This is an illustration that those who do not have their sin cleansed by Jesus will be destroyed by that sin in an eternal sense.

d. **But no sin offering from which any of the blood is brought into the tabernacle of meeting, to make atonement in the holy place, shall be eaten**: In chapter 4, a distinction is made between the sin offering for a priest, for Israel as a whole, for a ruler, and for the common person. For the sin offering made for a priest or for Israel as a whole, there was no portion of the animal that could be eaten.

Leviticus 7 – More Instructions for the Priests

A. The Trespass Offering.

1. (1-2) The killing of the trespass offering.

'Likewise this *is* the law of the trespass offering (it *is* most holy): In the place where they kill the burnt offering they shall kill the trespass offering. And its blood he shall sprinkle all around on the altar.

a. **This is the law of the trespass offering**: The procedure for the **trespass offering** was previously described in chapter 5. Here, a specific detail is added, explaining that the trespass offering had to be made at the altar of **burnt offering**; the central altar at the tabernacle and later the temple.

i. A **trespass** is a particular kind of sin. *Trespassing* is the unlawful crossing of a boundary. God has certain boundaries for humanity in general and for His people specifically, and when they cross those boundaries it is a sin of **trespass**. Leviticus 5:5 also explained that the trespass offering must begin with the confession of sin.

b. **Its blood he shall sprinkle all around on the altar**: The blood of the trespass offering did not need to be brought into the tabernacle or temple. It could simply be sprinkled **all around on the altar**.

i. **They shall kill the trespass offering**: "The verb *kill* actually means 'slaughter,' that is, to cut the throat of the animal." (Peter-Contesse)

2. (3-5) The offering of the fat of the trespass offering.

And he shall offer from it all its fat. The fat tail and the fat that covers the entrails, the two kidneys and the fat that *is* on them by the flanks, and the fatty lobe *attached* to the liver above the kidneys, he shall remove; and the priest shall burn them on the altar *as* an offering made by fire to the LORD. It *is* a trespass offering.

a. **He shall offer from it all its fat**: When the trespass offering is described in chapter 5, the focus is on the reasons why it would be necessary to make the offering. It said nothing of what to do with the blood or the fat of the sacrificial animal. Here, the priest is instructed to offer the fatty portions of the animal.

i. Adam Clarke clarified the sense of **all its fat**: "Chiefly the fat that was found in a *detached state*, not mixed with the muscles."

b. **The priest shall burn them on the altar as an offering**: As was normally done, the fatty portions of the trespass offering were burnt upon the altar.

3. (6-10) What belongs to the priests from the offerings.

Every male among the priests may eat it. It shall be eaten in a holy place. It *is* most holy. The trespass offering *is* like the sin offering; *there is* one law for them both: the priest who makes atonement with it shall have *it*. And the priest who offers anyone's burnt offering, that priest shall have for himself the skin of the burnt offering which he has offered. Also every grain offering that is baked in the oven and all that is prepared in the covered pan, or in a pan, shall be the priest's who offers it. Every grain offering, *whether* mixed with oil, or dry, shall belong to all the sons of Aaron, to one *as much* as the other.

a. **Every male among the priests may eat it**: The trespass offering followed a similar pattern to previous sacrifices. The blood and the fat belonged to God and the meat portions could be shared among the priests, with its distribution determined by the priest who actually performed the **trespass** offering or the **sin** offering (**the priest who makes atonement with it shall have it**).

b. **That priest shall have for himself the skin of the burnt offering which he has offered**: With the burnt offering (also described in chapter 1), the priest who made the sacrifice was also given the skin of the animal to use for leather or another purpose.

c. **Baked in the oven and all that is prepared in the covered pan, or in a pan**: The grain offerings prepared in the **oven**, the **covered pan**, and the **pan** were first mentioned in Leviticus 2:4-7. Here, it is made clear that a portion of those offerings belongs to the priest.

i. John Trapp noted how the ancient Christian writer Origen thought of these three items (the **oven**, the **covered pan**, and the **pan**) in an excessively allegorical way: "Here Origen, according to his manner, turns all into allegories and mysteries, and tells us of a threefold sense of Scripture, (1.) Literal; (2.) Moral; (3.) Mystical: comparing them to the gridiron, frying pan, and oven, used in dressing the meat offering. But this itch of allegorising dark and difficult texts hath no small danger in it. And I may doubt of Origen, as one doth of Jerome, whether he did more harm or good to the Church."

d. **Shall belong to all the sons of Aaron, to one as much as the other**: With the **grain offering** (previously described in chapter 2), the distribution was the responsibility of the priest who made the offering, but he was supposed to make sure that the portions were distributed equally.

B. The Peace Offering.

1. (11-14) Bread and cakes given with the peace offering.

'This *is* the law of the sacrifice of peace offerings which he shall offer to the LORD: If he offers it for a thanksgiving, then he shall offer, with the sacrifice of thanksgiving, unleavened cakes mixed with oil, unleavened wafers anointed with oil, or cakes of blended flour mixed with oil. Besides the cakes, *as* his offering he shall offer leavened bread with the sacrifice of thanksgiving of his peace offering. And from it he shall offer one cake from each offering *as* a heave offering to the LORD. It shall belong to the priest who sprinkles the blood of the peace offering.

a. **The law of the sacrifice of the peace offerings**: The **peace offerings** were previously mentioned in chapter 3. The peace offering was normally the sacrifice of an animal (Leviticus 3:1-2) and often made **for a thanksgiving**.

b. **He shall offer…unleavened cakes mixed with oil**: Along with the animal sacrifice of the **peace offering**, there was to be made an offering of some kind of baked good, either **unleavened cakes** or **wafers**, each made with **oil**.

c. **He shall offer leavened bread**: In addition to the **unleavened cakes** or **wafers**, the peace offering was to be made with **leavened bread**.

i. The prohibition of leaven in any offering (Leviticus 2:11) was apparently only relevant to those things which were burnt upon the altar. This leavened bread that was part of the peace offering ceremony was not offered upon the altar but presented in a heave offering. Leviticus 23:17 also describes leavened bread used in a wave offering.

ii. In the symbolism of the sacrificial system, this is fascinating. The peace offering was accompanied by the priest holding before God unleavened bread in one hand and leavened bread in the other. In some ritual manner, the unleavened and the leavened were waved before the LORD. From a New Testament perspective, we may connect this to the fact that Jesus Christ has made peace between Jew and Gentile, breaking down the wall that previously separated them (Ephesians

2:11-18), and Jesus Christ Himself *is our peace* (Ephesians 2:14) because of the sacrifice He made of His own flesh (Ephesians 2:15).

ii. "The Peace Offering is supremely the symbol of communion based on reconciliation. It is the offering which symbolises two sides to a great transaction; one of those is that of God, at the other is that of man. God and man are at peace. The Godward side can only be symbolised by that which is unleavened, free from all evil, separated from everything that tends to corruption. On the other hand, there remains in man much of imperfection. This is symbolised by the leavened cakes." (Morgan)

d. **He shall offer one cake from each offering as a heave offering to the LORD**: Apparently, when the peace offering was made (especially as a **sacrifice of thanksgiving**), there was also to be this **heave offering** made with both an unleavened cake or wafer, and with leavened bread.

i. Trapp on the **heave offering**: "So called, because it was heaved and lifted up before the Lord, in token that they received all from him, and did acknowledge all to be due to him."

ii. Adam Clarke says this regarding the **heave offering**, indicating that it comes from the Hebrew word "to *lift up*, because the offering was *lifted up* towards heaven, as the *wave*-offering, in token of the kindness of God in granting rain and fruitful seasons, and filling the heart with food and gladness. As the wave-offering was moved from *right* to *left*, so the heave-offering was moved *up* and *down*; and in both cases this was done several times."

2. (15-18) When to eat the meat of the peace offering.

'The flesh of the sacrifice of his peace offering for thanksgiving shall be eaten the same day it is offered. He shall not leave any of it until morning. But if the sacrifice of his offering *is* a vow or a voluntary offering, it shall be eaten the same day that he offers his sacrifice; but on the next day the remainder of it also may be eaten; the remainder of the flesh of the sacrifice on the third day must be burned with fire. And if *any* of the flesh of the sacrifice of his peace offering is eaten at all on the third day, it shall not be accepted, nor shall it be imputed to him; it shall be an abomination *to* him who offers it, and the person who eats of it shall bear guilt.

a. **His peace offering for thanksgiving shall be eaten the same day it is offered**: The **peace offering** could be made for a few different reasons, including for **thanksgiving** or for **a vow or a voluntary offering**.

b. **Shall be eaten the same day**: When the peace offering was made for thanksgiving, the meat had to be eaten on the day of the sacrifice. When it was made for a vow or a voluntary offering, it could also be eaten **on the next day**.

i. "Thanks must be returned while mercies are fresh; lest, as fish, they putrify with keeping." (Trapp)

c. **If any of the flesh of the sacrifice of his peace offering is eaten at all on the third day, it shall not be accepted**: Yet, the meat from a peace offering could never be eaten **on the third day** from the sacrifice. Any leftover meat had to **be burned with fire**. Perhaps this was God's way to emphasize His desire for a "fresh," current relationship with Him.

i. "Because in such a hot country it was apt to putrefy, and as it was considered to be *holy*, it would have been very improper to expose that to putrefaction which had been consecrated to the Divine Being." (Clarke)

3. (19-21) Who may eat of the peace offering.

'The flesh that touches any unclean thing shall not be eaten. It shall be burned with fire. And as for the *clean* flesh, all who are clean may eat of it. But the person who eats the flesh of the sacrifice of the peace offering that *belongs* to the LORD, while he is unclean, that person shall be cut off from his people. Moreover the person who touches any unclean thing, *such as* human uncleanness, *an* unclean animal, or any abominable unclean thing, and who eats the flesh of the sacrifice of the peace offering that *belongs* to the LORD, that person shall be cut off from his people.'"

a. **Flesh that touches any unclean thing shall not be eaten**: The meat that came from the peace offering that could be eaten had to be *kept* in a ceremonially clean manner.

b. **All who are clean may eat of it**: Ceremonial purity was required of anyone who wanted to participate in the fellowship meal associated with the peace offering. This illustrates the principle that we cannot enjoy the peace of God until we have received His cleansing grace.

c. **The person who touches any unclean thing…and who eats**: If a person who was ceremonially unclean *did* eat of the meat of a peace offering, it was a serious sin. Such disregard for the holiness of God's sacrifice meant **that person shall be cut off from his people**.

i. Presumably, the strong penalty of excommunication was reserved for those who *knowingly* ate of the peace offering while ceremonially unclean. If they did it accidentally or unknowingly, there was a sacrifice specifically accepted for it (Leviticus 5:2).

ii. It isn't that God demands perfection; the presence of the leavened loaf shows that isn't true. But when a believer today tries to receive spiritual things while *knowingly* unclean, there is some separation in regard to their fellowship with God. 1 John 1:6 says: *If we say that we have fellowship with Him, and walk in darkness, we lie and do not practice the truth.*

iii. "Moreover, in the partaking of the Lord's Supper, which closely approximates the eating of the fellowship offering, the believer must not participate if unconfessed sin is in his life. Like the Israelite who ate the sacrifice in a state of uncleanness, the believer who partakes of the Lord's Supper in an unworthy state may expect the direct judgment of God (1 Corinthians 11:27–32)." (Rooker)

C. Regarding the fat and blood of animals.

1. (22-25) The fat may not be eaten.

And the LORD spoke to Moses, saying, "Speak to the children of Israel, saying: 'You shall not eat any fat, of ox or sheep or goat. And the fat of an animal that dies *naturally,* and the fat of what is torn by wild beasts, may be used in any other way; but you shall by no means eat it. For whoever eats the fat of the animal of which men offer an offering made by fire to the LORD, the person who eats *it* shall be cut off from his people.

a. **You shall not eat any fat, of ox or sheep or goat**: Under the Old Covenant, an Israelite could not eat the large fatty portions of an animal. This was true of animals offered in sacrifice and even **an animal that dies naturally** or was dead and **torn by wild beasts**. The law was the same: **you shall by no means eat it.**

i. The **fat** of the animal represented its goodness and abundance, and that belonged to God. Additionally, the fat is the stored energy of the animal; that also belongs to God.

b. **Whoever eats the fat of the animal of which men offer an offering made by fire**: This shows that the prohibition against eating the fatty portions only applied to sacrificed animals, and to those animals which were otherwise forbidden for eating.

i. Leviticus 22:8 forbade the eating of any kind of animal that was killed by another animal (such as one **torn by wild beasts**).

c. **The person who eats it shall be cut off from his people**: As with the previous law against ceremonially unclean persons eating the meat from sacrifices, the penalty for violating this law was severe – excommunication from the community of God's people.

> i. "Nineteen offenses resulted in a person receiving the punishment of 'being cut off' in the Old Testament. Offenses that resulted in the offender being 'cut off' included violation of holy days (including the Sabbath), committing moral offenses, violating purity laws such as eating the blood, and failure to circumcise on the eighth day." (Rooker)

2. (26-27) The blood may not be eaten.

Moreover you shall not eat any blood in any of your dwellings, *whether* of bird or beast. Whoever eats any blood, that person shall be cut off from his people.'"

a. **You shall not eat any blood**: The law of the Old Covenant also prohibited the Israelite from the direct eating of blood of any kind (**of bird or beast**). The blood represents the life of the animal or person (Leviticus 17:11-14), and the life belongs to God.

b. **That person shall be cut off from his people**: As with the previous laws, the penalty for disobedience was severe: to be **cut off** from the community of God's people.

> i. "One would think this to be but a peccadillo [little sin]: yet how fearfully is it threatened! No sin can be little, because there is no little God to sin against." (Trapp)

D. The specific portions of the peace offering.

1. (28-31) The breast portion.

Then the LORD spoke to Moses, saying, "Speak to the children of Israel, saying: 'He who offers the sacrifice of his peace offering to the LORD shall bring his offering to the LORD from the sacrifice of his peace offering. His own hands shall bring the offerings made by fire to the LORD. The fat with the breast he shall bring, that the breast may be waved *as* a wave offering before the LORD. And the priest shall burn the fat on the altar, but the breast shall be Aaron's and his sons'.

a. **He who offers the sacrifice of his peace offering**: The following instructions relate to meat portions of the **peace offering**. The individual who brought the sacrifice to the priests actually brought **his offering to the LORD**.

b. **His own hands shall bring the offerings**: An Israelite could not delegate this to someone else. The **peace offering** had to be brought to the priest with **his own hands**.

c. **The breast may be waved as a wave offering before the LORD**: This was a specific waving of the portion of meat or bread dedicated to the LORD, waving it before the LORD in a specific pattern. In this way, even though the priest kept the portion, the one bringing the offering still dedicated it to God.

> i. Poole notes that it was the Israelite who brought the offering that made this waving motion with the breast of the sacrifice: "to and fro by his hands, which were supported and directed by the hands of the priest."

> ii. Adam Clarke says this regarding the wave offering, indicating that it comes from the Hebrew word "to *stretch out;* an offering of the first-fruits *stretched out before God,* in acknowledgment of his providential goodness. This offering was moved from the right hand to the left."

> iii. In his commentary on Exodus 29:27, Clarke wrote this regarding the heave and wave offerings: "As the *wave-offering* was agitated *to* and *fro,* and the *heave-offering up* and *down,* some have conceived that this twofold action represented the *figure of the cross,* on which the great *Peace-offering* between God and man was offered in the personal sacrifice of our blessed Redeemer." For this idea, Clarke cited the work of Charles Houbigant, a French Bible scholar of the 18th century.

2. (32-34) The thigh portion.

Also the right thigh you shall give to the priest *as* a heave offering from the sacrifices of your peace offerings. He among the sons of Aaron, who offers the blood of the peace offering and the fat, shall have the right thigh for *his* part. For the breast of the wave offering and the thigh of the heave offering I have taken from the children of Israel, from the sacrifices of their peace offerings, and I have given them to Aaron the priest and to his sons from the children of Israel by a statute forever.'"

a. **The right thigh you shall give to the priest**: This part of the animal belonged to the priest who carried out the sacrifice. Presumably, the *left thigh* of the animal was given to the Israelite who brought the offering, so they could enjoy the meat from the sacrifice in a fellowship meal.

b. **For the breast of the wave offering and the thigh of the heave offering**: There was some distinction between the ceremonial presentation of the breast and the thigh of the animal. The breast was presented in a **wave offering**, and the thigh was presented in a **heave offering**.

c. **I have taken**: Both portions belonged to the LORD. God was not visibly present at the sacrifice, yet God still received the offering through the work of the appointed, anointed priest. God received the offering, then gave it to the priest (**I have given them to Aaron the priest and to his sons**).

3. (35-36) The principle of portions given to the priest.

This *is* the consecrated portion for Aaron and his sons, from the offerings made by fire to the LORD, on the day when *Moses* presented them to minister to the LORD as priests. The LORD commanded this to be given to them by the children of Israel, on the day that He anointed them, *by* a statute forever throughout their generations.

a. **This is the consecrated portion for Aaron and his sons**: For emphasis, God repeated the idea that though these sacrifices were given to the LORD, portions of those sacrifices belonged to the priests by right and by command (**the LORD commanded this to be given to them by the children of Israel**).

i. Someone might object that this was a great benefit to the priests, and maybe even an excessive benefit. Meat was a luxury in the ancient world, and the priests had more meat to eat than most people. Yet, it should be remembered that the priests (as from the tribe of Levi), had no allotment of land given to them (Numbers 18:20). God was their inheritance, and they were provided for by the offerings and gifts of God's people.

ii. In a similar way, God says in the New Testament that those who serve God and His people in spiritual ways have the right to be supported in material ways (1 Corinthians 9:12). This is a right that can and should be set aside when it is to greater advantage to the cause of the gospel to set it aside, yet the right remains. As Paul wrote, *so the Lord has commanded that those who preach the gospel should live from the gospel* (1 Corinthians 9:14).

b. **On the day when Moses presented them to minister to the LORD as priests**: This ceremony was described in Exodus 29 and carried out in Leviticus 8. It was the ceremony that officially appointed and anointed Aaron and his sons as priests for Israel.

4. (37-38) Postscript on the sacrifices.

This *is* the law of the burnt offering, the grain offering, the sin offering, the trespass offering, the consecrations, and the sacrifice of the peace offering, which the LORD commanded Moses on Mount Sinai, on the day when He commanded the children of Israel to offer their offerings to the LORD in the Wilderness of Sinai.

a. **This is the law of the burnt offering**: This is a summary statement regarding the previous seven chapters, with the instructions for the sacrifices of Israel. These included:

- The **burnt offering**: Leviticus 1 and 6:8-13.

- The **grain offering**: Leviticus 2 and 6:14-23.

- The **sin offering**: Leviticus 4 and 6:24-30.

- The **trespass offering**: Leviticus 5 and 7:1-10.

- The **consecrations**: Perhaps a reference to the restitution offerings described in Leviticus 5:14-6:7, and the portions set aside for God and the priests in Leviticus 7:22-36.

- The **peace offering**: Leviticus 3 and 7:11-21.

b. **Which the LORD commanded Moses on Mount Sinai**: Moses received all these laws for Israel on Mount Sinai and brought them down to the people of Israel. They were an additional and important part of the Old Covenant, first established **in the Wilderness of Sinai**.

i. "These laws were probably given to Moses while he was on the mount with God; the time was quite sufficient, as he was there with God not less than fourscore days in all; forty days at the *giving*, and forty days at the *renewing*, of the law." (Clarke)

Jesus Christ and the Fulfillment of the Sacrificial System

But this Man, after He had offered one sacrifice for sins forever, sat down at the right hand of God. (Hebrews 10:12)

JESUS FULFILLED THE BURNT OFFERING (Leviticus 1)

As Christ also has loved us and given Himself for us, an offering and a sacrifice to God for a sweet-smelling aroma. (Ephesians 5:2)

JESUS FULFILLED THE GRAIN AND FIRSTFRUITS OFFERING (Leviticus 2)

But now Christ is risen from the dead, and has become the firstfruits of those who have fallen asleep. (1 Corinthians 15:20)

JESUS FULFILLED THE PEACE OFFERING (Leviticus 3)

Therefore, having been justified by faith, we have peace with God through our Lord, Jesus Christ. (Romans 5:1)

JESUS FULFILLED THE SIN OFFERING (Leviticus 4)

For He made Him who knew no sin to be sin for us, that we might become the righteousness of God in Him. (2 Corinthians 5:21)

JESUS FULFILLED THE GUILT OFFERING (Leviticus 5)

Who was delivered up because of our offenses, and was raised because of our justification. (Romans 4:25)

You make His soul an offering for sin. (Isaiah 53:10)

Jesus Christ has fulfilled every sacrifice for His people!

"He is the Burnt-offering, the Meat-offering, the Peace-offering, the Sin-offering, and the Trespass-offering for His people. By His one oblation of Himself once offered, He has stood in all these different relations." (Jukes)

We have been sanctified through the offering of the body of Jesus Christ once for all. (Hebrews 10:10)

Leviticus 8 – The Consecration of Priests

A. Prelude to the consecration of Aaron and his sons.

1. (1-3) The command given.

And the LORD spoke to Moses, saying: "Take Aaron and his sons with him, and the garments, the anointing oil, a bull as the sin offering, two rams, and a basket of unleavened bread; and gather all the congregation together at the door of the tabernacle of meeting."

a. **Take Aaron and his sons with him**: Exodus 29 records the command God gave to Moses to carry out this consecration ceremony with Aaron and his sons. Now that the tabernacle was built it was time to perform the ceremony.

i. Exodus 29:1 stated the purpose of the ceremony: *To hallow them for ministering to Me as priests.* That is, this ceremony was to set the priests aside for God's purpose and will.

ii. Since in Jesus we are *a holy priesthood... a royal priesthood* (1 Peter 2:5, 9), there is much for us to learn by analogy in this consecration ceremony. God wants us set apart for His purpose and will, and He uses these principles to accomplish that goal.

b. **Gather all the congregation together at the door of the tabernacle of meeting**: God gave a specific list of items needed in the consecration ceremony and commanded that **all the congregation together** witness this ceremony. It would not be performed secretly.

2. (4-5) Moses does as the LORD commands.

So Moses did as the LORD commanded him. And the congregation was gathered together at the door of the tabernacle of meeting. And Moses said to the congregation, "This *is* what the LORD commanded to be done."

a. **The congregation was gathered together at the door of the tabernacle of meeting**: We don't know if this was a large crowd, or certain representatives from the tribes, or both. This was a public ceremony.

i. "Ministers are to be ordained in the public assembly, (Acts 14:22) that the people may show their approbation, profess their purpose of obedience, and pray for God's Spirit to be poured upon them." (Trapp)

b. **This is what the LORD commanded to be done**: The entire consecration ceremony was God's plan, not the plan of Moses. In some ways this was a strange and messy plan, but it was God's plan for the process of consecration.

B. Preliminary aspects of the ceremony of priestly consecration.

1. (6) The washing of the priests.

Then Moses brought Aaron and his sons and washed them with water.

a. **Aaron and his sons**: This was not a ceremony for just anyone in Israel. There were special consecration ceremonies available to anyone – such as the Nazirite vow in Numbers 6. But this ceremony was for *priests*, for **Aaron and his sons**.

i. **Then Moses brought**: "In the sacred rites of consecration it is noticeable that Moses acted. It is an arresting thing to see him thus exercising all the functions of the priestly office, although he was not permanently appointed thereto. The explanation is that he was acting as in the very place of God. God, through His servant, anointed Tabernacle and priests." (Morgan)

b. **And washed them with water**: The process of consecration began with cleansing. All priestly ministries began with cleansing, and a cleansing that was *received*: **you shall wash them**. Aaron and his sons did not wash themselves; they *received* a washing.

i. This was humbling because it took place publicly at *the door of the tabernacle of meeting*. We cannot be cleansed from our sin without being humbled first.

ii. Rooker believed this washing was by full immersion, and Harrison also considered this point: "Some Jewish interpreters have maintained that the washing of Aaron and his sons was by immersion, as was required of the high priest on the day of atonement (Leviticus 16:4)."

iii. This great cleansing was a one-time thing. From then on, they just needed to cleanse their hands and their feet.

iv. Like these ancient priests, every Christian is washed by the work of God's word (Ephesians 5:26), by the regenerating work of the Holy Spirit (Titus 3:5). This cleansing work was accomplished by the death of Jesus for us (Revelation 1:5) and is appropriated by faith.

2. (7-9) The clothing of the high priest in priestly garments.

And he put the tunic on him, girded him with the sash, clothed him with the robe, and put the ephod on him; and he girded him with the intricately woven band of the ephod, and with it tied *the ephod* **on him. Then he put the breastplate on him, and he put the Urim and the Thummim in the breastplate. And he put the turban on his head. Also on the turban, on its front, he put the golden plate, the holy crown, as the LORD had commanded Moses.**

a. **And he put the tunic on him**: After being cleansed, the priest had to be clothed – but not in his own clothes. He had to put on garments given by God.

i. Like these ancient priests, every believer is clothed in Jesus Christ and in His righteousness (Revelation 3:5). These are clothes that are given freely by Jesus but received and "worn" by faith.

ii. "Note, that *these garments were provided for the*m. They were at no expense in buying them, nor labour in weaving them, nor skill in making them; they had simply to put them on. And you, dear child of God, are to put on the garments which Jesus Christ has provided for you, at his own cost, and freely bestows upon you out of boundless love." (Spurgeon)

b. **Girded with the sash...the ephod.... the breastplate.... the turban**: Each of these specific articles of clothing were made for the high priest, garments to show the *glory and for beauty* of the priesthood (Exodus 28:2).

- The **tunic** was woven from fine linen thread (Exodus 28:39).

- The **sash** was a broad, woven band tied around the midsection (Exodus 28:39).

- The **robe** was a blue, seamless robe, with bells and small decorative pomegranates around its bottom hem (Exodus 28:31-35).

- The **ephod** was essentially an ornate apron-like garment, made of gold, blue, purple and scarlet thread (Exodus 28:5-8).

- The **breastplate** was also made with gold, blue, purple, and scarlet thread. It was attached to the ephod with gold chains. On the breastplate were four rows of three gemstones, each stone having one of the names of the twelve tribes inscribed on it. In wearing the

breastplate, the high priest would *bear the names of the sons of Israel...
over his heart* (Exodus 28:15-30).

- The **Urim and the Thummim** seem to be a pair of stones, one light
  and another dark, and each stone indicated a "yes" or "no" from God.
  The high priest would ask God a question, reach into the breastplate,
  and pull out either a "yes" or a "no" (Exodus 28:30).

- The **turban** was a simple wound linen headpiece. More important
  than the turban itself was the **golden plate** with the inscription
  Holiness to the LORD (Exodus 28:36-38).

3. (10-13) The anointing of the priests.

**Also Moses took the anointing oil, and anointed the tabernacle and all
that *was* in it, and consecrated them. He sprinkled some of it on the
altar seven times, anointed the altar and all its utensils, and the laver
and its base, to consecrate them. And he poured some of the anointing
oil on Aaron's head and anointed him, to consecrate him. Then Moses
brought Aaron's sons and put tunics on them, girded them with sashes,
and put hats on them, as the LORD had commanded Moses.**

a. **Moses took the anointing oil**: The oil was **sprinkled** on non-living
things, to show that they were specially set apart for the service of the
LORD.

i. **On the altar seven times**: "**Seven times,** to signify the singular use
and holiness of it, which it was not only to have in itself, but also to
communicate to all the sacrifices laid upon it." (Poole)

b. **And he poured some of the anointing oil on Aaron's head and
anointed him, to consecrate him**: The priests of Israel also had to be
anointed. The oil (a picture of the Holy Spirit) was **poured** over their
heads, indicating that it was given in great measure, not in small measure
(Psalm 133:2). *Things* were **sprinkled**, but upon *people* the oil was **poured**
out.

i. **To consecrate him**: This means that the anointing oil set Aaron
apart. If something is *consecrated*, it is then set apart for God's service.
Once sprinkled with oil, then the tabernacle wasn't just a tent anymore;
the altar was no longer just a fire-pit; Aaron was no longer just a man.
He was a priest of the Living God and the high priest.

ii. "There is no statement in the OT as to why oil typified the Holy
Spirit. Oil was widely used in lamps. As the lamp burned, the oil
seemed to vanish into the air. Such a connection of oil and air possibly
may have made the typology natural in the Hebrew culture." (Kaiser)

iii. Like these ancient priests, every believer has an anointing (1 John 2:20) that they may receive and walk in by faith.

4. (14-17) The sacrifice of the sin offering.

And he brought the bull for the sin offering. Then Aaron and his sons laid their hands on the head of the bull for the sin offering, and Moses killed *it*. Then he took the blood, and put *some* on the horns of the altar all around with his finger, and purified the altar. And he poured the blood at the base of the altar, and consecrated it, to make atonement for it. Then he took all the fat that *was* on the entrails, the fatty lobe *attached to* the liver, and the two kidneys with their fat, and Moses burned *them* on the altar. But the bull, its hide, its flesh, and its offal, he burned with fire outside the camp, as the LORD had commanded Moses.

a. **Aaron and his sons laid their hands on the head of the bull**: The washing at the door of the tabernacle was only one aspect of the symbolic cleansing from sin. There also had to be the punishment of the guilty, and this happened in the **sin offering**. As Aaron and his sons **laid their hands on the head of the bull**, they symbolically transferred their sin to the bull.

i. "The Hebrew word means more than lightly placing the hand, it gives the idea of pressing hard upon the bullock's head. They came each one and leaned upon the victim, loading him with their burden, signifying their acceptance of its substitution, their joy that the Lord would accept that victim in their stead. When they put their hands on the bullock, they made a confession of sin." (Spurgeon)

ii. Like these ancient priests, every believer can only be consecrated to God through sacrifice. Our consecration should be greater because it was made through a far greater sacrifice – the sacrifice of God's own Son.

b. **Then he took the blood, and put some on the horns of the altar all around with his finger, and purified the altar**: The altar was sanctified with the blood of the sin offering, and the best of the animal was burnt before the LORD – the rest was destroyed outside the camp. The sin offering said, "We have failed to give our best to God. This animal now gives its best to atone for our failure, and we decide to live now giving our best, even as this animal which dies in our place."

i. The idea behind the ancient Hebrew word for **altar** is essentially, "killing-place." The ancient altar – a place of death – was made holy and was consecrated to God. Like that ancient altar, the altar of the New Covenant – the cross – is transformed from a place of death to a place set apart to bring life.

5. (18-21) The sacrifice of the burnt offering.

Then he brought the ram as the burnt offering. And Aaron and his sons laid their hands on the head of the ram, and Moses killed *it*. Then he sprinkled the blood all around on the altar. And he cut the ram into pieces; and Moses burned the head, the pieces, and the fat. Then he washed the entrails and the legs in water. And Moses burned the whole ram on the altar. It *was* a burnt sacrifice for a sweet aroma, an offering made by fire to the LORD, as the LORD had commanded Moses.

a. **Aaron and his sons laid their hands on the head of the ram**: As the sin offering before it, the **burnt offering** also symbolically received the sins of the priests and they laid their hands on the head of the animal and confessed their sin.

b. **Moses burned the whole ram on the altar**: The ram was completely burnt before the LORD, with its blood sprinkled on the altar. The burnt offering said, "We have failed to give our all to God. This animal now gives its all to atone for our failure, and we decide to live now giving our all, even as this animal which dies in our place."

i. This demonstration of total commitment to the LORD only came after the first three aspects of the ceremony: cleansing, anointing, and atonement. Without these things settled first, we cannot truly give ourselves to God.

C. The ceremony of priestly consecration.

1. (22-24) The sacrifice and the blood.

And he brought the second ram, the ram of consecration. Then Aaron and his sons laid their hands on the head of the ram, and Moses killed *it*. Also he took *some* of its blood and put it on the tip of Aaron's right ear, on the thumb of his right hand, and on the big toe of his right foot. Then he brought Aaron's sons. And Moses put *some* of the blood on the tips of their right ears, on the thumbs of their right hands, and on the big toes of their right feet. And Moses sprinkled the blood all around on the altar.

a. **The second ram, the ram of consecration.... Aaron and his sons laid their hands on the head of the ram**: After atonement for sin had been made through the sin offering and the burnt offering, it was then time for the sacrifices and ceremonies that would actually consecrate the priests. Like the previous sacrifices for atonement, these began with identification with the sacrificial victim, as they **laid their hands on the head of the ram**.

i. The theme of connection to and identification with the sacrificial victim did not end with the atoning of sin. It was the core principle of their consecration to priestly service. In the same way, our connection to and identification with Jesus Christ, and Him crucified, does in no way end when our sins are forgiven. It remains constant, especially in regard to any aspect of our priestly service.

b. **He took some of its blood and put it on the tip of Aaron's right ear**: To express the idea of consecration, blood from the ram was placed on the ear, thumb, and toe of the priest. It was blood from the ram – not the wool and not the fat. God wanted the *life* of the sacrificial victim to mark His consecrated priests.

i. Leviticus 17:11 is one of many instances that express this principle: *For the life of the flesh is in the blood*. God wanted the *life* of the sacrificial victim to be evident in the *body* of the priest.

c. **Tip of Aaron's right ear, on the thumb of his right hand, and on the big toe of his right foot**: These consecrated priests were stained with the blood of sacrifice. They should *hear* differently because the blood was on their **ear**. They should *work* differently because the blood was on their **thumb**. They should *walk* differently because the blood was on their **toe**.

i. Specifically, it was applied to the **right** ear, hand, and foot. This isn't because God felt they could do whatever they wanted to with their left ear, hand, and foot. It is because the **right** side was considered superior, with more strength and skill (because most people are right-handed). God wanted their *best* to be dedicated to Him.

2. (25-29) A wave offering to God.

Then he took the fat and the fat tail, all the fat that *was* on the entrails, the fatty lobe *attached to* the liver, the two kidneys and their fat, and the right thigh; and from the basket of unleavened bread that was before the LORD he took one unleavened cake, a cake of bread *anointed with* oil, and one wafer, and put *them* on the fat and on the right thigh; and he put all *these* in Aaron's hands and in his sons' hands, and waved them *as* a wave offering before the LORD. Then Moses took them from their hands and burned *them* on the altar, on the burnt offering. They *were* consecration offerings for a sweet aroma. That *was* an offering made by fire to the LORD. And Moses took the breast and waved it *as* a wave offering before the LORD. It was Moses' part of the ram of consecration, as the LORD had commanded Moses.

a. **He took the fat and the fat tail**: The second ram used in the consecration ceremony – the ram whose blood was applied to the ear, hand, and foot of the priest – was used as a **wave offering before the LORD**.

b. **Waved them as a wave offering before the LORD**: Part of this second ram – the best parts – was put together with the **bread**, **cake**, and the **wafer** and was first *waved* before God in an act of presentation. Then these portions were burnt on the altar as an act of complete devotion.

c. **Moses took them from their hands and burned them on the altar**: Normally, portions such as the **right thigh** belonged to the priests as their portion. But not in the consecration ceremony; it was inappropriate for them to personally benefit from this offering.

3. (30) Blood is sprinkled on the priestly garments.

Then Moses took some of the anointing oil and some of the blood which *was* on the altar, and sprinkled *it* on Aaron, on his garments, on his sons, and on the garments of his sons with him; and he consecrated Aaron, his garments, his sons, and the garments of his sons with him.

a. **Moses took some of the anointing oil and some of the blood which was on the altar, and sprinkled it**: The blood alone wasn't enough. God wanted **blood** mixed with **oil**, and to have the *mixture* sprinkled on the priests. There was to be a combination of both the sacrifice and the spirit (represented by the **anointing oil**).

i. "Yes, brethren, we need to know that double anointing, the blood of Jesus which cleanses, and the oil of the Holy Spirit which perfumes us. It is well to see how these two blend in one.... It is a terrible blunder to set the blood and the oil in opposition, they must always go together." (Spurgeon)

b. **And sprinkled it on Aaron, on his garments**: This mixture of oil and blood stained the garments of Aaron and his sons. It would be a long reminder of this ceremony of consecration.

i. "Thus we find that the high priest himself must be sprinkled with the blood of the sacrifice; and our blessed Lord, of whom Aaron was a type, was sprinkled with his own blood. 1. In his agony in the garden. 2. In his being crowned with thorns. 3. In the piercing of his hands and his feet. And, 4. In his side being pierced with the spear. All these were so many acts of atonement performed by the high priest." (Clarke)

4. (31-32) A fellowship meal with God.

And Moses said to Aaron and his sons, "Boil the flesh *at* the door of the tabernacle of meeting, and eat it there with the bread that *is* in the

basket of consecration offerings, as I commanded, saying, 'Aaron and his sons shall eat it.' What remains of the flesh and of the bread you shall burn with fire.

a. **Boil the flesh at the door of the tabernacle of meeting, and eat it there with the bread**: The remaining meat portions of this ram were given to Aaron and the other priests after those portions were presented to God as a **wave offering**. It was then cooked and eaten by the priests during the days of their consecration ceremony.

> i. The second ram – after the ram presented as a burnt offering – had its *life* applied to the consecrated priests. First, its life was applied with the application of blood to the ear, hand, and foot of the priest. Then through a ritual meal, its life was applied by the priest taking the ram into himself.

> ii. The eating did not *begin* the process of consecration. It came *after* the washing, the clothing, and the blood-atonement of the priests. The eating speaks of the *continuing relationship* of the priest with God. "Let not this distinction be forgotten; the eating of the sacrifice is not intended to give life, for no dead man can eat, but to sustain the life which is there already. A believing look at Christ makes you live, but spiritual life must be fed and sustained." (Spurgeon)

> iii. In this way, eating is a good picture of a healthy, continuing relationship with Jesus.

> - Eating is *personal*. No one can eat for you, and no one can have a relationship with Jesus on your behalf.

> - Eating is *inward*. It does no good to be around food or to rub food on the outside of your body – you must *take it in*. We must take Jesus to ourselves *inwardly*, not merely in an external way.

> - Eating is *active*. Some medicines are received passively – they are injected under the skin and go to work. Such medicines could even be received while one sleeps – but no one can eat while asleep. We must *actively* take Jesus to ourselves.

> - Eating arises *out of a sense of need* and produces *a sense of satisfaction*. We will have a healthy relationship with Jesus when we *sense our need* for Him and *receive the satisfaction* the relationship brings.

b. **What remains of the flesh and of the bread you shall burn with fire**: God did *not* want to fellowship with them over stale food. Even if they had the exact same meal, God wanted it made fresh. He wants our fellowship with Him to be *fresh*.

5. (33-36) Seven days of consecration.

And you shall not go outside the door of the tabernacle of meeting *for* seven days, until the days of your consecration are ended. For seven days he shall consecrate you. As he has done this day, *so* the LORD has commanded to do, to make atonement for you. Therefore you shall stay *at* the door of the tabernacle of meeting day and night for seven days, and keep the charge of the LORD, so that you may not die; for so I have been commanded." So Aaron and his sons did all the things that the LORD had commanded by the hand of Moses.

a. **You shall not go outside the door of the tabernacle of meeting for seven days**: With the coming generations, new descendants of Aaron would qualify for the priesthood and would be consecrated the same way. For Aaron and his descendants, the consecration process took **seven days**.

i. "Verse 35 indicates that on each of the next seven days Moses was to offer the same sacrifices on behalf of Aaron and his sons." (Harrison) See also Exodus 29:35-36 to clarify this point.

ii. **Seven days**: "This number was the number of *perfection* among the Hebrews; and the seven days' consecration implied a *perfect* and *full consecration* to the sacerdotal office." (Clarke)

b. **He shall consecrate you**: The **he** mentioned here may be a reference to Moses, who supervised the consecration ceremony. It may also be a reference to God, who does the true work of setting aside a person for ministry. Without God's consecration, all this would be an empty ceremony.

i. This was a complicated, long, repetitive, messy ceremony. God still has His own consecration and preparation process today for His servants. "Nothing is to be omitted which Jehovah commands. His priests must be washed, robed, anointed, sustained, separated, and all in His way, or they cannot exercise their functions in His service. To neglect anything, is to invalidate ministry." (Morgan)

c. **To make atonement for you**: Through the repetition of these sacrifices over seven days, it was emphasized again and again that these priests were sinners, they were fallible men who needed **atonement**. A high standard (indeed, a *higher* standard) should be expected of leaders among God's people, but not the standard of perfection.

i. "The contrast between the sinful lives of the high priests and the life and work of the Great High Priest, Jesus Christ, to which these priests pointed, was not lost to the writer of the Hebrews (Hebrews 9:7–14)." (Rooker)

d. **You shall stay at the door of the tabernacle of meeting day and night for seven days**: For **seven days** they lived at the tabernacle and ate the ram of the consecration and the bread of consecration. The consecration ceremony wasn't quick and easy. It took time, reflection, and a constant awareness of sacrifice and atonement.

> i. "The Lord's part was consumed with fire upon the altar, and another portion was eaten by man in the holy place. The peace offering was thus an open declaration of the communion which had been established between God and man, so that they ate together, rejoicing in the same offering." (Spurgeon)

> ii. "I know some good people who are very busy indeed in the services of God, and I am very delighted that they should be, but I would caution them against working and never eating. They give up attending the means of grace as hearers, because they have so much to do as workers." (Spurgeon)

e. **You shall stay at the door of the tabernacle...and keep the charge of the LORD**. After seven days of living in the tabernacle, they would either love the tabernacle of God and His presence, or they would hate them.

> i. If approached with the right heart, their consecration demonstrates the heart of the Psalmist: *How lovely is Your tabernacle, O LORD of hosts! My soul longs, yes, even faints for the courts of the LORD; My heart and my flesh cry out for the living God.* (Psalms 84:1-2)

> ii. **So that you may not die**: "If the threatening seem too severe for the fault, it must be considered both that it is the usual practice of lawgivers most severely to punish the first offences for the terror and caution of others, and for the maintenance of their own authority." (Poole)

Leviticus 9 – More on the Consecration of Priests

A. Introduction: God calls Aaron to minister.

1. (1) Moses calls to Aaron and his sons.

It came to pass on the eighth day that Moses called Aaron and his sons and the elders of Israel.

a. **It came to pass on the eighth day**: The whole ceremony of consecration lasted more than a week. It was not a quick and easy process. The call to the priesthood came **on the eighth day**, the day of new beginnings. After seven days of patient fellowship with the LORD in His tabernacle, God was ready to do a new work in and through the priests.

b. **Moses called Aaron and his sons and the elders of Israel**: This ceremony involved not only those who would be consecrated (**Aaron and his sons**). It also included the one who stood in God's place for the consecration process (**Moses**) and those whom the priests would serve (**the elders of Israel**, representing the people as a whole).

i. **The elders**: "In most cultures around the world age is still associated with authority and wisdom. The Hebrew term actually means 'the beards' or 'the bearded ones.'" (Peter-Contesse)

2. (2) Offerings for Aaron.

And he said to Aaron, "Take for yourself a young bull as a sin offering and a ram as a burnt offering, without blemish, and offer *them* before the LORD.

a. **Take for yourself a young bull as a sin offering**: As part of the consecration ceremony, Aaron and his sons lived for an entire week at the tabernacle of meeting. Yet they still had sin to atone for during that week. The consecration ceremony did not make Aaron perfect. During the seven days of just sitting in the tabernacle he added more sin to his account that had to be cleared.

i. Through the repetition of sacrifice, God also wanted to show that as useful as the animal sacrifices were, they were not complete and could not make an end of sins. Only the perfect sacrifice of the Messiah to come could do that.

ii. Some suggest (such as Trapp and Clarke) that there was a specific reason for this particular offering of **a young bull** – to answer for the sin with the golden calf that Aaron permitted (Exodus 32). "And this is supposed by the Jews to have been intended to make an atonement for his sin in the matter of the *golden calf*. This is very probable, as no formal atonement for that transgression had yet been made." (Clarke)

b. **And a ram as a burnt offering**: Even though Aaron just spent the prior week in special dedication to the LORD, there was still more to give. Though this was an important experience of dedication, the idea of consecration had to be *ongoing* in the life of Aaron and all of God's priests.

B. Aaron begins the priestly ministry.

1. (3-6) In a context of atonement and obedience, God will show His glory.

And to the children of Israel you shall speak, saying, 'Take a kid of the goats as a sin offering, and a calf and a lamb, *both* of the first year, without blemish, as a burnt offering, also a bull and a ram as peace offerings, to sacrifice before the LORD, and a grain offering mixed with oil; for today the LORD will appear to you.'" So they brought what Moses commanded before the tabernacle of meeting. And all the congregation drew near and stood before the LORD. Then Moses said, "This *is* the thing which the LORD commanded you to do, and the glory of the LORD will appear to you."

a. **Take a kid of the goats as a sin offering**: In one sense, this was the same kind of thing Aaron and his sons did in the previous week. They made several sacrifices a day, and now God commanded them to offer five more sacrifices (a **kid of the goats**, a **calf and a lamb**, and a **bull and a ram**). While all this repeated what had been done the previous days, on this eighth day something different would happen: **today the LORD will appear to you**.

b. **This is the thing which the LORD commanded you to do, and the glory of the LORD will appear to you**: Everything Aaron did in the previous week prepared him for this moment. This was the end goal of the week of separation and consecration to the LORD – the display of God's **glory**.

i. "The Hebrew word for glory (*kabod*) is from the root *kbd*, which denotes 'heaviness' or 'weightiness' and hence the extended meaning of 'significance, superior value, distinction, splendor.'" (Rooker)

2. (7) Aaron will begin to minister **for the people**.

And Moses said to Aaron, "Go to the altar, offer your sin offering and your burnt offering, and make atonement for yourself and for the people. Offer the offering of the people, and make atonement for them, as the LORD commanded."

a. **Offer your sin offering and your burnt offering, and make atonement for yourself and for the people**: Aaron had to first deal with his own sin, and only then he could truly function as a *priest*, ready to serve others.

b. **Make atonement for them, as the LORD commanded**: Aaron's priesthood existed for the glory of God and for the benefit of the people – not for his own personal benefit. The office of high priest was one of great authority, but of even greater responsibility.

3. (8-14) Aaron offers sacrifice for his own sin, along with a burnt offering.

Aaron therefore went to the altar and killed the calf of the sin offering, which *was* for himself. Then the sons of Aaron brought the blood to him. And he dipped his finger in the blood, put *it* on the horns of the altar, and poured the blood at the base of the altar. But the fat, the kidneys, and the fatty lobe from the liver of the sin offering he burned on the altar, as the LORD had commanded Moses. The flesh and the hide he burned with fire outside the camp. And he killed the burnt offering; and Aaron's sons presented to him the blood, which he sprinkled all around on the altar. Then they presented the burnt offering to him, with its pieces and head, and he burned *them* on the altar. And he washed the entrails and the legs, and burned *them* with the burnt offering on the altar.

a. **Aaron therefore went to the altar and killed the calf of the sin offering, which was for himself**: This was a display of honesty and humility before the people. Aaron, before offering a sacrifice of atonement for the people, publicly offered one for himself, identifying himself with the people. This sacrifice told the nation, "I am a sinner who needs atonement also."

i. "Aaron's first act was bringing the sin offering and the burnt offering for himself. He could not be the instrument of mediation between the people and God for worship save as he was brought into right relationship with God." (Morgan)

b. **He dipped his finger in the blood, put it on the horns of the altar**: This was the beginning of Aaron's service as a consecrated priest. He slaughtered the sacrifice, and with his **sons** carried out the commanded details of the sacrificial ritual.

4. (15-21) Aaron offers the sacrifice on behalf of the people.

Then he brought the people's offering, and took the goat, which *was* the sin offering for the people, and killed it and offered it for sin, like the first one. And he brought the burnt offering and offered it according to the prescribed manner. Then he brought the grain offering, took a handful of it, and burned *it* on the altar, besides the burnt sacrifice of the morning. He also killed the bull and the ram *as* sacrifices of peace offerings, which *were* for the people. And Aaron's sons presented to him the blood, which he sprinkled all around on the altar, and the fat from the bull and the ram; the fatty tail, what covers *the entrails* and the kidneys, and the fatty lobe *attached to* the liver; and they put the fat on the breasts. Then he burned the fat on the altar; but the breasts and the right thigh Aaron waved *as* a wave offering before the LORD, as Moses had commanded.

a. **Then he brought the people's offering**: Again, the idea is emphasized. Aaron, like every priest among God's people, must receive God's atoning sacrifice first. It was only **then** that he could properly bring **the people's offering**.

b. **The sin offering.... the burnt offering.... the grain offering.... peace offerings.... wave offering**: Aaron and his sons carried out the variety of offerings previously commanded in chapters 1 through 7. These were all done on behalf of Israel as a whole, as **the people's offering**. This was the beginning (or the training) for their priestly work for the people.

i. The atonement through the sacrifice of the calf in verses 8-14 was for the sake of Aaron and the priests, but not for their sake alone. It was to make them fit to be priests for **the people's offering**. It was so they could serve the people of Israel, not merely "be holy" for their own sake.

ii. We can assume the carrying out of these different sacrifices was a kind of training for their work, and it was all done under the watchful eye of Moses.

5. (22-24) God blesses Israel with a display of His glory.

Then Aaron lifted his hand toward the people, blessed them, and came down from offering the sin offering, the burnt offering, and peace offerings. And Moses and Aaron went into the tabernacle of meeting, and came out and blessed the people. Then the glory of the LORD appeared to all the people, and fire came out from before the LORD and consumed

the burnt offering and the fat on the altar. When all the people saw *it*, they shouted and fell on their faces.

a. **Then Aaron lifted his hand toward the people, blessed them**: Aaron's heart was turned towards the people. He longed to bless them, and so he **lifted his hand toward the people** [and] **blessed them**. His washing, sanctification, justification, consecration, waiting with and for the LORD, his identification with the people, and humility each made him desire a blessing for the people – more than a blessing for himself.

i. "In the Chaldee Version of the Pentateuch the words of the blessing are thus reported: 'May the Word of Jehovah accept your sacrifice with favour, and remit and pardon your sins.'" (Morgan)

ii. "It may also be of significance that blessing follows the sacrifices made on behalf of the people. This illustrates the New Testament truth that every spiritual blessing comes to the Christian as a result of the sacrifice of Jesus Christ upon the cross." (Rooker)

b. **Moses and Aaron went into the tabernacle of meeting**: After the sacrificial system had been instituted, Aaron now – perhaps for the first time – entered the tabernacle, as was now Aaron's right as a consecrated priest. Moses instructed him how to offer the incense, prepare the lamps, lay out the showbread, and so forth. They came out and once again **blessed the people**.

i. "The servants of God, whether prophets or priests, have no power to bless men save as they receive it in direct communion with God. Before we can go out and bless the people, we must go in to the Place of Meeting with God.... we are perpetually in danger of allowing our very eagerness to serve men, to interfere with our communion with God.... Forgetfulness of this is the secret of much futility in Christian work, of much fussiness, of much feverishness." (Morgan)

c. **Then the glory of the LORD appeared to all the people**: We don't know exactly what this looked like. Some think it was an extraordinary bright shining from the pillar of cloud (as in Exodus 16:10 and perhaps Numbers 14:10). It could also have been a strong and perhaps overwhelming sense of the presence of God, denoting the "weight" or "heaviness" of God's being.

d. **And fire came out from before the LORD**: God proved His presence by sending the fire. The priests were there, the offering was there, the tabernacle was there, and the nation was there, but it was all incomplete without the **fire** from God.

i. We don't know what form this **fire** appeared in. Many suppose that it was a bolt of lightning from the sky, igniting the altar of God (Job

1:6 uses this word "fire" to refer to lightning). The Jewish historian Josephus said that the fire actually came from the sacrifices on the altar itself, as if they ignited spontaneously (cited in Clarke).

ii. Whatever the exact manner of its appearing, it was essential that this **fire** should come in a manner that was not from man, or the product of trickery. The fire was not secretly given to Moses and Aaron in the tabernacle; it was publicly evident to the entire people of Israel. This was, beyond any doubt, *God's fire* and not from man.

iii. The Bible gives us seven examples of where God showed acceptance of a sacrifice with fire from heaven:

- Aaron (Leviticus 9:24).
- Gideon (Judges 6:21).
- Manoah (Judges 13:19-23).
- David (1 Chronicles 21:26).
- Solomon (2 Chronicles 7:1).
- Elijah (1 Kings 18:38).

iv. Fire was often associated with God's presence and work. Deuteronomy 4:24 tells us, *the LORD your God is a consuming fire, a jealous God.* John the Baptist promised Jesus would come with a baptism of the Holy Spirit and with *fire* (Matthew 3:11). The Holy Spirit manifested His presence on the day of Pentecost by tongues of fire (Acts 2:3). Jesus said: *I came to send fire on the earth, and how I wish it were already kindled!* (Luke 12:49)

e. **When all the people saw it, they shouted and fell on their faces**: When God revealed His **glory** and sent **fire** to the altar, it was a remarkable thing to see. The Israelites could not help shouting and falling in reverence and fear before God. This was, in one sense the goal of their worship: to encounter God in a way that honors Him, in obedience to Him.

i. **Fell on their faces**: "It involved bowing in such a way that the face actually touched the ground. In the Old Testament this gesture was an indication of the most profound and deepest respect before a superior." (Peter-Contesse)

ii. "The manifestation of the presence of God had specific relevance to this important day in Israel's history when the sacrificial system officially began; the manifestation of God's presence at the commencement of sacrificial offerings is a reminder that the goal of worship is to encounter God." (Rooker)

iii. It is also helpful to note the progression of the sacrifices made: The sin offering, then the burnt offering, then the grain offering, then the peace offerings, then the wave offering. "Carefully observe this order. Sin put away, life and work devoted, communion made possible; then the priestly blessing, speaking of acceptance, followed by a second blessing, which declared the divine satisfaction as it was accompanied by the manifestation of glory, and so finally the full worship of the people." (Morgan)

Leviticus 10 – The Conduct of Priests

A. Nadab and Abihu.

1. (1) The sin of Aaron's sons.

Then Nadab and Abihu, the sons of Aaron, each took his censer and put fire in it, put incense on it, and offered profane fire before the LORD, which He had not commanded them.

a. **Nadab and Abihu, the sons of Aaron, each took his censer and put fire in it**: In the afterglow of the consecration experience (which Nadab and Abihu were part of), these two sons of Aaron sought to connect with God their own way, apart from the specific ceremonies God revealed to Moses.

i. We don't know what their motivation was. Perhaps it was *pride*, perhaps it was *ambition*, perhaps it was *jealousy*, perhaps it was *impatience* that motivated them. Maybe they found the seven-day repetition of the sacrifices (8:35) to be tedious and wanted a new thrill to break what they considered boredom. Whatever their exact motivation, it wasn't holiness unto the LORD.

ii. Nadab and Abihu had a legacy of great spiritual experiences. As first-hand witnesses:

- They saw all the miracles God did in bringing the nation out of Egypt.
- They heard the voice of God and saw the fire, lightning, smoke, and felt the thunder and the earthquake with the rest of the nation at Mount Sinai.
- They went up with Moses, Aaron, and the seventy elders for a special meeting with God on Mount Sinai (Exodus 24:1-2),

where they *saw the God of Israel…. so they saw God, and they ate and drank* (Exodus 24:9-11).

iii. This shows that even a legacy of great spiritual experiences can't keep us right with God – only an abiding relationship grounded in the truth of God's word can.

b. **Which He had not commanded them**: They came in an unauthorized way, coming to God, but demanding to come according to their preference. Therefore, God considered this a **profane fire before the LORD**.

i. This was a misuse of special incense. This incense was regarded as *holy for the LORD* (Exodus 30:35-37). It wasn't to be used in someone's experiment with God.

ii. **Profane fire** was a fire not kindled from the altar of burnt offering; it was fire not associated with the atoning and redeeming work of sacrifice. It was easy to think, "fire is fire; as long as it burns, it's ok." In the case of Nadab and Abihu, that was literally a deadly mistake.

iii. The fire on the altar of burnt offering was sacred because it was kindled by God Himself (Leviticus 9:24). Nadab and Abihu offered a fire of their own making. Perhaps they thought that all fire was the same, and an undiscerning person may have agreed with them. But all fire isn't the same and there is a huge difference between the fire kindled by God and a fire conjured up by man.

iv. "Our censers are often flaming with 'strange fire.' How much so-called Christian worship glows with self-will or with partisan zeal! When we seek to worship God for what we can get, when we rush into His presence with hot, eager desires which we have not subordinated to His will, we are burning 'strange fire which He has not commanded.'" (Maclaren)

v. We also should not forget that Satan himself can deceive with fire. In the great tribulation the Antichrist and his associate will be able to make *fire come down from heaven on the earth in the sight of men* (Revelation 13:13). They will use this fire to deceive the undiscerning.

c. **Before the LORD**: This may have the sense that they dared even to go past the veil into the Holy of Holies, behind the veil to where the ark of the covenant was. Perhaps they thought they had accomplished so much during their time of consecration, and were now worthy to go right in.

i. In Leviticus 16:1-2, the sin of Nadab and Abihu is mentioned again in connection with the high priest entering the Holy of Holies on the Day of Atonement. This adds to the idea that one of the sins of Nadab and Abihu was going beyond the holy place into the Holy of Holies, which they were not permitted to do.

2. (2) The judgment of God upon Nadab and Abihu.

So fire went out from the LORD and devoured them, and they died before the LORD.

a. **So fire went out from the LORD**: The same fire that displayed God's glory in Leviticus 9:24 now showed His judgment of these unfaithful priests.

i. "Fire from heaven occurs twelve times in the Old Testament, six times in a beneficial way [Leviticus 9:24; Judges 6:21; Judges 13:20; 1 Chronicles 21:26; 2 Chronicles 7:1-2; and 1 Kings 18:38] and six times in judgment [Leviticus 10:2; Numbers 11:1; Numbers 16:35; Job 1:16; and 2 Kings 1:10, 12]." (Rooker)

b. **And devoured them**: The fire of Leviticus 9:24 was a fire of glory and this was a fire of judgment. Yet in many ways it was the *same fire*. In Leviticus 9:24, God sent fire that said, "I accept your sacrifice and approve of this priestly system." This same fire came from the LORD **and devoured them**, saying "I will not accept your man-based, fleshly attempt to imitate My fire; I will bring judgment."

i. Fire is a figure of searching judgment and purification. Our works for Jesus will be judged by fire (1 Corinthians 3:13-15), and Jesus is described as having *eyes like a flame of fire* (Revelation 1:14). He has eyes of searching judgment and discernment.

ii. "The surface of the sin was ceremonial impropriety; the heart of it was flouting Jehovah and His law. It was better that two men should die, and the whole nation perish not, as it would have done if their example had been followed. It is mercy to trample out the first sparks beside a powder-barrel." (Maclaren)

iii. Many of those who cry out to God, "send your fire among us" think only of a Leviticus 9:24 fire, without considering the same fire is present to purify and cleanse in Leviticus 10:2. Truth be known, many of us desperately beg God *not* to send His fire, so the purity of His judgments will not be known among us. God reads our hearts and not only our pious prayers to send revival fire.

iv. **Devoured** in 10:2 is the same word as *consumed* in 9:24. The fire that consumed the sacrifice in approval and acceptance is the same fire that **devoured** Nadab and Abihu in judgment.

v. **Devoured them**: "Destroyed their lives; for their bodies and garments were not consumed, as it appears from Leviticus 10:4,5.

Thus the sword is said to devour, 2 Samuel 2:26. Thus lightning many times kills persons, without any hurt to their bodies or garments." (Poole)

c. **They died before the LORD**: They may have been struck down in the tabernacle, the tent of meeting itself.

3. (3) God's warning to Moses and Aaron.

And Moses said to Aaron, "This is what the LORD spoke, saying:

'By those who come near Me
I must be regarded as holy;
And before all the people
I must be glorified.'"

So Aaron held his peace.

a. **By those who come near Me I must be regarded as holy**: Many think they can come their own way before God and do their own thing in His presence. But God demands to be **regarded as holy** by all those who come near to Him.

i. Make no mistake: We can come to God just as we are, but we may not come to Him any way we please. We must come the way He has provided, the way made by Jesus Christ.

- **I must be regarded as holy** means that God *will* show His holiness.

- **I must be regarded as holy** means that God's servants *must* honor Him in a way that is fitting for a holy God.

ii. "Sanctified he will be, either in the sincerity of men's conversation, or else in the severity of their condemnation." (Trapp)

b. **And before all the people I must be glorified**: This reminds us that *God* must be **glorified** in the meetings of His people. The focus must not be on man, on his cleverness, on his insight, or on his ingenuity. Those who fail to glorify God will not be rewarded.

- **I must be glorified** means that God *will* guard and proclaim His glory.

- **I must be glorified** means that God's servants *must* be concerned for His glory, not their own glory, thrill-seeking, or curiosity.

c. **So Aaron held his peace**: Aaron just saw two of his sons struck down dead before the LORD. It was natural for him to question, or even to lament – but God would not allow it. At this moment, the respect of God's holiness was more important than Aaron's right to grieve, and Aaron was able to see this wrong from God's standpoint, not only his own.

> i. "How elegantly expressive is this of his parental affection, his deep sense of the presumption of his sons, and his own submission to the justice of God!" (Clarke)

B. Aftermath of God's judgment on Nadab and Abihu.

1. (4-5) The bodies are removed.

Then Moses called Mishael and Elzaphan, the sons of Uzziel the uncle of Aaron, and said to them, "Come near, carry your brethren from before the sanctuary out of the camp." So they went near and carried them by their tunics out of the camp, as Moses had said.

> a. **The sons of Uzziel the uncle of Aaron**: The men chosen to remove the bodies of Nadab and Abihu were related to Aaron and his sons, but they were not of the priestly line.

> b. **They went near and carried them by their tunics out of the camp**: Moses would not send a consecrated priest (Aaron or one of his sons) to carry these dead bodies outside the tabernacle courts to burial. The work of burial had to be done instead by these relatives.

2. (6-7) Mourning is prohibited.

And Moses said to Aaron, and to Eleazar and Ithamar, his sons, "Do not uncover your heads nor tear your clothes, lest you die, and wrath come upon all the people. But let your brethren, the whole house of Israel, bewail the burning which the LORD has kindled. You shall not go out from the door of the tabernacle of meeting, lest you die, for the anointing oil of the LORD *is* upon you." And they did according to the word of Moses.

> a. **Do not uncover your heads nor tear your clothes, lest you die, and wrath come upon all the people**: This perhaps was the hardest day of Aaron's life. Two of his sons were suddenly killed under the judgment of God, and he could not mourn them. To mourn might have implied – even in the slightest way – that God was wrong in bringing this judgment upon Nadab and Abihu. Aaron or Moses could not communicate this; it would dishonor God.

> > i. "Because the priests were intermediaries between God and his people, they were required more than all others to avoid contact with death. This included both contact with dead bodies and with the whole mourning procedure." (Peter-Contesse)

b. **You shall not go out from the door of the tabernacle of meeting, lest you die**: Aaron perhaps also thought, "I did worse than this at the golden calf incident; why did God judge them?" But Aaron did that *before* his consecration as a priest. After his consecration, he and his sons had a greater accountability (**for the anointing oil of the LORD is upon you**).

3. (8-11) The prohibition of drunkenness.

Then the LORD spoke to Aaron, saying: "Do not drink wine or intoxicating drink, you, nor your sons with you, when you go into the tabernacle of meeting, lest you die. *It shall be* **a statute forever throughout your generations, that you may distinguish between holy and unholy, and between unclean and clean, and that you may teach the children of Israel all the statutes which the LORD has spoken to them by the hand of Moses."**

a. **Do not drink wine or intoxicating drink, you, nor your sons with you, when you go into the tabernacle of meeting, lest you die**: This commandment for the priests of Israel came immediately after the judgment of Nadab and Abihu. This causes us to believe they may have been drunk when they foolishly offered their profane fire before the LORD.

> i. "Indeed, common sense itself shows that neither a *drunkard* nor a *sot* should ever be suffered to minister in holy things." (Clarke)

> ii. There are some who believe that God did not prohibit the use of alcohol among the priests in all cases, but only when they were "on duty," performing their priestly service. On this principle, it is a great mystery why some modern churches make the serving of alcohol part of their church meetings.

> iii. "Nothing has more power to blur the sharpness of moral and religious insight than even a small amount of alcohol. God must be worshipped with clear brain and naturally beating heart.... Lips stained from the wine-cup would not be fit to speak holy words. Words spoken by such would carry no power." (Maclaren)

> iv. Significantly, these were words that **the LORD spoke to Aaron**. "This new paragraph begins with the common formulaic expression for the Lord's revelation in Leviticus, this time with the recipient being Aaron instead of Moses. This in fact is the only occurrence in Leviticus where Aaron is directly spoken to by the Lord." (Rooker)

b. **That you may distinguish between holy and unholy, and between unclean and clean**: This is the first of two priestly responsibilities listed in verse 11. The priest had to discern and explain the difference **between**

holy and unholy, and between unclean and clean. He had to know it for himself, and explain it to the people.

i. A priest needed all his abilities to think and discern between the good and the evil. God did not want the hearts and minds of His servants clouded with alcohol when they came to serve Him. Since alcohol is a depressant, it takes away the ability to completely give one's self to God.

c. **That you may teach the children of Israel all the statutes which the LORD has spoken**: The second priestly responsibility in verse 11 concerned teaching **the children of Israel**. They were to teach them God's word as revealed by Moses (**all the statutes which the LORD has spoken**). As time went on, it would also include what **the LORD has spoken** through God's additional appointed prophets and messengers.

i. This responsibility on the part of the priests is often overlooked. We tend to look at them as only those who offered sacrifices. They did that, of course but they also were called to be active Bible teachers. The "teaching priest" is seen in many Old Testament passages.

- Deuteronomy 33:10: *They shall teach Jacob Your judgments and Israel Your law.*

- 2 Chronicles 17:7: *Also in the third year of his reign he sent his leaders, Ben-Hail, Obadiah, Zechariah, Nethanel, and Michaiah, to teach in the cities of Judah.*

- 2 Chronicles 15:3: *For a long time Israel has been without the true God, without a teaching priest, and without law.*

- Nehemiah 8:7: *Also Jeshua, Bani, Sherebiah, Jamin, Akkub, Shabbethai, Hodijah, Maaseiah, Kelita, Azariah, Jozabad, Hanan, Pelaiah, and the Levites helped the people to understand the Law.*

- Micah 3:11: *Her heads judge for a bribe, her priests teach for pay, and her prophets divine for money.*

- Ezekiel 7:26: *Disaster will come upon disaster, and rumor will be upon rumor. Then they will seek a vision from a prophet; but the law will perish from the priest, and counsel from the elders.*

- Malachi 2:7: *For the lips of a priest should keep knowledge, and people should seek the law from his mouth; for he is the messenger of the LORD of hosts.*

- Ezra 7:25: *And you, Ezra* [a priest]*, according to your God-given wisdom, set magistrates and judges who may judge all the people who* *are in the region beyond the River, all such as know the laws of your God; and teach those who do not know them.*

- Hosea 4:6: *My people are destroyed for lack of knowledge. Because you have rejected knowledge, I also will reject you from being priest for Me; because you have forgotten the law of your God, I also will forget your children.*

- Jeremiah 18:18: *Then they said, "Come and let us devise plans against Jeremiah; for the law shall not perish from the priest, nor counsel from the wise, nor the word from the prophet."*

ii. "Related to this latter function is the involvement of the priests in copying biblical manuscripts since most of the scribes were also priests." (Rooker)

4. (12-15) The priest's portions defined.

And Moses spoke to Aaron, and to Eleazar and Ithamar, his sons who were left: "Take the grain offering that remains of the offerings made by fire to the LORD, and eat it without leaven beside the altar; for it *is* most holy. You shall eat it in a holy place, because it *is* your due and your sons' due, of the sacrifices made by fire to the LORD; for so I have been commanded. The breast of the wave offering and the thigh of the heave offering you shall eat in a clean place, you, your sons, and your daughters with you; for *they are* your due and your sons' due, *which* are given from the sacrifices of peace offerings of the children of Israel. The thigh of the heave offering and the breast of the wave offering they shall bring with the offerings of fat made by fire, to offer *as* a wave offering before the LORD. And it shall be yours and your sons' with you, by a statute forever, as the LORD has commanded."

a. **Take the grain offering that remains of the offerings made by fire to the LORD, and eat it without leaven beside the altar**: What was left over from a grain offering belonged to the priests, but they could not take it home to eat it. It had to be eaten **beside the altar**.

b. **The breast of the wave offering and the thigh of the heave offering you shall eat in a clean place**: These portions of a sacrifice belonged to a priest *and to his household*. They could be eaten in any clean place.

5. (16-20) Confusion regarding what the priests should eat.

Then Moses made careful inquiry about the goat of the sin offering, and there it was—burned up. And he was angry with Eleazar and Ithamar, the sons of Aaron *who were* left, saying, "Why have you not eaten the sin offering in a holy place, since it *is* most holy, and *God* has given it to you to bear the guilt of the congregation, to make atonement for them before

the LORD? See! Its blood was not brought inside the holy *place;* indeed you should have eaten it in a holy *place,* as I commanded." And Aaron said to Moses, "Look, this day they have offered their sin offering and their burnt offering before the LORD, and such things have befallen me! *If* I had eaten the sin offering today, would it have been accepted in the sight of the LORD?" So when Moses heard *that,* he was content.

a. **Moses made careful inquiry about the goat of the sin offering, and there it was; burned up**: Moses wanted to know why Eleazar and Ithamar didn't eat the portions of sacrifice that were given for the priests to eat. Since Aaron replied on their behalf in Leviticus 10:19, it seems they did not eat it because they followed their father's example.

i. "Apparently after the death of Nadab and Abihu the food on the altar had not been consumed." (Rooker)

ii. We often find it easy to burn the sin offering, and hard to eat it. Burning hard against sin in a judging manner is easy. To sit down with a brother or sister as a fellow sinner and partake of the sin offering with them means you realize you aren't any better than them. Only this kind of heart can minister to people.

iii. Jesus had this kind of heart, even though He had no sin! He still identified with His people in His humble birth, simple life, baptism, and death. Moses said the sin offering was given **to bear the guilt of the congregation, to make atonement for them before the LORD.** That's why he was upset when Aaron didn't eat it. But Jesus did "eat" the sin offering when He stood as a sinner in our place and received the judgment we deserved.

b. **And such things have befallen me**: Aaron did not eat of the sin offering because he mourned the loss of his sons. Though Aaron was not allowed to do any of the other signs of mourning, it was appropriate that he fast on the day of his sons' death – and so he did, and Moses was satisfied with this explanation (**he was content**).

i. "*He was content*: literally, 'and it was good in his eyes.' (Compare 'good in the eyes of the LORD' in verse 19, where the same verb is used)." (Peter-Contesse)

Leviticus 11 – Clean and Unclean Animals

A. Laws regarding eating animals of land, sea, and air.

1. (1-8) Land-living mammals that can be eaten and not eaten.

Now the LORD spoke to Moses and Aaron, saying to them, "Speak to the children of Israel, saying, 'These *are* the animals which you may eat among all the animals that *are* on the earth: Among the animals, whatever divides the hoof, having cloven hooves *and* chewing the cud— that you may eat. Nevertheless these you shall not eat among those that chew the cud or those that have cloven hooves: the camel, because it chews the cud but does not have cloven hooves, is unclean to you; the rock hyrax, because it chews the cud but does not have cloven hooves, *is* unclean to you; the hare, because it chews the cud but does not have cloven hooves, *is* unclean to you; and the swine, though it divides the hoof, having cloven hooves, yet does not chew the cud, *is* unclean to you. Their flesh you shall not eat, and their carcasses you shall not touch. They *are* unclean to you.

> a. **Now the LORD spoke to Moses and Aaron**: This begins a section over the next five chapters dealing with matters of ceremonial impurity and separation from impurity. God spoke this to **Moses and Aaron** because they involved both the government (**Moses**) and the priesthood (**Aaron**).

> > i. After 10 chapters of laws dealing with priests and sacrifices, "Here we come to the laws which touch the ordinary and everyday life of the people…. [God] is interested in every detail of their lives. He issues His commands as to what they may eat, and what they may not eat." (Morgan)

> b. **These are the animals which you may eat**: The laws God gave to Israel dealt with many aspects of life, and here begins a section with the laws

about what animals they **may eat** and what they were not permitted to eat. God gave these laws **to the children of Israel**, not to humanity in general.

i. Even in the days of Noah there was a distinction between clean and unclean animals (Genesis 7:2 and 8:20), but this may have only been for the purpose of sacrifice. Still, there was an early basis for these laws that God gave **to the children of Israel**.

ii. The reasons for the dietary laws are not clearly presented, and many have suggested the reasons. The suggested reasons fall into several categories: "symbolic, ethical, aesthetic, hygienic, morphological, and theological criteria" (Rooker). From all these, the purpose of these dietary laws can be summarized in three points.

iii. *The dietary laws gave the Israelites an opportunity to demonstrate obedience to God.* Overall, God's intent was to make Israel a holy nation, separate from the other nations – obedient to God, not only to their bellies. Just as the first law God gave to humanity had to do with what could and could not be eaten, so these laws were given to Israel as a test of their obedience and separation to God.

iv. *The dietary laws separated the Israelites from their Gentile, pagan neighbors.* This limited the true fellowship and connection an obedient Israelite could have with the surrounding peoples who did not worship or obey Yahweh. As well, some of these animals declared unclean for eating were animals that were idolized in pagan religions.

v. *The dietary laws helped to protect the health of the Jewish people.* Many diseases and problems were prevented by obedience to these dietary laws.

vi. This understanding is attacked based on the thinking that if this was the case, then it makes no sense for God to allow the eating of these animals under the New Covenant. However, it is reasonable to think that in the more than 1,500 years from the time of the giving of the Law of Moses to the first-century church, there was a better understanding of what made some meat dangerous and other meat safe.

vii. It is also reasonable to think that by protecting the health of the Jewish nation through dietary laws God ensured the continuation and prosperity of His covenant people.

c. **Among all the animals that are on the earth**: The dietary laws began with the animals most commonly eaten, mammals that are land based. For these animals, the rule was simple: **among the animals, whatever divides the hoof, having cloven hooves and chewing the cud; that you may**

eat. If an animal had a divided **hoof** (not a single hoof as a horse has) and chewed its **cud**, it could be eaten (**that you may eat**).

d. **These you shall not eat among those that chew the cud or those that have cloven hooves**: Here, many animals are mentioned that fit one requirement (**chew the cud**) or the other (**cloven hooves**), but not both.

i. For example, the **camel**, the **rock hyrax**, and the **hare** all chew the cud, but do not have divided hooves – instead, they have paws – they are considered **unclean** and are not to be eaten.

e. **And the swine, though it divides the hoof, having cloven hooves, yet does not chew the cud, is unclean to you**: Additionally, the **swine** has a divided hoof, but it does not chew the cud – so it is considered unkosher.

i. "The Hebrew term used here refers to the wild pig…. This animal is singled out perhaps because swine were considered especially offensive and to be avoided at all cost." (Peter-Contesse)

ii. "It is now known that the pig is the intermediate host for several parasitic organisms, some of which can result in tapeworm infestation. One of these worms, the *Taenia solium*, grows to about 2.5 m in length, and is found in poorly cooked pork." (Harrison)

f. **Their flesh you shall not eat, and their carcasses you shall not touch**: If an animal was considered unclean, it could not be used for food. Yet additionally, one could not touch an unclean animal, whether living or dead.

2. (9-12) Water creatures that can and cannot be eaten.

'These you may eat of all that *are* in the water: whatever in the water has fins and scales, whether in the seas or in the rivers—that you may eat. But all in the seas or in the rivers that do not have fins and scales, all that move in the water or any living thing which *is* in the water, they *are* an abomination to you. They shall be an abomination to you; you shall not eat their flesh, but you shall regard their carcasses as an abomination. Whatever in the water does not have fins or scales—that shall be an abomination to you.

a. **These you may eat of all that are in the water**: The rule again was simple: Any water creature having both **fins and scales** was kosher and could be eaten.

i. "There is evidence that fish without scales were also avoided by the Romans and Egyptians. These types of fish may have been regarded as scavengers, since they roamed the bottom of the sea. They were also the carriers of numerous parasites." (Rooker)

b. **Whatever in the water has fins and scales, whether in the seas or in the rivers; that you may eat**: On this principle, most fishes were considered clean – except a fish like the catfish, which has no scales. Shellfish would be unclean, because clams, crabs, oysters, and lobster all do not have fins and scales. Under these dietary laws given to Israel, these were to be regarded as an **abomination** and could not be eaten.

3. (13-19) Birds and other flying things that can and cannot be eaten.

'**And these you shall regard as an abomination among the birds; they shall not be eaten, they** *are* **an abomination: the eagle, the vulture, the buzzard, the kite, and the falcon after its kind; every raven after its kind, the ostrich, the short-eared owl, the sea gull, and the hawk after its kind; the little owl, the fisher owl, and the screech owl; the white owl, the jackdaw, and the carrion vulture; the stork, the heron after its kind, the hoopoe, and the bat.**

a. **These you shall regard as an abomination among the birds**: There was no rule given to determine if a bird was clean or unclean. Instead, specific birds (twenty in all) are mentioned as being unclean and therefore forbidden for eating.

b. **The eagle, the vulture, the buzzard**: The common thread through most of these birds is that they are either *predators* or *scavengers*. These birds were considered unclean.

i. "Many scholars maintain that it was the preying upon other animals with the real possibility that these animals would drink the blood of their victims that rendered them unclean." (Rooker)

4. (20-23) Insects that can and cannot be eaten.

'**All flying insects that creep on** *all* **fours** *shall be* **an abomination to you. Yet these you may eat of every flying insect that creeps on** *all* **fours: those which have jointed legs above their feet with which to leap on the earth. These you may eat: the locust after its kind, the destroying locust after its kind, the cricket after its kind, and the grasshopper after its kind. But all** *other* **flying insects which have four feet** *shall be* **an abomination to you.**

a. **All flying insects that creep on all fours shall be an abomination to you**: Among insects, any creeping insect was considered unclean (such as ants or grubs). Yet if there were a flying insect with legs jointed above their feet, these *could* be eaten. Good examples of clean insects include the **locust**, the **cricket**, and the **grasshopper**.

i. "The *locust* was eaten, not only in those ancient times, in the time of John Baptist, Matt. 3:4, but also in the present day. Dr. Shaw ate of them in Barbary 'fried and salted,' and tells us that 'they tasted very like crayfish.'" (Clarke)

b. That creeps on all fours: Some people think this means Moses was uninformed and did not understand that most insects have six legs. The phrase used for **creeps on all fours** doesn't necessarily mean that.

i. "This phrase can hardly describe insects as having four legs, since the *Insectae* as a class normally have six legs. The reference is evidently to their movements, which resemble the creeping or running of the four-footed animal." (Harrison)

ii. "The expression was probably used in a nonliteral sense, meaning 'to crawl,' and was used of any flying creature with more than two legs." (Peter-Contesse)

B. More on clean and unclean animals.

1. (24-28) Disposal of the carcasses of unclean animals.

'By these you shall become unclean; whoever touches the carcass of any of them shall be unclean until evening; whoever carries part of the carcass of any of them shall wash his clothes and be unclean until evening: *The carcass* **of any animal which divides the foot, but is not cloven-hoofed or does not chew the cud,** *is* **unclean to you. Everyone who touches it shall be unclean. And whatever goes on its paws, among all kinds of animals that go on** *all* **fours, those** *are* **unclean to you. Whoever touches any such carcass shall be unclean until evening. Whoever carries** *any such* **carcass shall wash his clothes and be unclean until evening. It** *is* **unclean to you.**

a. **Whoever touches the carcass of any of them shall be unclean until evening**: Unclean animals, when dead, couldn't just be left in the community to rot; they had to be disposed of. But the people who disposed of the unclean animals had to deal with their uncleanness by washing and a brief (**until evening**) quarantine.

i. This meant that if a dead rat was found in an Israelite village, it would be carefully and promptly disposed of, and the one disposing of it would wash afterward. This practice would help prevent disease in a significant way. When the bubonic plague – the Black Death – killed one-quarter of Europe's population in the 1300s, many Jewish communities were largely spared because they followed these hygienic regulations. Sadly, because these Jewish communities were often spared the high death count from the plague, they were many times accused and punished for having caused the plague. These were sad chapters in the history of Christianity.

b. **Whoever carries any such carcass shall wash his clothes and be unclean until evening**: This shows that ceremonial uncleanness was not the same as being in a state of sin. No sacrifice was required to remedy the condition of ceremonial uncleanness. It was a state of ceremonial impurity that needed to be addressed.

2. (29-30) More unclean animals: Reptiles and other creeping things.

"These also *shall be* unclean to you among the creeping things that creep on the earth: the mole, the mouse, and the large lizard after its kind; the gecko, the monitor lizard, the sand reptile, the sand lizard, and the chameleon.

a. **The mole, the mouse**: This brief grouping of animals that are **creeping things that creep on the earth** includes mammals such as the **mole** and the **mouse**. These are also excluded based on the requirements of verses 1-8 but are repeated here for clarity.

b. **The large lizard after its kind; the gecko**: In addition, these reptiles (also **creeping things that creep on the earth**) could not be eaten.

3. (31-38) The transmission of uncleanness from unclean animals.

These *are* unclean to you among all that creep. Whoever touches them when they are dead shall be unclean until evening. Anything on which *any* of them falls, when they are dead shall be unclean, whether *it is* any item of wood or clothing or skin or sack, whatever item *it is,* in which *any* work is done, it must be put in water. And it shall be unclean until evening; then it shall be clean. Any earthen vessel into which *any* of them falls you shall break; and whatever *is* in it shall be unclean: in such a vessel, any edible food upon which water falls becomes unclean, and any drink that may be drunk from it becomes unclean. And everything on which *a part* of *any such* carcass falls shall be unclean; *whether it is* an oven or cooking stove, it shall be broken down; *for* they *are* unclean, and shall be unclean to you. Nevertheless a spring or a cistern, *in which there is* plenty of water, shall be clean, but whatever touches any such carcass becomes unclean. And if a part of *any such* carcass falls on any planting seed which is to be sown, it *remains* clean. But if water is put on the seed, and if *a part* of *any such* carcass falls on it, it *becomes* unclean to you.

a. **Whoever touches them when they are dead shall be unclean until evening**: From a hygienic standpoint, these laws were very important. They required, for example, that if a rodent crawled inside a bowl, the bowl had to be broken. Therefore, any disease the rodent carried (such as bubonic plague) could not be passed on to the one who would use the bowl.

b. **It must be put in water**: Some things (an **item of wood or clothing or skin or sack**) could be cleansed by washing in water. A clay **vessel** had to be destroyed (**you shall break**). Contaminated food or drink had to be thrown out. Cooking tools were unclean if contaminated with dead, unclean animals.

i. These laws gave the Israelite household a reason to *prevent* pests and creeping things from coming into a house. No one wanted to destroy many earthen vessels and cooking tools or throw out a lot of food.

c. **Everything on which a part of any such carcass falls shall be unclean**: Therefore, these laws also promoted a general state of cleanliness inside the Israelite home. This certainly helped the health and the welfare of the family.

4. (39-40) Carcasses of clean animals.

'And if any animal which you may eat dies, he who touches its carcass shall be unclean until evening. He who eats of its carcass shall wash his clothes and be unclean until evening. He also who carries its carcass shall wash his clothes and be unclean until evening.

a. **If any animal which you may eat dies**: Seemingly, these laws apply to the natural death of clean animals, not to their butchering for food or death for sacrifice.

b. **Shall wash his clothes and be unclean until evening**: Those handling such carcasses were ceremonially unclean and needed to be cleansed by washing and a brief quarantine.

5. (41-43) Creeping animals considered unclean.

'And every creeping thing that creeps on the earth *shall be* an abomination. It shall not be eaten. Whatever crawls on its belly, whatever goes on *all* fours, or whatever has many feet among all creeping things that creep on the earth—these you shall not eat, for they *are* an abomination. You shall not make yourselves abominable with any creeping thing that creeps; nor shall you make yourselves unclean with them, lest you be defiled by them.

a. **Every creeping thing that creeps on the earth shall be an abomination**: Many of these animals were considered in verses 29-30. For clarity and emphasis, they are repeated.

b. **You shall not make yourselves abominable with any creeping thing**: It was considered highly sinful and even idolatrous to eat these forbidden

creeping things. In the Old Testament, the idea of **an abomination** is often linked to idolatry.

6. (44-47) The purpose of God's dietary laws.

For I *am* the LORD your God. You shall therefore consecrate yourselves, and you shall be holy; for I *am* holy. Neither shall you defile yourselves with any creeping thing that creeps on the earth. For I *am* the LORD who brings you up out of the land of Egypt, to be your God. You shall therefore be holy, for I *am* holy. "This *is* the law of the animals and the birds and every living creature that moves in the waters, and of every creature that creeps on the earth, to distinguish between the unclean and the clean, and between the animal that may be eaten and the animal that may not be eaten."'

a. **For I am the LORD your God**: God claims the right to speak to every area of our life, including what we eat. He had the right to tell Israel what to eat and what not to eat.

b. **You shall therefore consecrate yourselves**: One great purpose of the dietary laws of Israel was to **consecrate** them – to sanctify or set them apart – from the Gentile nations. It made fellowship with those who did not serve God far more difficult.

> i. We see this consecrating effect in Daniel 1, where Daniel and his friends refused to eat the unkosher food at the king of Babylon's table. God blessed them for being set apart for His righteousness.

c. **Neither shall you defile yourselves**: Not only did unclean animals defile the children of Israel spiritually, but there was also a hygienic defilement, and Israel was spared many diseases and plagues because of their kosher diet.

> i. Among the animals, most considered unclean fell into one of three categories: *Predators* (unclean because they ate both the flesh and the blood of animals), *scavengers* (unclean because they were carriers of disease, and they regularly contacted dead bodies), or *potentially poisonous or dangerous* foods such as shellfish and the like. Eliminating these from the diet of ancient Israel promoted good health among them.

> ii. "In general it can be said that the laws protected Israel from bad diet, dangerous vermin, and communicable diseases." (Harris)

d. **For I am the LORD who brings you up out of Egypt**: God had a claim to the obedience of the people of Israel because He was their *redeemer*. He freed them from 400 years of Egyptian slavery. Israel was also obligated to God because He was their *creator*, but He was also their *redeemer*.

i. Some Christians believe we are under obligation to observe these dietary laws of clean and unclean animals today. This is not true. First, these laws were specifically given *to the children of Israel* (verse 2). Second, this issue was settled once and for all at the Jerusalem Council in Acts 15. There, it was determined that obedience to the laws of Moses was not required of the followers of Jesus. So, as Paul wrote in Colossians 2:16: *So let no one judge you in food or in drink.*

ii. Paul also explained that for Christians, there is danger in legalistically declaring some foods forbidden for others: *Now the Spirit expressly says that in the latter times some will depart from the faith, giving heed to deceiving spirits and doctrine of demons...commanding to abstain from foods which God created to be received with thanksgiving by those who believe and know the truth. For every creature of God is good, and nothing is to be refused if it is received with thanksgiving; for it is sanctified by the word of God and prayer.* (1 Timothy 4:1, 3-5)

iii. Some people live under bondage when it comes to food; they are addicted to eating certain foods that aren't helpful for them. The principle of 1 Corinthians 6:12 teaches us that it is wise to eat what is helpful to us, and we should not be under the power of what we eat: *All things are lawful for me, but all things are not helpful. All things are lawful for me, but I will not be brought under the power of any.* Certainly, many would benefit from the attitude of self-denial and bodily discipline Paul spoke of in 1 Corinthians 9:24-27.

iv. Yet, apart from these considerations, Christians are free to eat or not eat whatever they please – and no one should think themselves more right with God because they eat or don't eat certain things. As Romans 14:14 says: *I know and am convinced by the Lord Jesus that there is nothing unclean of itself; but to him who considers anything to be unclean, to him it is unclean.*

v. "If today we are not to be governed by the actual rules of this Hebrew law, the principle involved in it finds expression in the words of Paul: 'Whatever therefore you eat, or drink, or whatsoever you do, do all to the glory of God' (1 Corinthians 10:31)." (Morgan)

Leviticus 12 – Cleansing After Childbirth

A. Ceremonial impurity after giving birth.

1. (1-4) When a male child is born.

Then the LORD spoke to Moses, saying, "Speak to the children of Israel, saying: 'If a woman has conceived, and borne a male child, then she shall be unclean seven days; as in the days of her customary impurity she shall be unclean. And on the eighth day the flesh of his foreskin shall be circumcised. She shall then continue in the blood of *her* purification thirty-three days. She shall not touch any hallowed thing, nor come into the sanctuary until the days of her purification are fulfilled.

a. **If a woman has conceived, and borne a male child, then she shall be unclean seven days**: After giving birth to a **male child**, a mother was considered ceremonially **unclean seven days**. The boy was then circumcised on the eighth day.

i. Mary, the mother of Jesus, brought Him to the temple on the eighth day after His birth (Luke 2:21). Jesus fulfilled the law in every respect, including His circumcision **on the eighth day**.

b. **On the eighth day the flesh of his foreskin shall be circumcised**: God commanded Abraham that his male covenant descendants (through Isaac and Jacob) should be circumcised when eight days old (Genesis 17:12). This was a sign of the covenant God made with Abraham and his covenant descendants (Genesis 17:11), and here is also commanded as an aspect of the Law of Moses.

i. Circumcision was not unknown in the ancient world. It was a ritual practice among various peoples. Yet for the Israelite, "Circumcision was to every man a *constant, evident* sign of the covenant into which he had entered with God, and of the moral obligations under which he was thereby laid." (Clarke)

101

ii. There were undoubtedly hygienic reasons for circumcision, especially making sense in the ancient world. In his book *None of These Diseases*, S.I. McMillen noted studies in 1949 and 1954 that showed a remarkably low rate of cervical cancer for Jewish women because they mostly have husbands who are circumcised.

iii. But more importantly, circumcision is a cutting away of the flesh and an appropriate sign of the covenant for those who should put no trust in the flesh. Also, because circumcision deals with the organ of procreation, it was a reminder of the special seed of Abraham, which would ultimately bring the Messiah.

iv. In Colossians 2:11-12, the Apostle Paul connected the ideas of circumcision and Christian baptism. His idea was that in Jesus we are *spiritually* circumcised, and we are also buried with Jesus in baptism. Paul did not say that baptism is the sign of the covenant Christians receive and live under, the New Covenant. Even if that connection is made, it is important to note that one was genetically born into the covenant described here and in Genesis 17. One is not genetically born into the New Covenant; one is born again into it by God's grace through faith. It is wrong and harmful to make the analogy, "babies were circumcised, so babies should be baptized."

c. **She shall then continue in the blood of her purification thirty-three days**: When a son was born, a mother's ceremonial uncleanness lasted an additional 33 days, for a total of 40 days of ceremonial impurity after giving birth to a male child. There were several reasons for this, but one important reason was to give an Israelite mother an ancient equivalent to the modern maternity leave. Here ceremonial uncleanness relieved her of many social obligations. Mothers welcomed these days of rest, seclusion, and bonding with the newborn.

i. In the law of ancient Israel, blood had sacred associations. It was understood that the life of a being was in their blood (Genesis 9:4, Leviticus 17:11); loss of blood can mean the loss of life. The blood of menstruation made a woman ritually unclean (Leviticus 15:19-24). Even animals had to be bled in a certain way in sacrifice or slaughter. Since childbirth is always associated with blood, it makes sense that there was a special ritual purification after childbirth. "Because life is in the blood (17:11), the loss of blood required some purification to acknowledge the sanctity of life." (Rooker)

ii. Mary, the mother of Jesus, also fulfilled these days of purification (Luke 2:22-24). It was on this occasion that Simeon (Luke 2:25-35) and Anna (Luke 2:36-38) met Jesus and His family and spoke their words of blessing and thanks.

iii. When Mary gave birth to Jesus, she was *not* responsible for bringing a sinner into the world. Nevertheless, Jesus identified with sinful humanity – even as an infant.

d. **She shall not touch any hallowed thing**: The commanded time of ceremonial impurity should not be regarded as a negative attitude towards birth or childbearing on God's part. God *commands* childbearing, in that humanity is commanded to be fruitful and multiply (Genesis 1:28), that children are regarded as a gift from God (Psalm 127:3), and that a woman with many children is considered blessed (Psalm 128:3).

i. The key to understanding this ceremony is to understand the idea of original sin. As wonderful as a new baby is, God wanted it to be remembered that with every birth another sinner was brought into the world, and in this symbolic picture, the mother was responsible for bringing a new sinner into the world.

ii. **She shall be unclean:** "Motherhood is one of the most sacred and beautiful things in the whole realm of human experience. This needs no argument. But motherhood is exercised in a race which is defiled. When the great singer of Israel, in his penitential psalm, said: 'Behold, I was shapen in iniquity, and in sin did my mother conceive me' (Psalm 51:5), he was casting no reflection upon his own mother, but rather stating a racial fact, from which no human being escapes." (Morgan)

2. (5) When a female child is born.

'But if she bears a female child, then she shall be unclean two weeks, as in her customary impurity, and she shall continue in the blood of *her* purification sixty-six days.

a. **If she bears a female child, then she shall be unclean two weeks**: The time period for each phase was double what was required when giving birth to a son. For the birth of a daughter, a woman was unclean for 14 days followed by 66 days. A mother of a **female child** received double of the ancient equivalent of maternity leave.

i. "On the purely physical side it will bear close and reverent consideration, providing as it did for the perfect repose of the new mother." (Morgan)

b. **She shall continue in the blood of her purification sixty-six days**: The longer period of ceremonial uncleanness for the birth of a daughter should not be understood as a penalty. Instead, it is linked to the idea stated in the previous verses – that the time of impurity is for the symbolic responsibility of bringing other sinners into the world. When giving birth to a female, a mother brings a sinner into the world who will bring still other sinners into the world.

i. It has also been suggested the longer period of time in connection with the birth of a girl was because girls are usually smaller at birth, and this would allow more time for the mother's focused care and attention on the child. As well, since sons were more prized, the longer time at home for a mother with a newborn girl would force the family to bond more deeply, over a more extended period of time with the newborn girl.

B. The purification rite for cleansing after childbirth.

1. (6-7) The sacrifice required.

'When the days of her purification are fulfilled, whether for a son or a daughter, she shall bring to the priest a lamb of the first year as a burnt offering, and a young pigeon or a turtledove as a sin offering, to the door of the tabernacle of meeting. Then he shall offer it before the LORD, and make atonement for her. And she shall be clean from the flow of her blood. This *is* the law for her who has borne a male or a female.

a. **Then he shall offer it before the LORD, and make atonement for her**: This was a fairly standard sacrifice for **atonement**, holding the woman symbolically responsible for bringing another sinner into this world. The mother had to bring **a lamb of the first year** to be a burnt offering, marking the dedication of the child to God. The mother also brought **a young pigeon or a turtledove** to be a sin offering, making **atonement**.

b. **For her who has borne a male or a female**: The mother's required sacrifice was the same whether she gave birth to a boy or a girl.

2. (8) Allowances for the poor.

'And if she is not able to bring a lamb, then she may bring two turtledoves or two young pigeons; one as a burnt offering and the other as a sin offering. So the priest shall make atonement for her, and she will be clean.'"

a. **If she is not able to bring a lamb**: God knew that not every family in Israel could afford to bring a lamb for sacrifice at the birth of a child. Therefore, He also allowed the lesser sacrifices of **two turtledoves or two young pigeons**.

i. Jesus' family offered only a pair of turtledoves (Luke 2:22-24) at birth. This shows that Jesus did not come from a wealthy family. It also means that the wise men, who gave costly gifts to Jesus (Matthew 2:11), had not yet visited the family of Jesus.

ii. "What a glimpse into our Master's humiliation! He owned the cattle on a thousand hills, yet He so emptied Himself that His parents were compelled to bring the poorest offering the law allowed. He stooped that we might rise; emptied Himself that we might be full; became poor that we might be made rich; was made human that we might be made Divine." (Meyer)

b. **So the priest shall make atonement for her**: This sacrifice marked the end of her time of ceremonial impurity; the mother was regarded as **clean**.

i. "If men are born in sin, through expiation and devotion a way is yet made for their restoration to the place of communion with God. Thus at the beginning of every life the appalling need and the gracious provision were brought freshly to mind." (Morgan)

Leviticus 13 – The Diagnosis of Leprosy

A. Instructions to the priests for diagnosing leprosy.

1. (1-8) The method of examination for leprosy.

And the LORD spoke to Moses and Aaron, saying: "When a man has on the skin of his body a swelling, a scab, or a bright spot, and it becomes on the skin of his body *like* a leprous sore, then he shall be brought to Aaron the priest or to one of his sons the priests. The priest shall examine the sore on the skin of the body; and if the hair on the sore has turned white, and the sore appears *to be* deeper than the skin of his body, it *is* a leprous sore. Then the priest shall examine him, and pronounce him unclean. But if the bright spot *is* white on the skin of his body, and does not appear *to be* deeper than the skin, and its hair has not turned white, then the priest shall isolate *the one who has* the sore seven days. And the priest shall examine him on the seventh day; and indeed *if* the sore appears to be as it was, *and* the sore has not spread on the skin, then the priest shall isolate him another seven days. Then the priest shall examine him again on the seventh day; and indeed *if* the sore has faded, *and* the sore has not spread on the skin, then the priest shall pronounce him clean; it *is only* a scab, and he shall wash his clothes and be clean. But if the scab should at all spread over the skin, after he has been seen by the priest for his cleansing, he shall be seen by the priest again. And *if* the priest sees that the scab has indeed spread on the skin, then the priest shall pronounce him unclean. It *is* leprosy.

a. **When a man has on the skin of his body a swelling, a scab, or a bright spot**: This larger part of Leviticus (chapters 11 through 15) deals with laws of purity. In chapter 11, the laws of purity regarding the eating of animals were given. In chapter 12, the laws of purity regarding childbirth were given. In chapters 13 and 14, we have laws regarding growths and sores on the skin, walls, and fabrics. These were investigated for the presence of leprosy.

b. The priest shall examine the sore on the skin of the body: It was the job of the priests of Israel to **examine** these potentially diseased areas. In this sense, the priests served as public health officers and diagnosed the disease from these carefully defined criteria, not from intuition or guessing.

i. "The Hebrew priest-physicians appear to have been the first in the ancient world to isolate persons suspected of infectious or contagious diseases." (Harrison)

ii. "The law provided that there should be most careful distinction made between actual leprosy and that which may appear to be leprosy. When the case was a clearly defined one, the method was drastic in the extreme." (Morgan)

c. If the hair on the sore has turned white, and the sore appears to be deeper than the skin of his body, it is a leprous sore: The methodology in this passage erred on the side of safety. If a person could not be pronounced **clean** (free from leprosy) with certainty, they were then isolated until they could be pronounced **clean**.

i. These judgments were based on sound medical diagnosis and concern. These judgments were made with a concern for the benefit of the afflicted person, but with an even greater concern for the health of the community from the outbreak of disease. "These two principles are perpetual in their application. The State should ever have the right of inspection and examination. It should, however, use its right with the greatest care that no wrong be done to any individual." (Morgan)

ii. "The type of infectious disease is not specified but has often been associated with leprosy (Hansen's disease), since the noun *sara at* was translated *lepra* in the LXX and thus 'leprosy' in earlier English translations." (Rooker)

iii. "The Hebrew word does not exactly correspond to what we call 'leprosy' today. It is rather a very general term that perhaps includes ringworm, psoriasis, leucoderma, as well as 'Hansen's disease' (the modern medical terminology used to refer to what is commonly called 'leprosy' today)." (Peter-Contesse)

iv. Illnesses such as smallpox, measles, and scarlet fever might start out with a skin condition considered to be leprosy – and the person would be isolated for the necessary time until the condition cleared up. This quarantine helped prevent the spread of these kinds of diseases among the people of Israel.

d. **It is leprosy**: Leprosy was dealt with so seriously because it was such a horrible disease. It was also a dramatic picture of sin and its spiritual operation in human beings.

i. When leprosy first appears on a victim's skin, it begins as small, red spots. Before too long they get bigger, start to turn white, having a shiny or scaly appearance. Soon the spots spread over the entire body and the hair begins to fall out – first from the head, then even from the eyebrows. As things get worse, the fingernails and toenails become loose; they start to rot and eventually fall off. Then the joints of fingers and toes begin to rot and start to fall off piece by piece. In the mouth, the gums start shrinking and are unable to hold teeth, so several teeth are often lost. Leprosy keeps eating away at the face until the nose is literally gone, and the palate and even eyes rot – and the victim wastes away until death.

ii. "Even until to-day leprosy is so dire a disease that it completely baffles the skill of the physician. Much may be done to alleviate the distress which it causes, but there is no cure for it. In countries where sanitary laws obtain, it is almost eliminated, but that is done by removing causes, not by curing those suffering from it." (G. Campbell Morgan in 1926)

iii. "Leprosy was indeed nothing short of a living death, a poisoning of the springs, a corrupting of all the humours of life; a dissolution little by little of the whole body, so that one limb after another actually decayed and fell away." (Trench in *Notes on the Miracles*)

iv. "These precautions were taken not merely for sanitary reasons, or to guard against contagion, for it is not certain that leprosy was contagious, but in order that the people might be taught through the parable of leprosy, what a fearful and loathsome thing sin is in the sight of God." (Taylor)

v. Leprosy is like sin in many ways. There are some good reasons why many ancient rabbis considered a leper as someone already dead. Leprosy is like sin in that:

- It begins as nothing.
- It is painless in its first stages.
- It grows slowly.
- It often remits for a while and then returns.
- It numbs the senses – one cannot feel in the afflicted area.
- It causes decay and deformity.

- It eventually gives a person a repulsive appearance.

vi. "Every man by nature is like a leper, loathsome in his person, infected in all his actions and in all that he does; he is incapable of fellowship with God's people, and he is shut out utterly and entirely by his sin from the presence and acceptance of God." (Spurgeon)

vii. "In the light of these considerations, we remember that there came in the fulness of time One Who could not only look at, but touch the leper – One Who could cure. That is also the story of His dealing with sin." (Morgan)

2. (9-11) Examining a swollen sore.

"When the leprous sore is on a person, then he shall be brought to the priest. And the priest shall examine *him;* and indeed *if* the swelling on the skin *is* white, and it has turned the hair white, and *there is* a spot of raw flesh in the swelling, it *is* an old leprosy on the skin of his body. The priest shall pronounce him unclean, and shall not isolate him, for he *is* unclean.

a. **And the priest shall examine him**: This section clearly shows the very specific rules for making an exact diagnosis of leprosy. The details given in so many different situations emphasize that God did not want this to be guesswork but the result of careful examination. Such a serious diagnosis should not be guessed.

i. **A spot of raw flesh in the swelling**: This "showed that this was not a superficial leprosy, but one of a deeper and more malignant nature, that had eaten into the very flesh, for which cause it is in the next verse called *an old, or inveterate, or grown leprosy.*" (Poole)

b. **The priest shall pronounce him unclean, and shall not isolate him**: If a man or a woman was diagnosed with leprosy, they were no longer in isolation under the supervision of the priests. They lived on their own, excluded from the larger community of Israel (as described in verses 45-46).

i. "The only thing that the priest could do, was to discover whether or not the disease was actual leprosy. If it were not, then there might be a period of separation, and presently a restoration to the community. If it were leprosy, nothing could be done other than to separate the sufferer completely from others." (Morgan)

3. (12-17) Examining an outbreak over the entire body.

"And if leprosy breaks out all over the skin, and the leprosy covers all the skin of *the one who has* the sore, from his head to his foot, wherever

the priest looks, then the priest shall consider; and indeed *if* **the leprosy has covered all his body, he shall pronounce** *him* **clean** *who has* **the sore. It has all turned white. He** *is* **clean. But when raw flesh appears on him, he shall be unclean. And the priest shall examine the raw flesh and pronounce him to be unclean;** *for* **the raw flesh** *is* **unclean. It** *is* **leprosy. Or if the raw flesh changes and turns white again, he shall come to the priest. And the priest shall examine him; and indeed** *if* **the sore has turned white, then the priest shall pronounce** *him* **clean** *who has* **the sore. He** *is* **clean.**

a. **If leprosy breaks out all over the skin**: It is apparent in this chapter that the Biblical term **leprosy** covered a broader range of skin diseases than the modern technical diagnosis of leprosy.

b. **If the leprosy has covered all his body, he shall pronounce him clean**: This is counter-intuitive but apparently dealing with these ancient skin diseases, this stage of the disease gave hope for recovery. In addition, it provides a powerful spiritual picture, given the association of leprosy with humanity's sinful condition.

i. Rooker sees that the key phrase in regard to the one whose **leprosy has covered all his body** is, **it has turned all white**. "White skin indicated that a healing of the disease had taken place since the white skin would be new skin that had grown over the raw flesh."

ii. "At first sight this seems a very extraordinary provision. When the leprosy was beginning to show itself, and whilst the marks were hardly distinguishable, the poor patient was treated as unclean; but, when it had fully developed, from the crown of the head to the sole of the foot, the priest pronounced the leper clean." (Meyer)

iii. "As long as we palliate and excuse our sins, and dream that there is much in us which is noble and lovely, we are not fit subjects for God's saving grace.... we must confess that from the crown of our head to the sole of our foot we are full of need and sin – then we are nearest Christ, and in a fit condition to be richly blest, and made the channel of blessing to others." (Meyer)

c. **He is clean…. he shall be unclean**: The priest was to pronounce the afflicted person either **clean** or **unclean**, based on the instructions in this chapter.

4. (18-23) Examining a boil on the skin.

"If the body develops a boil in the skin, and it is healed, and in the place of the boil there comes a white swelling or a bright spot, reddish-white, then it shall be shown to the priest; and *if,* **when the priest sees**

it, it indeed *appears* deeper than the skin, and its hair has turned white, the priest shall pronounce him unclean. It *is* a leprous sore which has broken out of the boil. But if the priest examines it, and indeed *there are* no white hairs in it, and it *is* not deeper than the skin, but has faded, then the priest shall isolate him seven days; and if it should at all spread over the skin, then the priest shall pronounce him unclean. It *is* a leprous sore. But if the bright spot stays in one place, *and* has not spread, it *is* the scar of the boil; and the priest shall pronounce him clean.

> a. **If the body develops a boil in the skin**: The priests were given the criteria to examine and judge the severity of boils and their aftermath.

5. (24-28) Examining a burn on the skin.

"Or if the body receives a burn on its skin by fire, and the raw *flesh* of the burn becomes a bright spot, reddish-white or white, then the priest shall examine it; and indeed *if* the hair of the bright spot has turned white, and it appears deeper than the skin, it *is* leprosy broken out in the burn. Therefore the priest shall pronounce him unclean. It *is* a leprous sore. But if the priest examines it, and indeed *there are* no white hairs in the bright spot, and it *is* not deeper than the skin, but has faded, then the priest shall isolate him seven days. And the priest shall examine him on the seventh day. If it has at all spread over the skin, then the priest shall pronounce him unclean. It *is* a leprous sore. But if the bright spot stays in one place, *and* has not spread on the skin, but has faded, it *is* a swelling from the burn. The priest shall pronounce him clean, for it *is* the scar from the burn.

> a. **If the body receives a burn on its skin by fire**: The priests were given the criteria to examine and judge the severity of burns and their aftermath.

> b. **The raw flesh of the burn becomes a bright spot**: The examination and diagnosis of the skin diseases associated with a burn were the same as those associated with a boil (verses 18-23).

6. (29-37) Examining sores in the midst of hair.

"If a man or woman has a sore on the head or the beard, then the priest shall examine the sore; and indeed if it appears deeper than the skin, *and there is* in it thin yellow hair, then the priest shall pronounce him unclean. It *is* a scaly leprosy of the head or beard. But if the priest examines the scaly sore, and indeed it does not appear deeper than the skin, and *there is* no black hair in it, then the priest shall isolate *the one who has* the scale seven days. And on the seventh day the priest shall examine the sore; and indeed *if* the scale has not spread, and there is no yellow hair in it, and the scale does not appear deeper than the skin, he

shall shave himself, but the scale he shall not shave. And the priest shall isolate *the one who has* the scale another seven days. On the seventh day the priest shall examine the scale; and indeed *if* the scale has not spread over the skin, and does not appear deeper than the skin, then the priest shall pronounce him clean. He shall wash his clothes and be clean. But if the scale should at all spread over the skin after his cleansing, then the priest shall examine him; and indeed *if* the scale has spread over the skin, the priest need not seek for yellow hair. He *is* unclean. But if the scale appears to be at a standstill, and there is black hair grown up in it, the scale has healed. He *is* clean, and the priest shall pronounce him clean.

a. **If a man or a woman has a sore on the head or the beard**: The priests were given the criteria to examine and judge the severity of skin problems associated with hairy parts of the body.

i. **A man or a woman**: "The additional specification referring to the woman does not indicate that women were excluded from the previous cases but that rather because the following case involves specifically an infection on the beard it could be assumed that women were exempt. The text indicates that they were not." (Rooker)

ii. **It is a scaly leprosy**: "The word used here literally means 'a tearing off,' something so annoying that the person who has it cannot keep his hands off it." (Peter-Contesse)

b. **He is clean, and the priest shall pronounce him clean**: The priest had the power to declare someone **clean** or unclean, but only on the basis of what God had specifically commanded. The true power was not in the priest's pronouncement but in his application of what God's word instructed.

i. "If the priest had partially pronounced one clean who was not clean, his sentence had been null. And therefore it is a fond and dangerous conceit to think that the absolution given to any sinner by a priest will stand him in any stead if he do not truly repent." (Poole)

7. (38-39) Examining bright spots on the skin.

"If a man or a woman has bright spots on the skin of the body, *specifically* white bright spots, then the priest shall look; and indeed *if* the bright spots on the skin of the body *are* dull white, it *is* a white spot *that* grows on the skin. He *is* clean.

a. **If a man or a woman has bright spots on the skin of the body**: The priests were given the criteria to examine and judge the severity of **white bright spots** and their aftermath.

8. (40-44) Examining skin associated with hair loss.

"As for the man whose hair has fallen from his head, he *is* bald, *but* he *is* clean. He whose hair has fallen from his forehead, he *is* bald on the forehead, *but* he *is* clean. And if there is on the bald head or bald forehead a reddish-white sore, it *is* leprosy breaking out on his bald head or his bald forehead. Then the priest shall examine it; and indeed *if* the swelling of the sore *is* reddish-white on his bald head or on his bald forehead, as the appearance of leprosy on the skin of the body, he is a leprous man. He *is* unclean. The priest shall surely pronounce him unclean; his sore *is* on his head.

> a. **As for the man whose hair has fallen from his head**: The scriptures pronounce such a man to be **bald**, yet **he is clean**. Through the centuries, this has been a comfort to men who lose their hair.

> > i. **He is bald on the forehead**: "The Hebrew had a special word for this type of baldness as opposed to the baldness on the top of the head. It is related to the verb meaning 'to be high' and is always used in contrast with the baldness of the top of the head. Compare the English expression 'to have a high forehead.'" (Peter-Contesse)

> b. **If there is on the bald head or bald forehead a reddish-white sore**: The priests were given the criteria to examine and judge the severity of sores that appear where the hair has been lost, and their aftermath.

9. (45-46) The result of leprosy.

"Now the leper on whom the sore *is*, his clothes shall be torn and his head bare; and he shall cover his mustache, and cry, 'Unclean! Unclean!' He shall be unclean. All the days he has the sore he shall be unclean. He *is* unclean, and he shall dwell alone; his dwelling *shall be* outside the camp.

> a. **His clothes shall be torn and his head bare**: Once the diagnosis of leprosy was confirmed, everything changed for the leper. They lived in a perpetual state of mourning and in a perpetual state of public disgrace (**he shall...cry "Unclean! Unclean!"**). Furthermore, they were commanded to live in a perpetual state of exclusion (**he shall dwell alone**).

> > i. "The leprous person is required to be as one that mourned for the dead, or for some great and public calamity." (Clarke)

> > ii. **He shall dwell alone**: "The emphasis is not on complete separation from all others, since people with this condition were permitted to live with each other, but they had to be away from the rest of the community (see 2 Kings 7:3–10)." (Peter-Contesse)

b. **He is unclean, and he shall dwell alone**: As strict as all this was, eventually many of the Jewish people went further in excluding lepers from society. In the days of Jesus many Jews thought two things about a leper: *You are the walking dead* and *you deserve this because this is the punishment of God against you.*

i. Jewish custom said that you should not even greet a leper, and you had to stay six feet (two meters) away from them. One rabbi bragged that he would not even buy an egg on a street where he saw a leper, and another boasted that he threw rocks at lepers to keep them from coming close. Some rabbis didn't even allow a leper to wash his face.

ii. But Jesus was different. He loved lepers; He touched them and healed them when they had no hope at all (such as in Matthew 8:1-4 and Luke 17:11-19).

iii. Because of modern drugs and treatments, leprosy is almost unknown in the western world. At one time there were two leper colonies in the United States, but they have been closed. Yet, worldwide there are some 15 million lepers, almost all of them in developing nations.

B. Diagnosing fabrics and leather contaminated by leprosy.

1. (47-52) Contaminated garments to be destroyed.

"Also, if a garment has a leprous plague in it, *whether it is* a woolen garment or a linen garment, whether *it is* in the warp or woof of linen or wool, whether in leather or in anything made of leather, and if the plague is greenish or reddish in the garment or in the leather, whether in the warp or in the woof, or in anything made of leather, it *is* a leprous plague and shall be shown to the priest. The priest shall examine the plague and isolate *that which has* the plague seven days. And he shall examine the plague on the seventh day. If the plague has spread in the garment, either in the warp or in the woof, in the leather *or* in anything made of leather, the plague *is* an active leprosy. It *is* unclean. He shall therefore burn that garment in which is the plague, whether warp or woof, in wool or in linen, or anything of leather, for it *is* an active leprosy; *the garment* shall be burned in the fire.

a. **If a garment has a leprous plague in it**: In Old Testament times, the term *leprosy* had a broad definition and could include some forms of mold, mildew, or fungus.

i. **In the warp or woof**: "While the interpretation is far from certain, the meaning of these words is probably 'any woven or knitted material.'" (Peter-Contesse)

b. **The priest shall examine the plague**: The priests had to make careful determination to see if a garment might pass on a contagious disease or if it could still be used. Fabrics were presented to the priest and isolated for seven days. If the mildew had spread after seven days, the fabric was burned.

2. (53-58) Garments that can be washed and preserved.

"But if the priest examines *it*, and indeed the plague has not spread in the garment, either in the warp or in the woof, or in anything made of leather, then the priest shall command that they wash *the thing* in which *is* the plague; and he shall isolate it another seven days. Then the priest shall examine the plague after it has been washed; and indeed *if* the plague has not changed its color, though the plague has not spread, it *is* unclean, and you shall burn it in the fire; it continues eating away, *whether* the damage *is* outside or inside. If the priest examines *it*, and indeed the plague has faded after washing it, then he shall tear it out of the garment, whether out of the warp or out of the woof, or out of the leather. But if it appears again in the garment, either in the warp or in the woof, or in anything made of leather, it *is* a spreading *plague;* you shall burn with fire that in which is the plague. And if you wash the garment, either warp or woof, or whatever is made of leather, if the plague has disappeared from it, then it shall be washed a second time, and shall be clean.

a. **And indeed the plague has not spread in the garment**: If the mold or mildew or fungus had not spread, the garment could be washed and isolated for another seven days. If the mildew remained after that seven days, the item was burned.

b. **The plague has faded after washing**: If the mold or mildew or fungus had faded, the infected portion could be torn away.

c. **If it appears again**: If the mold or mildew or fungus returned, the article was to be burned.

d. **If the plague has disappeared from it**: If after a washing the mold or mildew or fungus was gone, the garment or fabric could be used again after a **second** washing.

3. (59) Summary of the law regarding leprous garments and in leather.

"This *is* the law of the leprous plague in a garment of wool or linen, either in the warp or woof, or in anything made of leather, to pronounce it clean or to pronounce it unclean."

Leviticus 14 – Rituals on the Cleansing of a Leper

A. The first seven days of the ritual performed upon the cleansing of a leper.

1. (1-3) The examination of the leper.

Then the LORD spoke to Moses, saying, "This shall be the law of the leper for the day of his cleansing: He shall be brought to the priest. And the priest shall go out of the camp, and the priest shall examine *him*; and indeed, *if* the leprosy is healed in the leper,

> a. **The priest shall go out of the camp**: When it was believed that someone was healed of **leprosy**, arrangements were made for the priest to examine the afflicted person. The leper did not come to the tabernacle; the **priest** went **out of the camp** to the community of lepers to make the examination.

> > i. It should be remembered that the Old Testament word translated **leprosy** includes the modern diagnosed disease of leprosy (Hansen's Disease), but also many other skin diseases.

> b. **The priest shall examine him**: The priest made the examination according to the principles explained in chapter 13. The leper was declared to be clean or unclean based on those principles.

2. (4-7) The two birds: one sacrificed, one set free.

Then the priest shall command to take for him who is to be cleansed two living *and* clean birds, cedar wood, scarlet, and hyssop. And the priest shall command that one of the birds be killed in an earthen vessel over running water. As for the living bird, he shall take it, the cedar wood and the scarlet and the hyssop, and dip them and the living bird in the blood of the bird *that was* killed over the running water. And he shall sprinkle it seven times on him who is to be cleansed from the leprosy, and shall pronounce him clean, and shall let the living bird loose in the open field.

a. **Two living and clean birds, cedar wood, scarlet, and hyssop**: These were the items used in this part of the ritual upon the cleansing of the leper. This ritual was not done in the hope of healing the leper; it was done when the leper was healed. They used two **birds**, clean for either eating or sacrifice, a stick or piece of **cedar wood**, a piece of **scarlet** yarn or thread, and a **hyssop** branch.

> i. Since the priest went outside the camp (verse 3) to meet the cleansed leper, and there is no mention of the tabernacle until a second ritual in verses 10 and 11, this unusual ceremony did not take place at the tabernacle. It happened at the community of lepers, outside the camp.

> ii. **Cedar wood**: Cedar is extremely resistant to disease and rot, and these qualities may be the reason for including it here.

> iii. Most commentators believe that the **scarlet** here is yarn, not cloth itself. "This material was used for making the curtains and the veil of the tabernacle (Exodus 25:4; 26:1, 31; 28:5). Its color may have symbolized blood." (Rooker)

> iv. **Hyssop** branches were used for the sprinkling of blood or water (Exodus 12:22, Numbers 19:18). When David said *purge me with hyssop* in Psalm 51:7, he admitted that he was as bad as a leper – but *a cleansed leper*.

b. **One of the birds be killed**: In the ritual, the first bird was killed in a clay bowl (**an earthen vessel**) that also contained water from a spring, creek, or river (**running water**). The blood of this sacrificed bird was collected together with the water in the clay bowl in which the bird was killed.

> i. "The Hebrew preposition implies that the action is rather to be performed over the clay pot so that the blood of the bird falls into the pot and is mixed with the spring water." (Peter-Contesse)

> ii. **Running water** is literally, "living water." It refers to water that comes from a flowing source, such as a spring, river, or creek. It did not come from a well or a cistern. It was thought to be pure, fresh water.

c. **Dip them and the living bird in the blood**: Then, the second **bird** (still alive), together with the piece of **cedar wood**, the **scarlet** yarn, and the **hyssop** branch, were dipped in the blood of the sacrificed bird.

> i. "The *cedar-wood* served for the *handle*, the *hyssop* and *living bird* were attached to it by means of the *scarlet wool* or *crimson fillet*. The bird was so bound to this handle as that its tail should be downwards, in order to be dipped into the blood of the bird that had been killed. The whole of this made an instrument for the sprinkling of this blood." (Clarke)

d. **Sprinkle it seven times**: Apparently, as the priest held the blood-dipped living bird, the wood, the yarn, and the branch together, he waved it at or towards the cleansed leper, sprinkling the sacrificed bird's blood on the leper **seven times**.

e. **Let the living bird loose in the open field**: After declaring the leper **clean** (based on the previous examination, verse 3), the priest let the blood-stained, **living bird** fly away.

i. "This [living bird] might as well be called the *scape-bird;* as the *goat*, in chapter 16, is called the *scape-goat*. The rites are similar in both cases, and probably had nearly the same meaning." (Clarke)

ii. This unusual ritual can be summarized with these points:

- This happened outside the camp, away from the normal conduct of the system of sacrifice.

- There, a living thing of the heavens was sacrificed in an earthen vessel.

- Even as the bird was killed, it was cleansed (by the running water).

- This death, associated with water and blood, was applied to the leper, and applied perfectly (seven times) in connection with a living bird.

- The sacrificial blood was also applied to scarlet yarn and a piece of wood, together with hyssop.

- Bearing the mark of sacrifice, the living bird flew away, ascending to the heavens and out of sight.

iii. In a remarkable way, this unusual ritual points to the future work of the Messiah, who would cleanse those stained with the leprosy of sin.

- Jesus was sacrificed outside the camp (Hebrews 13:11-13).

- Jesus was the Man from heaven (John 3:13, 6:38).

- Jesus remained cleansed and holy (Acts 2:27) even in His death, becoming sin (2 Corinthians 5:21) without becoming a sinner.

- Jesus came by water and blood (1 John 5:6) and died in association with blood and water (John 19:34-35).

- Jesus died in association with scarlet cloth (Matthew 27:28).

- Jesus died in association with wood (John 19:17-18).

- Jesus died in association with hyssop (John 19:29).

- Jesus lived, bearing the marks of His death (John 20:27).

- Jesus ascended to heaven, out of human sight (Acts 1:9).

iv. There is a sense in which the living bird set free points to the resurrected Jesus. But it also points to the one healed and free from their leprosy, including the leprosy of sin; they are resurrected and free in the resurrected Jesus Christ.

3. (8-9) The cleansing of the leper's body.

He who is to be cleansed shall wash his clothes, shave off all his hair, and wash himself in water, that he may be clean. After that he shall come into the camp, and shall stay outside his tent seven days. But on the seventh day he shall shave all the hair off his head and his beard and his eyebrows; all his hair he shall shave off. He shall wash his clothes and wash his body in water, and he shall be clean.

a. **Shall wash his clothes, shave off all his hair, and wash himself in water**: After the ritual with the two birds, the recovered leper was to completely cleanse himself. Then he could **come into the camp** of Israel, and spend a week living in public view (**stay outside his tent**).

i. That the recovered leper could not live his first week in his own tent was uncomfortable, but the public nature of it proved to the whole community that he really was healed and should be accepted and restored to the community.

ii. "**Shave off all his hair**; partly, to discover his perfect soundness; partly, to preserve him from relapse through any seeds or relics of it which might remain in his hair, or in his clothes; and partly, to teach him to put off his old lusts, and become a new man." (Poole)

b. **He shall shave all the hair off his head and his beard and his eyebrows**: At the end of the week outside his tent, he was to **shave** and **wash** completely again. This shaving was to include even his **beard** and **eyebrows**. The recovered leper would start all over again as if he was a newborn baby – as if he was born again.

B. The eighth day ritual upon the cleansing of a leper.

1. (10-11) Presentation at the tabernacle.

"And on the eighth day he shall take two male lambs without blemish, one ewe lamb of the first year without blemish, three-tenths *of an ephah* of fine flour mixed with oil as a grain offering, and one log of oil. Then the priest who makes *him* clean shall present the man who is to be made clean, and those things, before the LORD, *at* the door of the tabernacle of meeting.

a. **Two male lambs without blemish**: On the eighth day from the start of the rituals upon the cleansing of a leper, the leper brought three lambs (two male and one female), along with flour and oil for sacrifice.

i. This was a considerable expense, and since most lepers were not prosperous (the disease was isolating from the community and normally lasted a long time), provision was made for the poor leper (14:21-32).

ii. The amount **three-tenths of an ephah** is given as anywhere between five pounds (2.25 kilos) and 20 pounds (9 kilos).

iii. **One log of oil** is given as being about 10 ounces or one-third of a liter.

b. **The priest who makes him clean**: It was the priest who declared a leper clean or unclean (as in 13:3, 13:6, 13:8, 13:11, 13:13, 13:17, 13:20 and so on). It is in this sense that the priest "made" a leper clean; by judging his condition in light of God's revealed word.

i. Even so, a priest, minister, bishop, pastor, or any other such person cannot *make* another person either righteous or unrighteous before God. They can, on the basis of God's revealed word, judging the condition of another (their professed faith and conduct of life), declare them to be righteous or unrighteous.

c. **Shall present the man who is to be made clean**: Even though this leper had been declared clean, there was still cleansing to be done. Lepers still had to follow the sacrifices and rituals (which pointed to the perfect work of the Messiah to come) and they would be **made clean**.

d. **Before the LORD, at the door of the tabernacle of meeting**: The unusual ceremony of 14:1-7 took place outside the camp. The washing of 14:8-9 took place at the leper's normal living place. This sacrifice took place at **the tabernacle**.

i. "The movement of the cleansed man from outside the camp (14:3), to the camp (14:8), to the Tent of Meeting (14:11) is another way of describing the cleansed man's full restoration." (Rooker)

2. (12-14) One male lamb as a trespass offering; the application of the blood.

And the priest shall take one male lamb and offer it as a trespass offering, and the log of oil, and wave them *as* a wave offering before the LORD. Then he shall kill the lamb in the place where he kills the sin offering and the burnt offering, in a holy place; for as the sin offering *is* the priest's, so *is* the trespass offering. It *is* most holy. The priest shall take *some* of the blood of the trespass offering, and the priest shall put

it **on the tip of the right ear of him who is to be cleansed, on the thumb of his right hand, and on the big toe of his right foot.**

a. **The priest shall take one male lamb and offer it as a trespass offering**: The first male lamb was offered according to the instructions in chapter 5 and chapter 7:1-10. The meat from this offering belonged to **the priest**, not to the restored leper.

b. **The priest shall take some of the blood of the trespass offering**: Here was a dramatic break from the normal **trespass offering**. In the case of the restored leper, the priest took **some of the blood** of the first sacrificed lamb, and applied it to the right ear, the right thumb, and the right big toe, to sanctify and consecrate the cleansed leper. This was the same action that was used in the consecration of priests (Leviticus 8:22-24).

i. The blood on the right ear said, "this one should hear God first." The blood on the right thumb said, "this one should put his hand to do God's will first." The blood on the big toe of the right foot said, "this one should follow God's path first."

ii. Therefore, a cleansed leper had a special calling and a special anointing – *just as the priests did*. This ritual affirmed and declared the radical change of life that happened to the restored leper. He was a new person, born again as it were and his life belonged to God in a special way.

iii. "To signify that all Christ's sanctified ones have a hearing ear, an active hand, a nimble foot to walk in the way that is called holy." (Trapp)

iv. Since leprosy is a picture of sin, we see how this ritual has spiritual application to every sinner that Jesus cleanses, restores, and sets free. We are bought with a price and should therefore glorify God with our bodies (1 Corinthians 6:20).

3. (15-18) The application of the oil.

And the priest shall take *some* **of the log of oil, and pour** *it* **into the palm of his own left hand. Then the priest shall dip his right finger in the oil that** *is* **in his left hand, and shall sprinkle some of the oil with his finger seven times before the LORD. And of the rest of the oil in his hand, the priest shall put** *some* **on the tip of the right ear of him who is to be cleansed, on the thumb of his right hand, and on the big toe of his right foot, on the blood of the trespass offering. The rest of the oil that** *is* **in the priest's hand he shall put on the head of him who is to be cleansed. So the priest shall make atonement for him before the LORD.**

a. **The priest shall dip his right finger in the oil**: After the application of the blood, then the priest sprinkled oil with **his finger seven times before the LORD** (not upon the restored leper). Then, the priest applied the **rest of the oil** to the right ear, right thumb, and right big toe of the restored leper.

i. Oil has a consistent association with the Holy Spirit in the Bible (such as in Zechariah 4:1-7). Olive oil was essential and valued in Biblical culture and was a worthy representation of the Holy Spirit.

- Oil *heals* and was used as a medicinal treatment in Biblical times (Luke 10:34) – the Spirit of God brings healing and restoration.

- Oil *lights* when it is burned in a lamp – where the Spirit of God is there is light.

- Oil *warms* when it is used as fuel for a flame – where the Spirit of God is there is warmth and comfort.

- Oil *invigorates* when used to massage – the Holy Spirit invigorates us for His service.

- Oil *adorns* when applied as a perfume – the Holy Spirit adorns us and makes us more pleasant to be around.

- Oil *polishes* when used to shine metal – the Holy Spirit wipes away our grime, smoothing out our rough edges.

- Oil *lubricates* when used for that purpose – there is little friction and wear among those who truly walk in the Spirit.

ii. Significantly, the oil was applied **on the blood of the trespass offering**. The anointing of the Holy Spirit could not come unless it was *upon* the work of a blood sacrifice.

iii. This was unique; in the priestly consecration, ritual blood was applied to the ear, thumb, and big toe – but not oil. This was a powerful way to say that all that the restored leper heard, all he did with the work of his hands, and every path he walked should be under the anointing and influence of the Holy Spirit.

iv. This has special relevance as a picture of what God does for those restored from their leprous-like sin in the New Covenant. One of the significant promises of the New Covenant is an outpouring of the Holy Spirit upon all those who take part in the covenant (Ezekiel 36:27).

b. **The rest of the oil…he shall put on the head of him who is to be cleansed**: After the application of the oil upon the ear, thumb, and toe of the restored leper, it was the applied in a more customary way, anointing **the head** of the restored leper in the same manner that priests and kings were anointed.

i. This dramatic act said to the leper, "There is a sense in which God regards you as a king and a priest."

ii. The repetition of the phrase, **him who is to be cleansed** reminds us that there was a sense in which the leper *was already* cleansed, and another sense in which he was *still* **to be cleansed**.

4. (19-20) The remaining sin offering, burnt offering, and grain offering.

"Then the priest shall offer the sin offering, and make atonement for him who is to be cleansed from his uncleanness. Afterward he shall kill the burnt offering. And the priest shall offer the burnt offering and the grain offering on the altar. So the priest shall make atonement for him, and he shall be clean.

a. **Then the priest shall offer the sin offering**: The second of the three lambs was offered as a **sin offering**. This sacrifice is described in Leviticus 4 and 6:24-30.

b. **The priest shall offer the burnt offering**: The priest offered the third of the three lambs as a **burnt offering**. This sacrifice is described in Leviticus 1 and 6:8-13.

c. **And the grain offering**: The priest offered the fine flour (14:10). This offering is described in Leviticus 2 and 6:14-23.

i. "The sin offering would put an individual in good standing with God, while the burnt offering and grain offering symbolized the renewed dedication of the worshiper and of his devotion to God." (Rooker)

d. **So the priest shall make atonement for him, and he shall be clean**: These remarkable sacrifices were rarely used. In fact, there is no record in the Old Testament of an Israelite leper being restored, apart from Miriam (Numbers 12).

i. "The despair that resulted when one suspected that he may have contracted an infectious disease must have been intense. By contrast the joy of being declared clean was unspeakable." (Rooker)

ii. When Jesus restored a leper and commanded him to go to the temple priests and make the appropriate offerings (Luke 5:12-14), it must have gained much attention and provided a striking testimony.

C. Provisions for the poor to fulfill the ritual for a cleansed leper.

1. (21-23) Provisions for the poor to fulfill the ritual for a cleansed leper.

"But if he *is* poor and cannot afford it, then he shall take one male lamb *as* a trespass offering to be waved, to make atonement for him,

one-tenth *of an ephah* of fine flour mixed with oil as a grain offering, a log of oil, and two turtledoves or two young pigeons, such as he is able to afford: one shall be a sin offering and the other a burnt offering. He shall bring them to the priest on the eighth day for his cleansing, to the door of the tabernacle of meeting, before the LORD.

a. **But if he is poor and cannot afford it**: Because a diagnosis of leprosy separated the leper from the community, and because diseases diagnosed as leprosy often lasted a long time, we can suppose that many lepers were **poor** and could not afford the three lambs for sacrifice called for in the ritual described in verses 1-20. God graciously made provision for those who were **poor** and could not **afford it**.

b. **He shall take one male lamb…and two turtledoves or two young pigeons, such as he is able to afford**: Instead of requiring three sacrificial lambs, God required only one. The other two lambs could be replaced with two birds, either **turtledoves** or **pigeons**.

c. **To the door of the tabernacle of meeting, before the LORD**: The poor man brought his offering to the same place, in the same manner, and to the same priests as the richer man who could afford a more substantial offering.

2. (24-25) The application of the blood of the trespass offering.

And the priest shall take the lamb of the trespass offering and the log of oil, and the priest shall wave them *as* a wave offering before the LORD. Then he shall kill the lamb of the trespass offering, and the priest shall take *some* of the blood of the trespass offering and put *it* on the tip of the right ear of him who is to be cleansed, on the thumb of his right hand, and on the big toe of his right foot.

a. **The priest shall take the lamb of the trespass offering**: The offering of the lamb for the trespass offering for the poor man and the application of the sacrificial blood was the same as described in verses 12-14.

3. (26-29) The application of the oil in the ritual.

And the priest shall pour some of the oil into the palm of his own left hand. Then the priest shall sprinkle with his right finger *some* of the oil that *is* in his left hand seven times before the LORD. And the priest shall put *some* of the oil that *is* in his hand on the tip of the right ear of him who is to be cleansed, on the thumb of the right hand, and on the big toe of his right foot, on the place of the blood of the trespass offering. The rest of the oil that *is* in the priest's hand he shall put on the head of him who is to be cleansed, to make atonement for him before the LORD.

a. **The priest shall pour some of the oil**: The application of the oil in the ritual for the poor was the same as was described in verses 15-18.

4. (30-32) The presentation of the sin offering, burnt offering, and grain offering.

And he shall offer one of the turtledoves or young pigeons, such as he can afford—such as he is able to afford, the one *as* a sin offering and the other *as* a burnt offering, with the grain offering. So the priest shall make atonement for him who is to be cleansed before the Lord. This *is* the law *for one* who had a leprous sore, who cannot afford the usual cleansing."

a. **He shall offer one of the turtledoves or young pigeons**: The carrying out of the sin offering and the burnt offering was the same as described in verses 19-20 except that birds were substituted for lambs. The presentation of the grain offering was the same as mentioned in verse 20.

D. Mold, mildew, fungus in a house.

1. (33-35) Suspected leprous plague (mold, mildew, fungus) in a house.

And the Lord spoke to Moses and Aaron, saying: "When you have come into the land of Canaan, which I give you as a possession, and I put the leprous plague in a house in the land of your possession, and he who owns the house comes and tells the priest, saying, 'It seems to me that *there is* some plague in the house,'

a. **When you have come into the land of Canaan**: The following section deals with **leprous plague** on the walls of a structure. It did not apply to the tents that Israel lived in during their wilderness years on the way to Canaan. Outbreaks of what was broadly termed leprosy on the fabric or leather walls of a tent was dealt with in Leviticus 13:47-58.

b. **I put the leprous plague in the house of the land of your possession**: The Israelites inherited the land and property of the Canaanites when they came into the land. The idea here seems to be that some of that property would have been under the judgment of God, and therefore it could be said that God **put** the plague there. Or, this may simply be a Hebraic way of expressing the truth that in an ultimate sense God directs or allows all things.

i. "It is well known that in Scripture God is frequently represented as *doing* what, in the course of his providence, he only *permits* or suffers to be done." (Clarke)

c. **It seems to me that there is some plague in the house**: Just as with the instructions regarding leprosy in garments in Leviticus 13, the idea of **the**

leprous plague or simply **plague** in this context covers a broad range of things. In that broad range, mold, mildew, and fungus can be included.

i. "From the modern scientific point of view, mildew and skin disease have little in common, but they do both affect the surface of various objects." (Peter-Contesse)

2. (36-38) The initial examination of the house.

Then the priest shall command that they empty the house, before the priest goes *into it* to examine the plague, that all that *is* in the house may not be made unclean; and afterward the priest shall go in to examine the house. And he shall examine the plague; and indeed *if* the plague *is* on the walls of the house with ingrained streaks, greenish or reddish, which appear to be deep in the wall, then the priest shall go out of the house, to the door of the house, and shut up the house seven days.

a. **The priest shall command that they empty the house**: Many molds, mildews, or fungi can be dangerous if touched or breathed in. This was a sound, sanitary practice and promoted the health of the community of Israel.

i. "It reveals the interest of God in the physical wellbeing of His people and His unceasing antagonism to everything likely to harm them... teaching us among other things that it is impossible for men to be loyal to God and careless in any measure concerning the laws of sanitation." (Morgan)

b. **The priest shall go in to examine the house**: With the house cleared, the priest would examine the walls and the plague, noting the color and nature of the mold, mildew, or fungus. If he determined it was severe enough, the house would be **shut up** for **seven days**.

3. (39-42) The remedy for the plague that remains on the walls.

And the priest shall come again on the seventh day and look; and indeed *if* the plague has spread on the walls of the house, then the priest shall command that they take away the stones in which *is* the plague, and they shall cast them into an unclean place outside the city. And he shall cause the house to be scraped inside, all around, and the dust that they scrape off they shall pour out in an unclean place outside the city. Then they shall take other stones and put *them* in the place of *those* stones, and he shall take other mortar and plaster the house.

a. **If the plague has spread on the walls of the house**: If the mold, mildew, or fungus had become worse, the priest commanded **that they take away the stones in which is the plague**. They would be removed from the house.

i. The fact that only **stones** are mentioned (and not wood or other building materials) indicates what archaeologists confirm: that ancient homes in that part of the world were largely built from stone.

ii. Jude wrote that believers should be *hating even the garment defiled by the flesh* (Jude 1:23). "Whatever in our life has been associated with and contaminated by the leprosy of past sin, it is good to destroy without compromise or pity." (Morgan)

b. **He shall cause the house to be scraped inside**: The interior stone of a home would commonly be coated with some kind of plaster. This would be **scraped** and disposed of. The house would then receive new **mortar and plaster**.

4. (43-47) Dealing with a chronic infestation in a house.

"Now if the plague comes back and breaks out in the house, after he has taken away the stones, after he has scraped the house, and after it is plastered, then the priest shall come and look; and indeed *if* the plague has spread in the house, it *is* an active leprosy in the house. It *is* unclean. And he shall break down the house, its stones, its timber, and all the plaster of the house, and he shall carry *them* outside the city to an unclean place. Moreover he who goes into the house at all while it is shut up shall be unclean until evening. And he who lies down in the house shall wash his clothes, and he who eats in the house shall wash his clothes.

a. **If the plague comes back and breaks out in the house**: If the infestation of mold, mildew, or fungus is chronic, the priest declared the house **unclean** and the house would be broken down and the remains carried out of **the city to an unclean place**.

i. **An active leprosy**: "The whole expression in this context means something like 'it is fungus that cannot be eliminated.'" (Peter-Contesse)

b. **He who goes into the house at all while it is shut up shall be unclean**: If someone went into a house that was quarantined, they were **unclean** and had to take the appropriate measures.

i. By spiritual analogy, we can say that our homes can be infected with sin. When this is the case, we should not just continue to live as before; radical changes must be made. Things may need to be removed and discarded. Furthermore, the work of the crucified and resurrected Christ in all its dimensions must be applied to the home, with a sense of repentance and renewed dedication.

5. (48-53) What to do when a house was cleansed from plague of mold, mildew, or fungus.

"But if the priest comes in and examines *it,* and indeed the plague has not spread in the house after the house was plastered, then the priest shall pronounce the house clean, because the plague is healed. And he shall take, to cleanse the house, two birds, cedar wood, scarlet, and hyssop. Then he shall kill one of the birds in an earthen vessel over running water; and he shall take the cedar wood, the hyssop, the scarlet, and the living bird, and dip them in the blood of the slain bird and in the running water, and sprinkle the house seven times. And he shall cleanse the house with the blood of the bird and the running water and the living bird, with the cedar wood, the hyssop, and the scarlet. Then he shall let the living bird loose outside the city in the open field, and make atonement for the house, and it shall be clean.

a. **Indeed the plague has not spread in the house**: If the priest determined that the plague was **healed**, the house was pronounced **clean**.

b. **Two birds, cedar wood, scarlet, and hyssop**: The same ritual described in verses 4-7 upon the cleansing of a leper was also to be performed when a house was declared clean from a plague of mold, mildew, or fungus.

6. (54-57) Summation of the laws of leprosy.

"This *is* the law for any leprous sore and scale, for the leprosy of a garment and of a house, for a swelling and a scab and a bright spot, to teach when *it is* unclean and when *it is* clean. This *is* the law of leprosy."

a. **This is the law**: This summary statement concludes the section of chapters 13 and 14 dealing with skin diseases, other diseases, mold, mildew, and fungus categorized as **leprosy** for the people of Israel.

b. **To teach when it is unclean and when it is clean**: These laws were given to make the distinction between **unclean** and **clean**; to protect the health and strength of Israel.

i. "To teach; to direct the priest when to pronounce a person or house clean or unclean. So it was not left to the priest's power or will, but they were tied to plain rules, such as the people might discern no less than the priest." (Poole)

Leviticus 15 – Laws Concerning Bodily Discharges

A. Bodily discharges from a man.

1. (1-3) The general principle regarding an abnormal bodily discharge.

And the LORD spoke to Moses and Aaron, saying, "Speak to the children of Israel, and say to them: 'When any man has a discharge from his body, his discharge *is* unclean. And this shall be his uncleanness in regard to his discharge—whether his body runs with his discharge, or his body is stopped up by his discharge, it *is* his uncleanness.

a. **When any man has a discharge from his body, his discharge is unclean**: The idea is of some obviously abnormal genital discharge, indicating some type of disease. When this occurs, the man was to be somewhat isolated in order not to pass on the infection to anyone else.

i. "This refers to an abnormal fluid that comes out of the male sexual organ as a result of some kind of sickness." (Peter-Contesse)

ii. "The exact nature of this discharge is not stated, although the most frequently suggested opinion is that it refers to gonorrhea." (Rooker)

iii. **From his body**: From the context, it is clear that this is a polite reference to the penis, the male sexual organ. God and His word deal with all manner of private and sexual matters but do so in an appropriate, dignified way. There is no coarse or inappropriate reference here.

b. **And this shall be his uncleanness**: In contrast to the previous chapters regarding the broad definition of leprosy, there is no mention made of priestly inspection or monitoring. This was done by the individual, supported by the expectation of the culture.

i. **His body is stopped up by his discharge**: "One way of understanding this passage is that the discharge caused by the infection may block the opening in the penis." (Peter-Contesse)

c. **It is his uncleanness**: The status of "unclean" did not completely take the unclean one out of the community. It placed restrictions on them and required a ceremonial purification if and when the infection was gone.

2. (4-12) The spread of the uncleanness of an abnormal bodily discharge.

Every bed is unclean on which he who has the discharge lies, and everything on which he sits shall be unclean. And whoever touches his bed shall wash his clothes and bathe in water, and be unclean until evening. He who sits on anything on which he who has the discharge sat shall wash his clothes and bathe in water, and be unclean until evening. And he who touches the body of him who has the discharge shall wash his clothes and bathe in water, and be unclean until evening. If he who has the discharge spits on him who is clean, then he shall wash his clothes and bathe in water, and be unclean until evening. Any saddle on which he who has the discharge rides shall be unclean. Whoever touches anything that was under him shall be unclean until evening. He who carries *any of* those things shall wash his clothes and bathe in water, and be unclean until evening. And whomever the one who has the discharge touches, and has not rinsed his hands in water, he shall wash his clothes and bathe in water, and be unclean until evening. The vessel of earth that he who has the discharge touches shall be broken, and every vessel of wood shall be rinsed in water.

a. **Every bed is unclean on which he who has the discharge lies**: Essentially, the uncleanness associated with an abnormal genital discharge from a man was spread through contact. Therefore, it could be transmitted to a **bed**, to a place **on which he sits**, and by direct touch (**he who touches**).

b. **Whoever touches his bed**: In this context, there were three ways a person or thing might be made unclean. The first level was the uncleanness of the man afflicted with the abnormal genital discharge (15:1-3). The second level was an object or person who came into contact with the afflicted one. The third level was someone who came in contact with an object made unclean.

c. **If he who has the discharge spits on him who is clean**: The uncleanness could also be spread through saliva. The general principle was that when the unclean comes into contact with the clean, it is the clean that is made unclean.

i. This general principle was completely reversed in the person and work of Jesus the Messiah. When Jesus – who was "clean" in every sense – touched an unclean person, He made them clean (Luke 5:12-14). They didn't make Him unclean.

d. **Whoever touches his bed shall wash his clothes and bathe in water**: People and things made unclean on the second or third level could be purified by a ceremonial washing of the object and the person involved. Then their uncleanness ended when the day ended (**until evening**).

3. (13-15) The offering regarding an abnormal bodily discharge.

'And when he who has a discharge is cleansed of his discharge, then he shall count for himself seven days for his cleansing, wash his clothes, and bathe his body in running water; then he shall be clean. On the eighth day he shall take for himself two turtledoves or two young pigeons, and come before the LORD, to the door of the tabernacle of meeting, and give them to the priest. Then the priest shall offer them, the one *as* a sin offering and the other *as* a burnt offering. So the priest shall make atonement for him before the LORD because of his discharge.

a. **When he who has a discharge is cleansed**: When the abnormal genital discharge ended, the man could be made ceremonially clean. After a period of seven days (presumably without the discharge), there was a ceremonial cleansing.

b. **He shall take for himself two turtledoves or two young pigeons**: A small offering was brought to the **priest** at the **tabernacle**. They were offered as a **sin offering** and as a **burnt offering**.

4. (16-18) Regarding a normal bodily discharge from a man.

'If any man has an emission of semen, then he shall wash all his body in water, and be unclean until evening. And any garment and any leather on which there is semen, it shall be washed with water, and be unclean until evening. Also, when a woman lies with a man, and *there is* an emission of semen, they shall bathe in water, and be unclean until evening.

a. **If any man has an emission of semen**: When a man discharged semen (either accidentally or in sex), he had to cleanse himself and respect a brief time of ceremonial impurity.

i. The fact that even normal and permitted sexual activity made a man ceremonially unclean was not God's condemnation of sex. It was a powerful way to prevent an aspect of sexual and spiritual corruption common in the ancient world: ritual prostitution, often practiced at a sacred place. Under this principle of the Law of Moses, any emission of semen was ceremonially unclean and could not be associated with the working of the tabernacle or temple. In a radical way, this separated Israel from the spiritual and sexual practices of the surrounding peoples.

ii. "The declaration of semen as unclean in this passage illustrates the sharp distinction between Israelite religion and the pagan religions of the ancient Near East. In pagan religion sexual activity among worshipers was believed to activate the gods into fertilizing the soil with rain." (Rooker)

b. **They shall bathe in water, and be unclean until evening**: In the case of **an emission of semen**, both the man and his wife needed to ceremonially cleanse themselves and respect a brief time of ceremonial impurity.

i. It is the habit of many today – even many believers – to consider their sexual life and practices to be *their own* business and *not* God's business. Here we see that God has a part in even natural, permitted, blessed expressions of sexuality.

ii. "We must bring the thought of God into the simplest, the commonest, and the most secret acts. Nothing is outside His jurisdiction. Though hid from sight, yet He is ever near the child of God. His grace, and blood, and cleansing, are always requisite, and ever ready." (Meyer)

B. Bodily discharges from a woman.

1. (19-24) Impurity during menstruation.

'**If a woman has a discharge, *and* the discharge from her body is blood, she shall be set apart seven days; and whoever touches her shall be unclean until evening. Everything that she lies on during her impurity shall be unclean; also everything that she sits on shall be unclean. Whoever touches her bed shall wash his clothes and bathe in water, and be unclean until evening. And whoever touches anything that she sat on shall wash his clothes and bathe in water, and be unclean until evening. If *anything* is on *her* bed or on anything on which she sits, when he touches it, he shall be unclean until evening. And if any man lies with her at all, so that her impurity is on him, he shall be unclean seven days; and every bed on which he lies shall be unclean.**

a. **If a woman has a discharge**: In the case of a bloody discharge from a woman (her normal menstruation), her ceremonial impurity could be spread through direct contact or through an object that she lay or sat upon.

b. **She shall be set apart seven days**: The woman's ceremonial impurity lasted seven days. There is no specific washing commanded at the end of the **seven days**, but it was either implied or considered unnecessary.

i. There was at least one other additional benefit: "The laws would also provide the woman a break from housework, caring for children, and marital relations." (Rooker)

c. **If any man lies with her**: A man who had sex with a woman during her days of normal menstruation was also **unclean seven days**, following the course of the woman's uncleanness. The man made unclean could spread his uncleanness through contact (**every bed on which he lies shall be unclean**).

i. The avoidance of intercourse during menstruation was later mentioned in Ezekiel 18:6 as an evidence of a righteous man. As an aspect of the law given to Israel under the Old Covenant, under the New Covenant this is no longer binding on Christians, whatever other reasons there may be for avoiding intercourse during menstruation.

ii. Yet a principle behind this command is universal, for every Christian and even every person: *God commands sexual restraint.* The command forced the obedient Israelite man or woman to say "no" to their sexual desires in certain situations. This does not mean that God regards sex itself as inherently sinful or impure, but it does mean that the sexual ethic of "if it feels good, do it" is an ungodly and destructive approach.

iii. The principle of sexual restraint is often stated in the New Testament. The mere presence of both desire and opportunity do not mean that a sexual act is obedient or pure before God. It is significant that the Apostle Paul made a close connection between uncleanness and sexual immorality, as in 2 Corinthians 12:21, Ephesians 5:3, Colossians 3:5 and other passages.

iv. Beyond building a culture of appropriate sexual restraint, there were additional benefits to these commands. "These laws, in addition to rendering the Israelites as a distinct nation, would undeniably provide a measure of good hygiene as well." (Rooker)

2. (25-30) Unusual or abnormal bodily discharge.

'If a woman has a discharge of blood for many days, other than at the time of her *customary* impurity, or if it runs beyond her *usual time of impurity*, all the days of her unclean discharge shall be as the days of her *customary* impurity. She *shall be* unclean. Every bed on which she lies all the days of her discharge shall be to her as the bed of her impurity; and whatever she sits on shall be unclean, as the uncleanness of her

impurity. Whoever touches those things shall be unclean; he shall wash his clothes and bathe in water, and be unclean until evening.

a. **If a woman has a discharge of blood for many days**: In the case of blood discharge **other than** normal menstruation (either longer in duration or out of her normal menstrual cycle), a woman was also ceremonially **unclean**.

b. **Whatever she sits on shall be unclean**: The woman's ceremonial uncleanness could be spread to any object upon which she lay or sat. That uncleanness would be spread to any person touching those objects made unclean.

3. (28-30) The offering made upon the cleansing of a woman with an abnormal genital discharge.

But if she is cleansed of her discharge, then she shall count for herself seven days, and after that she shall be clean. And on the eighth day she shall take for herself two turtledoves or two young pigeons, and bring them to the priest, to the door of the tabernacle of meeting. Then the priest shall offer the one *as* a sin offering and the other *as* a burnt offering, and the priest shall make atonement for her before the LORD for the discharge of her uncleanness.

a. **If she is cleansed**: When the abnormal discharge ended, there was an additional seven days of ceremonial impurity. This was the same procedure followed after the cleansing of a man with an abnormal genital discharge (verses 13-15).

b. **She shall take for herself two turtledoves or two young pigeons**: A small offering was brought to the **priest** at the **tabernacle**. They were offered as a **sin offering** and as a **burnt offering**.

i. "The reason offerings had to be made for these discharges and not for the discharges of semen and menstruation was because they were considered abnormal." (Rooker)

4. (31-33) Summation of the laws of bodily discharge.

'Thus you shall separate the children of Israel from their uncleanness, lest they die in their uncleanness when they defile My tabernacle that *is* among them. This *is* the law for one who has a discharge, and *for him* who emits semen and is unclean thereby, and for her who is indisposed because of her *customary* impurity, and for one who has a discharge, either man or woman, and for him who lies with her who is unclean.'"

a. **When they defile My tabernacle**: None of these discharges made a man or a woman *sinful*, only ceremonially unclean. Normal discharges of semen and menstruation made one ceremonially unclean, not because there was anything inherently wrong with them, but because the two are connected with symbols of redemption and life, **blood** and **semen**.

i. This presented a powerful and consistent message. It said that there is something broken and inherently impure in us, even in what comes from us normally. It also said that there is a significant aspect of our brokenness and impurity that is, in some way, connected to our sexuality.

ii. We have a tendency to think that if something is *natural*, it is *pure*. That may not be true. "The ordinary processes of life are not necessarily clean because they are natural. The foul heart may vitiate the most natural functions." (Meyer)

iii. "A careful perusal of these requirements reminds us that the procreative faculties are all underneath the curse.... Whether the exercise of such faculties be natural or unnatural, in the sight of a God of absolute holiness they are tainted with sin." (Morgan)

b. **When they defile My tabernacle that is among them**: This made an obvious separation between sex and the worship of God. To the modern world this seems normal, but in the ancient world it was common to worship the gods by having sex with temple prostitutes. God did not want this association in His worship.

i. "Thus it would be an abomination to engage in sexual activity in the tabernacle precinct." (Rooker)

ii. It is important for us to regard these laws of cleanliness from a New Testament perspective. In Mark 7:1-9 Jesus criticized the Pharisees for their over-emphasis on ceremonial cleanliness and their lack of regard for *internal* cleanliness. These laws were meant to have both hygienic benefits and spiritual applications; they were never intended as the way to be right with God.

iii. In Acts 15, the early Christian community properly discerned the work and will of God in the New Covenant: that under the New Covenant, the believer was not bound to these laws of ritual purity. One could be a follower of Jesus without the ritual conformity to the Mosaic Law.

iv. Yet we need to remember that spiritual cleanliness in worship is important today. We also remember that Jesus is the One who makes us clean and fit for fellowship: *You are already clean because of the word which I have spoken to you* (John 15:3). As we receive from the word of

God, we are being cleansed. As G. Campbell Morgan wrote, "For us the way of perpetual cleansing is provided in Christ."

v. Our cleanliness is complete as we abide in Jesus: 1 John 1:7-9 – *But if we walk in the light as He is in the light, we have fellowship with one another, and the blood of Jesus Christ His Son cleanses us from all sin. If we say that we have no sin, we deceive ourselves, and the truth is not in us. If we confess our sins, He is faithful and just to forgive us our sins and to cleanse us from all unrighteousness.*

Leviticus 16 – The Day of Atonement

A. Preparation for sacrifice on the Day of Atonement.

1. (1-2) How Aaron should not come into the Most Holy Place.

Now the LORD spoke to Moses after the death of the two sons of Aaron, when they offered *profane fire* before the LORD, and died; and the LORD said to Moses: "Tell Aaron your brother not to come at *just* any time into the Holy *Place* inside the veil, before the mercy seat which *is* on the ark, lest he die; for I will appear in the cloud above the mercy seat.

a. **The LORD spoke to Moses after the death of the two sons of Aaron**: Nadab and Abihu were struck down by the LORD because they came into the Holy Place and offered *profane fire* before the LORD (Leviticus 10). In chapter 16, God explained the proper way to come before Him.

b. **Tell Aaron your brother not to come at just any time into the Holy Place inside the veil**: Aaron (or any other high priest) could not come into the Holy Place any time he pleased, but only at God's invitation and at the appointed time and place. This was so important that God added the warning, **lest he die**. Apparently, it was possible for the high priest to **die** in the Holy of Holies, where the ark of the covenant and the **mercy seat** were.

i. The same is true today: We can *only* come into God's Holy Place at His invitation. Blessedly, the access has been opened wide because of Jesus' work on the cross for us. Romans 5:1-2 specifically says that because of Jesus' work on our behalf, we have standing access to God.

2. (3-5) What Aaron needs to bring with him when he goes into the Holy Place.

"Thus Aaron shall come into the Holy *Place*: with *the blood of* a young bull as a sin offering, and *of* a ram as a burnt offering. He shall put the holy linen tunic and the linen trousers on his body; he shall be girded with a linen sash, and with the linen turban he shall be attired. These

are holy garments. Therefore he shall wash his body in water, and put them on. And he shall take from the congregation of the children of Israel two kids of the goats as a sin offering, and one ram as a burnt offering.

a. **Thus Aaron shall come into the Holy Place**: After the warning in verses 1-2, God began instructions for the Day of Atonement. Though this chapter describes the ritual for the Day of Atonement, that phrase is not used in this chapter. The phrase comes from Leviticus 23:27-28.

i. "The day was the most solemn of all the Old Testament rituals. So significant was it that in later Jewish tradition it came to be called just that, 'The Day' (*Yoma*)." (Rooker)

ii. "Every arrangement was intended to impress the mind with the solemnity of approach to God and to emphasise the fact that man as a sinner has no right of access save as he approaches through sacrifice." (Morgan)

b. **With the blood of a young bull as a sin offering**: On the Day of Atonement, Aaron started with **the blood of a young bull** to atone for his own sin and the sin of his house.

c. **He shall put the holy linen tunic and the linen trousers on his body**: Aaron must come clothed with garments of humility. He did not wear his normal priestly garments for *glory and for beauty* (Exodus 28:2). Instead, the high priest wore a **holy linen tunic and the linen trousers**. He was clothed in simple, humble white.

i. "He was not to dress in his [priestly] garments, but in the simple sacerdotal vestments, or those of the Levites, because it was a day of *humiliation;* and as he was to offer sacrifices for his *own sins*, it was necessary that he should appear in habits suited to the occasion." (Clarke)

d. **He shall wash his body in water**: Aaron must come washed. Traditionally, this washing was done by immersion.

e. **He shall take from the congregation of the children of Israel two kids of the goats**: Aaron must come with two goats and one ram to complete the offering of atonement.

i. **As a sin offering**: "The two goats are regarded as one sacrifice. They are a 'sin offering.' Hence, to show how unimportant and non-essential is the distinction between them, the 'lot' is employed; also, while the one is being slain, the other stands before the 'door of the Tabernacle.' This shows that both are parts of one whole, and it is only from the impossibility of presenting both halves of the truth to be symbolised in one that two are taken." (Maclaren)

B. What the high priest does on the Day of Atonement.

1. (6-10) Casting lots to choose between the two goats.

"Aaron shall offer the bull as a sin offering, which *is* for himself, and make atonement for himself and for his house. He shall take the two goats and present them before the Lord *at* the door of the tabernacle of meeting. Then Aaron shall cast lots for the two goats: one lot for the Lord and the other lot for the scapegoat. And Aaron shall bring the goat on which the Lord's lot fell, and offer it *as* a sin offering. But the goat on which the lot fell to be the scapegoat shall be presented alive before the Lord, to make atonement upon it, *and* to let it go as the scapegoat into the wilderness."

a. **Aaron shall offer the bull as a sin offering, which is for himself**: The sacrifice of this bull is described in verses 11-14.

i. The emphasis in this chapter is that **Aaron** (or every high priest after him) was to do this *by himself*. The phrase **Aaron shall** or **he shall** is repeated more than 20 times in this chapter. Not until the very end of the ritual was there any assistance to Aaron.

ii. Normally the tabernacle was a busy place, with many priests and Levites and those bringing their offerings, and many people about. But on this day the tabernacle was empty, except for one man doing his work.

iii. This was a preview of the perfect work of atonement to be made by Jesus the Messiah. "There was none with our Lord: he trod the winepress alone. He his own self bare our sins in his own body on the tree. He alone went in where the thick darkness covered the throne of God, and none stood by to comfort him." (Spurgeon)

b. **He shall take two goats**: There were **two goats** used in the sacrifices made on the Day of Atonement. Aaron presented them before the Lord. According to some, the two goats were to be as alike as possible – similar in size, color, and value.

c. **Then Aaron shall cast lots for the two goats: one lot for the Lord and the other lot for the scapegoat**: One goat was **for the Lord** and would be sacrificed as a sin offering. The other goat was **the scapegoat** and would be released to the wilderness. Each goat had an important role on the Day of Atonement.

i. There are many theories as to the nature of the **lots** that were **cast** to choose between the goats. Some believe that one lot had the name of the LORD, and the other the name *Azazel* – the literal Hebrew that is translated **scapegoat**. Rooker gives another theory: "According to Gerstenberger, a yes-stone and a no-stone were placed in a container. The one that fell out first would provide the answer to the posed question."

ii. The **scapegoat** was literally the "escape goat." It escaped death and went into the wilderness. **Scapegoat** translates the Hebrew word *azazel*. "The meaning of this word is far from certain.... The word may perhaps signify 'removal' or 'dismissal'.... Probably the best explanation is that the word was a rare technical term describing 'complete removal.'" (Harrison)

iii. "There are three possible interpretations for the meaning of this term: (1) It may mean 'the goat that departs' (that is, a scapegoat).... (2) It may refer to 'the place where the animal is dispatched' or 'the Precipice,'.... (3) It may be considered the proper name of a demon inhabiting the desert (that is, *Azazel*)." (Peter-Contesse)

2. (11-14) The bull for the sin offering.

"And Aaron shall bring the bull of the sin offering, which is for himself, and make atonement for himself and for his house, and shall kill the bull as the sin offering which *is* for himself. Then he shall take a censer full of burning coals of fire from the altar before the LORD, with his hands full of sweet incense beaten fine, and bring *it* inside the veil. And he shall put the incense on the fire before the LORD, that the cloud of incense may cover the mercy seat that *is* on the Testimony, lest he die. He shall take some of the blood of the bull and sprinkle *it* with his finger on the mercy seat on the east *side;* and before the mercy seat he shall sprinkle some of the blood with his finger seven times.

a. **The bull of the sin offering, which is for himself:** The idea was that Aaron could only make atonement for the sins of the people of Israel after his own sins (and the sins of **his house**) were dealt with.

i. "According to tradition he prayed the following prayer: 'O God, I have committed iniquity, transgressed, and sinned before thee, I and my house. O God, forgive the iniquities and transgressions and sins which I have committed and transgressed and sinned before thee, I and my house, as it is written in the Law of thy servant Moses, *For on this day shall atonement be made for you to cleanse you; from all your sins shall ye be clean before the Lord* (Leviticus 16:30) (*Yoma* 3:8)." (Rooker)

ii. The high priest in Leviticus 16 stands as a preview picture of the great work of Jesus the Messiah. Here is an important point of contrast: Aaron, and every high priest descended from him, was a sinner and must make atonement for his own sin *first*.

iii. *For such a high priest was fitting for us, who is holy, harmless, undefiled, separate from sinners, and has become higher than the heavens; who does not need daily, as those high priests, to offer up sacrifices, first for His own sins and then for the people's, for this He did once for all when He offered up Himself.* (Hebrews 7:26-27)

b. **He shall put the incense on the fire before the LORD:** This created more than a pleasant smell. As the high priest entered the Most Holy Place, it created a cloud of smoke to **cover the mercy seat.** This shielded the high priest from full exposure to the glory of the LORD and was necessary **lest he die.**

i. "Would not his heart beat faster as he laid his hand on the heavy veil, and caught the first gleam of the calm light from the Shechinah?" (Maclaren)

c. **He shall take some of the blood of the bull and sprinkle it with his finger on the mercy seat:** Once the high priest entered the Holy of Holies, he sprinkled **some of the blood of the bull** upon the **mercy seat,** even as it was hidden in the cloud of incense. This was the lid on top of the ark of the covenant.

i. The idea was that God was *above* **the mercy seat** (*I will appear in the cloud above the mercy seat,* Leviticus 16:2), and as He looked down upon the ark of the covenant, He saw the sin of man. Man's sin was represented by the items in the ark of the covenant: Manna Israel complained about, tablets of law Israel broke, and a budding almond rod given as a response to Israel's rebellion. Then, the high priest sprinkled atoning blood seven times on the mercy seat – covering over the emblems of Israel's sin. God saw the blood cover over the sin, and atonement was made.

ii. This captures the thought behind the Hebrew word for atonement: *Kipper,* which means, "to cover." Sin was not *removed* but *covered over* by sacrificial blood. The New Testament idea of atonement is that our sin is not merely covered, but removed – taken away, so there is no barrier between God and man any longer.

d. **Before the mercy seat he shall sprinkle some of the blood:** Because of this phrase, some believe that this blood was put on the mercy seat itself, and on the ground in front of the mercy seat and ark of the covenant.

3. (15-19) The goat selected for sacrifice is offered to make atonement for the tabernacle.

"Then he shall kill the goat of the sin offering, which *is* for the people, bring its blood inside the veil, do with that blood as he did with the blood of the bull, and sprinkle it on the mercy seat and before the mercy seat. So he shall make atonement for the Holy *Place*, because of the uncleanness of the children of Israel, and because of their transgressions, for all their sins; and so he shall do for the tabernacle of meeting which remains among them in the midst of their uncleanness. There shall be no man in the tabernacle of meeting when he goes in to make atonement in the Holy *Place*, until he comes out, that he may make atonement for himself, for his household, and for all the assembly of Israel. And he shall go out to the altar that *is* before the Lord, and make atonement for it, and shall take some of the blood of the bull and some of the blood of the goat, and put it on the horns of the altar all around. Then he shall sprinkle some of the blood on it with his finger seven times, cleanse it, and consecrate it from the uncleanness of the children of Israel.

a. **Then he shall kill the goat of the sin offering**: The bull provided atonement for the sin of the high priest and **the goat of the sin offering** was brought **inside the veil** and sprinkled seven times on and before the mercy seat. This made atonement for **the Holy Place**.

i. The goat that was sacrificed was also like Jesus, in that the goat was spotless, was from the people of Israel (Leviticus 16:5), was chosen by God (Leviticus 16:8), and the goat's blood was taken to the Holy Place to provide atonement.

ii. "The two goats made only *one sacrifice*, yet only one of them was slain. *One* animal could not point out both the *Divine* and *human* nature of Christ, nor show both his *death* and *resurrection*, for the goat that was *killed* could not be made *alive*." (Clarke)

iii. According to some Jewish traditions, it was on the Day of Atonement that the high priest – and only the high priest – could pronounce the name of God, the sacred Tetragrammaton, YHWH (Yahweh). When he entered the Holy Place with the blood of the goat set apart to the Lord, he uttered the name. He was the only one, and that was the only time, when the name could be spoken, and the high priest was to pass on the exact pronunciation of the name of God to his successor with his dying breath.

b. **So he shall make atonement for the Holy Place, because of the uncleanness of the children of Israel**: This blood was applied to the mercy seat, but also the tabernacle and altar itself. This blood cleansed the house of God itself, which was made ceremonially unclean by man's constant touch.

   i. **Atonement for the Holy Place**: Both the *priest* of God and the *house* of God needed to be cleansed by atoning blood before atonement for Israel as a nation could be made. "The priest who cleanses others is himself unclean, and he and his fellows have tainted the sanctuary by the very services which were meant to atone and to purify." (Maclaren)

   ii. The use of the three terms **their transgressions**, **their sins**, **their uncleanness** give extreme emphasis to the idea of Israel's sinfulness. This was atonement for the depths of sin.

   iii. The first used term may be the most important. "The word *pesa*, translated [**transgressions**], is the most grievous word for sin in the Old Testament. The term refers to sin in its grossest manifestation. It indicates a breach of relationship between two parties and was probably borrowed from the diplomatic realm, where it indicated a covenant-treaty violation." (Rooker)

4. (20-22) The release of the scapegoat.

"And when he has made an end of atoning for the Holy *Place*, the tabernacle of meeting, and the altar, he shall bring the live goat. Aaron shall lay both his hands on the head of the live goat, confess over it all the iniquities of the children of Israel, and all their transgressions, concerning all their sins, putting them on the head of the goat, and shall send *it* away into the wilderness by the hand of a suitable man. The goat shall bear on itself all their iniquities to an uninhabited land; and he shall release the goat in the wilderness.

   a. **He shall bring the live goat**: After the high priest's sin was dealt with and after the tabernacle itself was cleansed, Aaron then dealt with the sin of the people through the transference of sin and release of the scapegoat.

   b. **Aaron shall lay both his hands**: As the high priest did this, he confessed **all the iniquities of the children of Israel**. This confession of sins was an important part of the Day of Atonement ritual, linking the concept of the confession of sin and atonement.

   i. The confession of sin was to be complete. The triple use of **all the iniquities...all their transgressions...all their sins** gives a strong emphasis.

   ii. "According to the Mishnah, the high priest said the following prayer as he placed his hands upon the scapegoat: 'O God, thy people, the House of Israel, have committed iniquity, transgressed, and sinned before thee. O God, forgive, I pray, the iniquities and transgressions and sins which thy people, the House of Israel, have committed and transgressed and sinned before thee; as it is written in the law of thy servant Moses, *For on this day shall atonement be made for you to cleanse you: from all your sins shall ye be clean before the Lord* (Leviticus 16:30; *Yoma* 6:2)." (Rooker)

c. **He shall release the goat in the wilderness**: This was a perfect demonstration of atonement under the Old Covenant, before the completed work of Jesus on the cross. Sin could be put away, but never really eliminated. The sin-bearing goat, bearing the sin of Israel, was alive somewhere but put away.

i. Charles Spurgeon explained that Rabbi Jarchi said the goat was taken ten miles out of Jerusalem, and there were refreshment stations each mile along the way for the man who escorted the goat out of the city. He finally went the ten miles and then watched the goat wander off until he could see the goat no more. Then the sin was gone, and the Day of Atonement was considered complete.

ii. "The picture of the goat going away, and away, and away, a lessening speck on the horizon, and never heard of more is the divine symbol of the great fact that there is full, free, everlasting forgiveness, and on God's part, utter forgetfulness. 'Though your sins be as scarlet, they shall be white as snow.' 'I will remember them no more at all for ever.'" (Maclaren)

iii. The first goat was a picture of *how* atonement is granted: sins are forgiven because punishment has been put on an innocent party. The second goat, the scapegoat, was a picture of the *effect* of atonement: the penalty of our sins is cast far away, never to return.

iv. Sin was put away – but not completely. How could one know for certain that God had accepted the sacrifice on the Day of Atonement? What if someone accidentally encountered the scapegoat in the wilderness? What if the scapegoat wandered back among the people of Israel? Through their traditions, the Jews began to deal with these concerns. "On the head of the *scape-goat* a piece of scarlet cloth was tied, and the tradition of the Jews states that if God accepted the sacrifice the scarlet cloth turned *white* while the goat was led to the desert; but if God had not accepted this expiation, the *redness* continued, and the rest of the year was spent in mourning." (Clarke) Through this, they thought to have a *certainty* about the work of atonement.

v. It seems that later the ceremony was altered, so the goat would be killed and have no chance of contacting Israel again. "The Jews write, that this goat was carried to the mountain called Azazel, whence the goat is so called; and that there he was cast headlong; and that the red string by which he was led turned white when God was pleased with the Israelites, otherwise it remained red; and they mourned all that year." (Poole)

vi. When Jesus' rose from the dead, clothed with white garments, it was proof forever that the red had changed to white – and atonement Jesus made at the cross was perfect and complete.

vii. "And the ancient Hebrews write, that forty years before the destruction of the temple, which was about the time of Christ's death, this red string turned no more white" (Poole).

5. (23-28) Completion of the sacrifices.

"Then Aaron shall come into the tabernacle of meeting, shall take off the linen garments which he put on when he went into the Holy *Place,* and shall leave them there. And he shall wash his body with water in a holy place, put on his garments, come out and offer his burnt offering and the burnt offering of the people, and make atonement for himself and for the people. The fat of the sin offering he shall burn on the altar. And he who released the goat as the scapegoat shall wash his clothes and bathe his body in water, and afterward he may come into the camp. The bull *for* the sin offering and the goat *for* the sin offering, whose blood was brought in to make atonement in the Holy *Place,* shall be carried outside the camp. And they shall burn in the fire their skins, their flesh, and their offal. Then he who burns them shall wash his clothes and bathe his body in water, and afterward he may come into the camp.

a. **He shall wash his body with water in a holy place**: After releasing the scapegoat, the high priest and the one who released the scapegoat washed, and the sin offering and burnt offering would be completed.

b. **Take off the linen garments.... put on his garments**: When atonement was finished, the high priest emerged from the tabernacle in glory – with the humble garments taken off and in his normal clothes for glory and beauty.

i. On the Day of Atonement, the high priest was humble (Leviticus 16:4), he was spotless (Leviticus 16:11), and he was alone (Leviticus 16:11-14), and he emerged victorious. Each of these aspects was perfectly fulfilled by Jesus Messiah in accomplishing the ultimate work of atonement.

6. (29-31) What the people did on the Day of Atonement.

"*This* shall be a statute forever for you: In the seventh month, on the tenth *day* of the month, you shall afflict your souls, and do no work

at all, *whether* a native of your own country or a stranger who dwells among you. For on that day *the priest* shall make atonement for you, to cleanse you, *that* you may be clean from all your sins before the LORD. It *is* a sabbath of solemn rest for you, and you shall afflict your souls. *It is* a statute forever.

a. **You shall afflict your souls**: In contrast to other national days of gathering, the Day of Atonement was a day to **afflict your souls**. That is, it was a day of fasting and rest – **a sabbath of solemn rest**.

i. God wanted them to afflict themselves, to show the humility and repentance appropriate for those who need forgiveness. It was also an identification with the sacrifice for sin. Afflicting the soul brought the Israelite into sympathy with the afflicted sacrificial victim, even as the believer identifies with Jesus Christ on the cross.

ii. **Afflict your souls**: "The admonition…has been traditionally understood to refer to fasting. This is thus the only fast day in the Mosaic Law." (Rooker)

iii. Modern Jews who do observe the Day of Atonement (Yom Kippur) typically fast for that day. The Mishna gives four more things to abstain from: bathing, the use of oil on the body, wearing shoes, and sexual intercourse (cited in Rooker). Even if a Jewish person today were to observe all those things on Yom Kippur, they still have no *sacrifice* for sins.

• Some Jewish people consider *their own sacrifice* to be a suitable substitute; today some sacrifice a rooster for every male in the family, and a hen for every female, on the Day of Atonement – a vague shadow of obedience to Leviticus 16.

• Some Jewish people consider *charity* a suitable substitute for sacrifice; the word "charity" in modern Hebrew is the same as the word for "righteousness."

• Some Jewish people consider *sufferings* a suitable substitute for sacrifice; among the Jews of Eastern Europe there used to be custom to inflict 39 lashes upon themselves on the Day of Atonement.

• Some Jewish people consider *good works* or *the study of the law* as suitable substitutes for sacrifice.

b. **That you may be clean from all your sins before the LORD**: The afflicting of one's soul, the taking of rest, and the observance of a sabbath of solemn rest were important aspects of the Day of Atonement. Yet, fundamentally, the basis of atonement was sacrifice; the atonement made by the priest.

i. "The shallow dream that God's forgiveness can be extended without a sacrifice having been offered does not exalt but detracts from the divine character. It invariably leads to an emasculated abhorrence of evil, and detracts from the holiness of God, as well as introduces low thoughts of the greatness of forgiveness and of the infinite love of God." (Maclaren)

c. **It is a sabbath of solemn rest for you**: This **sabbath of solemn rest** demanded a cessation of works, even as the believer is justified and finds atonement apart from his own works, being justified by the work of another. This means that all the charity, all the sufferings, all the study of the law in the world cannot atone for sin – we must rest in the finished work of Jesus Christ on our behalf.

i. Yom Kippur ends with the blowing of the Shofar, the trumpet that heralds the coming of the Messiah. The following prayer for a Jewish Day of Atonement liturgy is attributed to Rabbi Eleazer Kalir in the 9th Century, and is often repeated today in some form:

Our righteous Messiah has departed from us,
We are horror-stricken, and have none to justify us.
Our iniquities and the yoke of our transgressions
He carries who is wounded because of our transgressions
He bears on His shoulder the burden of our sins.
To find pardon for all our iniquities.
By His stripes we shall be healed –
O Eternal One, it is time that thou should create Him anew!

ii. Charles Spurgeon suggested three things that Christian believers should do as we appreciate the perfect atonement that Jesus the Messiah made for His people:

- Afflict our souls in humility and repentance.

- Rest from our works of self-justification and self-righteousness.

- Behold our High Priest in His glorious garments.

7. (32-34) What the high priest does on the Day of Atonement.

"And the priest, who is anointed and consecrated to minister as priest in his father's place, shall make atonement, and put on the linen clothes, the holy garments; then he shall make atonement for the Holy Sanctuary, and he shall make atonement for the tabernacle of meeting and for the altar, and he shall make atonement for the priests and for all the people of the assembly. This shall be an everlasting statute for you, to make atonement for the children of Israel, for all their sins, once a year." And he did as the LORD commanded Moses.

a. **He shall make atonement for the Holy Sanctuary**: This meant the priest and only the priest. *Only* once a year could any man – and then, only one man – enter into the Holy Place and come near the presence of God.

b. **For all their sins, once a year**: To this summary of what was previously described in the chapter is the reminder that this is to be done **once a year**.

i. *Every* year, year after year, this atonement had to be made, showing it was never completed. In contrast, Jesus provided a finished work: *For Christ has not entered the holy places made with hands, which are copies of the true, but into heaven itself, now to appear in the presence of God for us; not that He should offer Himself often, as the high priest enters the Most Holy Place every year with blood of another; He then would have had to suffer often since the foundation of the world; but now, once at the end of the ages, He has appeared to put away sin by the sacrifice of Himself. And as it is appointed for men to die once, but after this the judgment, so Christ was offered once to bear the sins of many. To those who eagerly wait for Him He will appear a second time, apart from sin, for salvation.* (Hebrews 9:24-28)

ii. "For us there is no waiting for an annual day of atonement. We need not wait, with sin undealt with for an hour. Our Priest abides in the holiest, and we have access there through Him at all times." (Morgan)

Leviticus 17 – The Sanctity of Blood

A. Prohibition of sacrifice outside the tabernacle.

1. (1-4) Sacrifice must be at the tabernacle and by the appointed priests.

And the LORD spoke to Moses, saying, "Speak to Aaron, to his sons, and to all the children of Israel, and say to them, 'This *is* the thing which the LORD has commanded, saying: "Whatever man of the house of Israel who kills an ox or lamb or goat in the camp, or who kills *it* outside the camp, and does not bring it to the door of the tabernacle of meeting to offer an offering to the LORD before the tabernacle of the LORD, the guilt of bloodshed shall be imputed to that man. He has shed blood; and that man shall be cut off from among his people,

a. **Who kills an ox or lamb or goat in the camp**: This refers not to the mere slaughter of animals for meat, but specifically killing for the sake of sacrifice.

   i. "Indeed the technical term for sacrificing an animal, *sht* is the term used in v. 3 (see 1:5; 3:2; 4:4; 14:13). This word never refers to the mere killing of an animal when it occurs in sacrificial contexts." (Rooker)

b. **Bring it to the door of the tabernacle of meeting**: In the pagan world at that time, it was customary to offer sacrifice wherever one pleased. Altars were often built on high hills, in forested areas, or at other special places.

c. **The guilt of bloodshed shall be imputed to that man**: With the building of the tabernacle (Exodus 40), Israel had a centralized place of worship. Therefore, they were not allowed to offer sacrifice in any place or in any way they pleased. They had to come to the tabernacle and have their sacrifice performed by the priests. If they disobeyed, they would be **cut off from among** the **people** – exiled from their community.

   i. This command runs completely contrary to the way most people come to God in our culture. The modern world emphasizes an individualistic way of coming to God, where everyone does according to their own preference in how and when and where and with whom they will meet with God.

ii. This thinking runs deep in the modern western world and is rarely even questioned. As described in the book *Habits of the Heart* (1985) Robert Bellah and his colleagues interviewed a young nurse named Sheila Larson, whom they described as representing the experience and views of many Americans on religion. Speaking about her own faith and how it worked in her life, she said: "I believe in God. I'm not a religious fanatic. I can't remember the last time I went to church. My faith has carried me a long way. It is 'Sheilaism.' Just my own little voice." This way of thinking dominates spirituality in the modern western world – but it is not the Biblical pattern for seeking God, pleasing Him, or becoming right with God.

2. (5-7) The right way to bring sacrifice – to the tabernacle, through the priest.

To the end that the children of Israel may bring their sacrifices which they offer in the open field, that they may bring them to the LORD at the door of the tabernacle of meeting, to the priest, and offer them *as* peace offerings to the LORD. And the priest shall sprinkle the blood on the altar of the LORD *at* the door of the tabernacle of meeting, and burn the fat for a sweet aroma to the LORD. They shall no more offer their sacrifices to demons, after whom they have played the harlot. This shall be a statute forever for them throughout their generations.'"

a. **That they may bring them to the LORD at the door of the tabernacle of meeting**: God established a place for Israel to bring their sacrifices – **the tabernacle of meeting**. To honor God, an Israelite could not simply follow their heart, their feelings, or their opinions. They had to come the way God made for them.

i. There were times when, under the leadership of His appointed priests, *God* authorized sacrifices at places other than **the tabernacle** (as in 1 Samuel 7:9 and 11:15, 2 Samuel 24:18, 1 Kings 18:20-23). "But though men were tied to this law, God was free to dispense with his own law, which he did sometimes to the prophets, as 1 Samuel 7:9, 11:15; etc." (Poole)

b. **They shall no more offer their sacrifices to demons**: When one came to the tabernacle of meeting and God's appointed priests, it was to offer the sacrifice to the LORD – Yahweh, the covenant God of Israel. They were to stop **their sacrifices to demons** and bring their sacrifice to Yahweh only, at the tabernacle of Yahweh, performed by the priest of Yahweh.

i. The same word here translated **demons** (*sair*) is also translated *wild goats* in Isaiah 13:21 and 34:14. The word can be literally understood as "hairy ones," referring to male goats. The English Standard Version translates this as *goat demons*. The New International Version and the New Living Translation have *goat idols*.

ii. "The Hebrew word actually means 'goats' and is so translated by at least three French translations. But it refers to something more than an ordinary goat. It is a kind of demonic being in the form of a goat." (Peter-Contesse)

iii. Herodotus (*The Histories*, 2.46) notes that many ancient cultures worshipped goats or goat-gods in some form. The "goat-gods" can rightly be understood as representative of all idols. Later, the Apostle Paul would specifically say that sacrifice to idols was, in some sense, a sacrifice to the **demons** that were identified with and were the inspiration of those gods (1 Corinthians 10:20-21).

c. **After whom they have played the harlot**: The idea was that Israel was the covenant "wife" of Yahweh. When Israel worshipped, honored, and sacrificed to idols it was like committing adultery or even prostitution with those gods – and the **demons** they represented.

i. **Played the harlot**: "The Hebrew term *zana* literally refers to 'going astray' and is most often employed in reference to an unfaithful wife. The term is used to describe such offenses as the apostasy of the worship of Molech and of consulting spiritists (Leviticus 20:5–6). Metaphorically the term applies to Israel's unfaithfulness to the Lord." (Rooker)

3. (8-9) Repeating the command to bring sacrifice to the tabernacle.

Also you shall say to them: 'Whatever man of the house of Israel, or of the strangers who dwell among you, who offers a burnt offering or sacrifice, and does not bring it to the door of the tabernacle of meeting, to offer it to the LORD, that man shall be cut off from among his people.

a. **Whatever man of the house of Israel, or of the strangers who dwell among you**: The command to bring *every* sacrifice to the tabernacle was not only for the covenant descendants of Abraham, Isaac, and Jacob (**the house of Israel**). It was also for foreigners who were proselytes, either full or partial converts to the worship of the God of Israel.

i. Because of the way this phrase is used in verses 13 and 15 of this chapter, there is reason to believe that **strangers** here refers to foreigners who were full or partial converts to the worship of the God of Israel.

ii. "The alien who lived in the land of Israel after the conquest may have in fact been what we would call a proselyte. As such he was subject to many of the same Old Testament laws and regulations as the Israelite." (Rooker)

b. **That man shall be cut off from among his people**: As was previously stated in verse 4, those who refused to sacrifice only to the LORD and only at the **tabernacle** were to be **cut off** – that is, put out of the community of Israel.

i. This perhaps would happen by force of law, or simply by community rejection. "The New Jerusalem Bible translates here 'that man will be outlawed from his people.' Other possible translations are 'he shall be isolated' or 'his people shall have nothing more to do with him.'" (Peter-Contesse)

B. Prohibition against eating blood.

1. (10-12) The command against eating blood and the reason for the command.

'And whatever man of the house of Israel, or of the strangers who dwell among you, who eats any blood, I will set My face against that person who eats blood, and will cut him off from among his people. For the life of the flesh *is* in the blood, and I have given it to you upon the altar to make atonement for your souls; for it *is* the blood *that* makes atonement for the soul.' Therefore I said to the children of Israel, 'No one among you shall eat blood, nor shall any stranger who dwells among you eat blood.'

a. **Whatever man of the house of Israel, or of the strangers who dwell among you**: Again, this command was for those who lived in ancient Israel, under the unique kingdom where God was recognized as king and His word was the law of the land.

i. **I will set My face against**: "The basic meaning is 'to reject' or 'to repudiate,' implying hostile action." (Peter-Contesse)

b. **Who eats any blood**: Since ancient times, people might eat or drink blood either as food, or often as a ritual or spiritual practice. Often, the idea was that the one who consumed the blood received the life strength of the being that supplied the blood. God strongly commanded that this should not be done in Israel, and that He would **set His face against that person who eats blood**.

i. Thus, as a matter of practice, all animals that were butchered in Israel were drained of blood as much as possible. Not all nations did this. "It appears from history that those nations who lived most on it [blood] were very fierce, savage, and barbarous, such as the *Scythians, Tartars, Arabs* of the desert, the *Scandinavians*, [and so forth], some of whom drank the blood of their enemies, making cups of their skulls!" (Clarke)

ii. "The prohibition against eating the blood became an important aspect of 'Kosher' food. For food to be kosher the animal's carotid artery was cut, and the animal had to bleed for a designated amount of time." (Rooker)

iii. In Acts 15, the Jerusalem Council told Gentile Christians in Antioch, Syria, and Cilicia that they should not eat blood or meat that was not killed by draining the blood. This was not a universal command for all Christians in all places and at all times. It was to those specific Gentile Christians, for the specific reason that they would not needlessly offend their Jewish neighbors; for the sake of evangelism (Acts 15:18-21).

c. **For the life of the flesh is in the blood**: God agreed that there was spiritual significance **in the blood** of an animal or person. The difference was that among pagans, they said: "The life is in the blood; I must eat or drink it and take that life for myself." The godly Israelite said, "**The life of the flesh is in the blood**, and it therefore belongs to God and not to me."

i. This emphasized a powerful idea: *life belongs to God*. God sets His **face against that person** who takes authority over life for themselves. Life depends on blood, is preserved by blood, and is nourished by blood. When enough blood leaves a body, life leaves a body.

ii. "Because the life of a creature is in the blood, blood makes atonement for one's life. One life is sacrificed for another. The shedding of substitutionary blood on the altar makes atonement, since the blood of the innocent victim was given for the life of the one who has sinned." (Rooker)

iii. The idea of **life** being **in the blood** is directed to sacrifice. "Most of the occurrences of the word 'blood' in the Old Testament indicate a death by violence. The focal point of the mention of blood was thus not of blood flowing through the veins but rather on blood shed, which indicated that life had ended." (Rooker)

d. **And I have given it to you upon the altar to make atonement for your souls**: Additionally, blood was the means by which atonement was made – therefore, to eat blood was to profane it, to make it a common thing.

2. (13-14) Respecting the blood of animals hunted and caught.

"Whatever man of the children of Israel, or of the strangers who dwell among you, who hunts and catches any animal or bird that may be eaten, he shall pour out its blood and cover it with dust; for *it is* the life of all flesh. Its blood sustains its life. Therefore I said to the children of Israel, 'You shall not eat the blood of any flesh, for the life of all flesh is its blood. Whoever eats it shall be cut off.'

a. **Whatever man of the house of Israel, or of the strangers who dwell among you**: Once more, this command was for those who lived in ancient Israel, under the unique kingdom where God was recognized as king and His word was the law of the land.

i. The commands of verses 13-14 and 15-16 seem to apply only to foreign proselytes or converts to the worship of the God of Israel, and not all foreigners in Israel (such as a traveler through the land). One reason to believe this is based on Deuteronomy 14:21, which says that it *was* permitted for a foreigner to eat an animal that died naturally. Therefore, the command of verses 15-16 likely applies not to every foreigner, but to those who were proselytes or converts to the worship of the God of Israel.

b. **He shall pour out its blood and cover it with dust**: If an animal was caught and killed in a hunt and could not be properly bled as in a regular butchering, then the blood was to be poured out on the ground and covered **with dust**.

i. **Who hunts and catches**: "Hunting was carried out by various means in the Old Testament, including the use of arrows, lances, swords, clubs, and pits and nets (Job 41:26-29; Isaiah 24:17-18; 51:20; Ezekiel 19:4, 8; Psalms 7:15; 140:5). In addition numerous devices were used for catching birds (Job 18:8-10)." (Rooker)

ii. It is easy to think that allowing the blood to drip on the ground and to cover it with dirt was to disrespect the blood of that animal; to profane it. When we think like that, we make the same mistake Uzzah made in 2 Samuel 6:6. Uzzah thought that somehow, the ground was more profane than his own touch.

iii. Instead, pouring out the blood on the ground in this manner *honored* the blood of the animal. The blood was "buried" and could not be defiled. "The life had thus returned to the ground from which it had come, and the hunters and others who chanced to be in the vicinity were protected from the possibility of communicable disease or infection." (Harrison)

iv. This respect for the blood of animals should make us consider how we regard the blood of Jesus. If, under the Old Covenant, the blood of animals was to be respected, what of the precious blood of Jesus which makes a New Covenant? *Of how much worse punishment, do you suppose, will he be thought worthy who has trampled the Son of God underfoot, counted the blood of the covenant by which he was sanctified a common thing, and insulted the Spirit of grace?* (Hebrews 10:29)

3. (15-16) Respecting the blood of animals that die in nature.

"And every person who eats what died *naturally* or what was torn *by beasts, whether he is* a native of your own country or a stranger, he shall both wash his clothes and bathe in water, and be unclean until evening. Then he shall be clean. But if he does not wash *them* or bathe his body, then he shall bear his guilt."

a. **Every person who eats what died naturally or what was torn by beasts**: If one came upon an animal that had died naturally or by accident, one could eat it.

i. "Or a stranger; understand of the proselytes; either of the proselytes of the gate, who were obliged to observe the precepts of Noah, whereof this was one; or of the proselytes of righteousness, or converts to the Jewish religion; for other strangers were allowed to eat such things, Deuteronomy 14:21." (Poole)

b. **He shall both wash his clothes and bathe in water, and be unclean until evening**: It was permitted to eat animals that died under some kind of natural cause, but it made someone ceremonially unclean. They had to wash and wait for the new day (**until evening**) to once again be ceremonially clean. If that one refused to do this, they would remain in a state of ceremonial impurity (**he shall bear his guilt**).

Leviticus 18 – Laws of Sexual Morality

A. Commands against incest.

1. (1-5) Introduction to the commands regarding sexual conduct.

Then the LORD spoke to Moses, saying, "Speak to the children of Israel, and say to them: 'I am the LORD your God. According to the doings of the land of Egypt, where you dwelt, you shall not do; and according to the doings of the land of Canaan, where I am bringing you, you shall not do; nor shall you walk in their ordinances. You shall observe My judgments and keep My ordinances, to walk in them: I *am* the LORD your God. You shall therefore keep My statutes and My judgments, which if a man does, he shall live by them: I *am* the LORD.

a. **Then the LORD spoke to Moses**: This chapter is one of the most extensive and direct passages in the Bible reflecting God's stated will and commands regarding the expression of human sexuality. These are the words of God, and as such they have immeasurably more authority than the words, opinions, theories, desires, feelings, longings, or wishes of any person or persons.

i. We know that as a whole, Christians are not under the law (Romans 6:14-15, Galatians 5:18). While obedience to God's law is *not* the basis of our right standing before Him, the principles of the law remain useful. One important use of the law is to be something of a *guardrail* for humanity, showing us the heart and desire of God for humanity in general and His people in particular.

ii. This chapter stands in the midst of commands that were uniquely directed to Israel, the only kingdom that specifically recognized Yahweh as their king and covenant God. Yet, it still expresses the mind and heart of God regarding the expression of sexuality. This is evident in the many *New Testament* commands to abstain from sexual immorality and uncleanness (2 Corinthians 12:21, Ephesians 5:3, Colossians 3:5, 1 Thessalonians 4:3-8, and many other passages). When the New Testament writers wrote of sexual immorality and uncleanness, they did so from a context that understood the commands of Leviticus 18 as one of the important passages that *defined* sexual immorality and impurity.

iii. In addition, Jesus Himself affirmed the goodness of these commands when He said in the Sermon on the Mount: *Do not think that I came to destroy the Law or the Prophets. I did not come to destroy but to fulfill. For assuredly, I say to you, till heaven and earth pass away, one jot or one tittle will by no means pass from the law till all is fulfilled. Whoever therefore breaks one of the least of these commandments, and teaches men so, shall be called least in the kingdom of heaven; but whoever does and teaches them, he shall be called great in the kingdom of heaven.* (Matthew 5:17-19)

iv. Furthermore, Jesus summarized the entire law in two points: *"You shall love the* LORD *your God with all your heart, with all your soul, and with all your mind." This is the first and great commandment. And the second is like it: "You shall love your neighbor as yourself." On these two commandments hang all the Law and the Prophets.* (Matthew 22:37-40) Obedience to the commands of Leviticus 18 is not only an expression of love to God (recognizing His wisdom and submitting to His will). It is also an expression of love for our neighbor; whom we will not sin against by participating with them in behavior that is against God's will and ultimately destructive to a blessed, happy, flourishing life.

v. "Although the laws in Leviticus 18 set forth moral/ceremonial principles, the sexual prohibitions enumerated are still in effect today. The New Testament echoes the teaching of Leviticus 18, for it also prohibits incest (Mark 6:17-29; 1 Corinthians 5:1-5), adultery (Romans 13:9; 1 Corinthians 6:9; Hebrews 13:4), and homosexuality (Romans 1:27; 1 Corinthians 6:9-11; 1 Timothy 1:10)." (Rooker)

b. **I am the** LORD **your God. According to the doings of the land of Egypt, where you dwelt, you shall not do**: Before God gave a single command in this area, He first established a foundation for the whole matter. He declared this principle: "You belong to Me; you shall not do as the world does." They were not to do what they saw among the Egyptians in the past, or what they would see among the Canaanites in the future (**the doings of the land of Egypt…the doings of the land of Canaan**).

i. "The Persians, for example, encouraged marital unions with mothers, daughters and sisters, on the ground that such relationships had special merit in the eyes of the gods." (Harrison)

ii. In many ways, the modern western world is moving further and further from a Biblically guided sexual morality. Yet every person has some sense of right and wrong when it comes to sexual matters. In our modern culture it often appears that the strongest idea shaping the sense of right and wrong is, *if it feels good, then it is right for me*. This twisted sense of sexual right and sexual wrong has done tremendous damage in our culture, as it has throughout all history. It is important that Christians live according to God's sense of right and wrong when it comes to sexual matters, and not do **according to the doings** of the surrounding culture.

iii. "Seven times in the introduction and conclusion [of Leviticus 18] the Israelites are commanded not to act as the other nations (see 18:3 [2x], 24, 26, 27, 29, 30)." (Rooker)

iv. There is a sense in which the Apostle Paul gave the same idea in Romans 12:2: *Do not be conformed to this world, but be transformed by the renewing of your mind, that you may prove what is that good and acceptable and perfect will of God.*

v. In radical contrast to the thinking of much of the modern western culture, Christianity has the important message: *sexual activity has profound meaning for people and before God.* The broader culture has emptied sex of all meaning and has reduced it to only a way to experience personal pleasure. God's desire is that people should experience sexual fulfillment not only in pleasure, but in the fulfillment of the highest purpose for sex: as part of what bonds together a man and a woman in a one-flesh relationship in their covenant of marriage (Genesis 2:24, Matthew 19:4-6).

vi. Strangely, **the doings of the** culture around us want us to trade God's purpose for sex (full of meaning and fulfillment) for the culture's confusion regarding sex (empty of meaning). Stranger still, many professing Christians willingly make the trade.

c. **If a man does, he shall live by them**: The standard of right and wrong in sexual matters given by God in this chapter (and the entire Bible) was not given to hurt, deprive, or restrict life, joy, or happiness for humanity. They were given to ultimately build the best life for society and individuals; we can **live by them**, and live *better* **by them**.

i. When it comes to sexual morality, Christians have a thrilling message of hope and life for the world. We can speak to a world that is battered, broken, hurting, and empty from their confused, misguided rebellion against God's standard for right and wrong in sexual matters – and to those who have suffered much abuse from others. We can speak to them and say, "There is life and hope in God's way." We can say, "When you are hurt and tired from a sexual morality that takes life from you, God has a sexual morality that will bring life to you."

ii. In a day when more and more people seem to abandon God's clearly stated standard of right and wrong regarding sexual matters – *including* many who profess to be faithful Christians – one must ask: "If I will not accept God's standard for right and wrong when it comes to sexual behavior, then what standard or whose standard do I accept?"

iii. Every person has some sense of right or wrong regarding sexual matters but not every person's sense of right or wrong brings ultimate blessing to humanity, either in general or in individual lives.

iv. The sickness and disease associated with sexual immorality is only one obvious way that disobedience to God's wisdom takes away from life and does not add to it. One might say, "**if a man does, he shall live by them**; if he does not, he may die by them."

v. "*By doing which a man shall live*: literally, 'which a man will do and he will live.' The idea that obedience to God's commandments is a source of life is found throughout the Bible (see, for example, Ezekiel 18:9; Nehemiah 9:29; Luke 10:28; Romans 10:5; Galatians 3:12)." (Peter-Contesse)

2. (6-9) Sexual relations among immediate family (incest) prohibited.

'None of you shall approach anyone who is near of kin to him, to uncover his nakedness: I *am* the LORD. The nakedness of your father or the nakedness of your mother you shall not uncover. She *is* your mother; you shall not uncover her nakedness. The nakedness of your father's wife you shall not uncover; it *is* your father's nakedness. The nakedness of your sister, the daughter of your father, or the daughter of your mother, *whether* born at home or elsewhere, their nakedness you shall not uncover.

a. **None of you shall approach anyone who is near of kin to him**: The first section of this chapter defining sexual sin prohibits sin among close relatives, those **near of kin**. This is known as incest, and the specifically prohibited relationships will be described in the following verses.

i. The very first command of this chapter shows that God's standard for right and wrong rises above what brings physical pleasure in a sexual act. Speaking from a purely physical perspective, the physical pleasure from a sexual act with someone **near of kin** is not any different than the pleasure received from a sexual act with someone else. But God never intended that the pursuit of physical pleasure be the highest purpose and good of the sexual act. God intended it to mean more; to be an important part of what binds together a husband and a wife in a one-flesh relationship (Genesis 2:24, Matthew 19:4-6).

ii. "Leviticus 18 defines specific boundaries for the family. This instruction is critical if the promise that Abraham was to be the ancestor of a great and mighty nation was to be fulfilled. A nation cannot exist if the family unit is not well defined, for the family is the foundation of society." (Rooker)

iii. Adam Clarke spoke to the issue of some of the marriages earlier in the Bible between relatives (such as Abraham and Sarah): "Notwithstanding the prohibitions here, it must be evident that in the infancy of the world, persons very near of kin must have been joined in matrimonial alliances; and that even brothers must have matched with their own sisters. This must have been the case in the family of Adam. In these first instances necessity required this; when this necessity no longer existed, the thing became inexpedient and improper."

b. **To uncover his nakedness**: This phrase (used 17 times in this chapter) is a polite way to speak of sexual activity. The emphasis is not so much on nudity (especially casual, accidental nudity), but on sexual activity. However, the term **to uncover...nakedness** is broad enough to include the idea of inappropriate activity short of actual sexual intercourse (such as oral sex). It would also include molestation and inappropriate fondling.

i. The words **to uncover...nakedness** "simply mean 'to have sexual intercourse' or 'to commit a sex act.'" (Peter-Contesse)

ii. There is a literal sense in which the viewing, reading, or hearing of pornography is to **uncover** the **nakedness** of another person.

c. **The nakedness of your father or the nakedness of your mother you shall not uncover**: In these verses, sexual activity between parents and children, parents and stepchildren, and between siblings (by birth or marriage) is prohibited. It is not to be done, and apart from the husband and wife relationship, the family relationship should not and must not be sexualized.

i. Significantly, sex among people in these relationships is condemned even if they are adults. These are not merely commands against sexual activity between children and adults. For example, it is sin for a man to have sex with his stepmother, even if they are both adults (as was the case in 1 Corinthians 5:1). It is wrong for a man to have sex with his adopted sister, even if they are consenting adults.

ii. "Sexual impulse is a potent desire. If gratified incestuously within the family, it blurs family lines and leads to the destruction of the family unit." (Rooker)

iii. There was *both* a moral and genetic reason for these commands. "Surveys in different parts of the world where inbreeding occurs have shown that it is accompanied by an increase in congenital malformations and perinatal mortality, for which recessive genes and environmental factors respectively would be responsible." (Harrison)

iv. "In those instances where the parents are siblings, or where the relationship is one between parent and child, the resultant offspring incur approximately at a 30% risk of retardation or some other serious defect." (Harrison)

d. **The nakedness of your father's wife you shall not uncover; it is your father's nakedness**: In a sense, the **nakedness** of a husband or wife *belongs* to their spouse, and to no one else. The legal spouse is the only one with whom God intends them to be *naked and unashamed*, in the Genesis 2:25 sense of restoring some of what the curse has taken away.

3. (10-18) Other applications of the command against incest.

The nakedness of your son's daughter or your daughter's daughter, their nakedness you shall not uncover; for theirs *is* your own nakedness. The nakedness of your father's wife's daughter, begotten by your father— she *is* your sister—you shall not uncover her nakedness. You shall not uncover the nakedness of your father's sister; she *is* near of kin to your father. You shall not uncover the nakedness of your mother's sister, for she *is* near of kin to your mother. You shall not uncover the nakedness of your father's brother. You shall not approach his wife; she *is* your aunt. You shall not uncover the nakedness of your daughter-in-law— she *is* your son's wife—you shall not uncover her nakedness. You shall not uncover the nakedness of your brother's wife; it *is* your brother's nakedness. You shall not uncover the nakedness of a woman and her daughter, nor shall you take her son's daughter or her daughter's daughter, to uncover her nakedness. They *are* near of kin to her. It *is* wickedness. Nor shall you take a woman as a rival to her sister, to uncover her nakedness while the other is alive.

a. **The nakedness of your son's daughter or your daughter's daughter, their nakedness you shall not uncover**: In these verses, God condemns sexual relations between many different family members:

- Grandparents and grandchildren (by blood or by marriage).

- Uncles, aunts, nieces, and nephews.

- Parents and the spouses of their children.
- Siblings and the spouses of their other siblings.
- The children of a spouse.
- The sibling of a spouse.

> i. "The group of relatives the Israelite was forbidden to marry would largely coincide with the relatives who would have lived in a single household in ancient Israel." (Rooker)

b. **It is your brother's nakedness**: The principle is related again. There is an important sense in which the **nakedness** of an individual *belongs* to their spouse and no one else. It goes against God's wisdom and law to *give* that nakedness to anyone else, or for anyone else to *take* it.

> i. A man and a woman become "one flesh" in marriage (Genesis 2:24, Matthew 19:4-6), so there is a real sense in which the **nakedness** of a husband or wife *belongs* to their spouse, and to no one else. The Apostle Paul expressed a similar thought in 1 Corinthians 7:4: *The wife does not have authority over her own body, but the husband does. And likewise the husband does not have authority over his own body, but the wife does.*

> ii. **It is wickedness**: "The term translated here as *wickedness* is a very general one which is also found in 19:29 and 20:14 and about twenty times in the rest of the Old Testament. It is used to describe any kind of morally unacceptable or detestable action." (Peter-Contesse)

> iii. **You shall not take a woman as a rival to her sister**: The Puritan commentator John Trapp was among those who believed that this was also a command against polygamy, but this is not clear from the text itself.

B. Other laws regarding sexual morality.

1. (19) The command against sex during menstruation.

'Also you shall not approach a woman to uncover her nakedness as long as she is in her *customary* impurity.

a. **In her customary impurity**: This command is an echo of Leviticus 15:19-24, where the penalty for breaking this observance of ceremonial cleanliness was described. The penalty was to perform a ritual washing.

> i. There is no specific mention of a marriage relationship in this verse. A **woman** includes a wife but goes beyond the marriage relationship. In marriage, this was a command for sexual restraint and honor even within a marriage relationship.

ii. The idea of some aspect of sexual restraint in marriage may seem strange or even offensive to those who feel that in regard to sex, a marriage relationship eliminates any need for restraint. Yet one aspect of the New Testament ethic of sex in marriage is expressed in 1 Corinthians 7:3: *Let the husband render to his wife the affection due her, and likewise also the wife to her husband.* The universal Christian values of servanthood and self-sacrifice demand that a spouse practice restraint of their sexual expectations when love and care for the other would require it.

b. **You shall not approach a woman to uncover her nakedness**: The use of this familiar phrase in Leviticus 18, in this particular context, emphasizes the idea that to **uncover** the **nakedness** was more than looking upon a nude body. The implication is of some kind of sexual act.

2. (20) The command against adultery.

Moreover you shall not lie carnally with your neighbor's wife, to defile yourself with her.

a. **You shall not lie carnally with your neighbor's wife**: To **lie carnally** (a polite way to speak of sexual intercourse or activity) with **your neighbor's wife** is to violate the marriage bond. God's intention for sexual expression is within a marriage covenant between one man and one woman (Genesis 2:18-25, Matthew 19:4-6). Sexual acts outside of the marriage covenant, or *breaking* the marriage covenant, do not fulfill this intention. They go against God's design and the ultimate benefit of humanity, both collectively and individually.

i. This is an echo of the seventh commandment (Exodus 20:14). We see the *act itself* is condemned and there is no justification allowed under the ways people often seek to justify adultery.

ii. To hope to justify adultery with excuses such as, "My partner doesn't understand me" or "we are in love" or "God led us to be with each other" goes against the clear command here and throughout the Scriptures and it ignores the destructive nature of this sin against the marriage covenant.

iii. "Adultery is an assault on the nuclear family. It was called 'the great sin' in the ancient Near East." (Rooker)

b. **To defile yourself with her**: Many people who are tempted to adultery do not consider how the sin will **defile** themselves. They *might* think about how their sin obviously affects their spouse, children, and other family members. But adultery also defiles the individual committing the sin, showing them to be an *unfaithful* and *uncontrolled* person.

3. (21) The command against Molech worship.

And you shall not let any of your descendants pass through *the fire* to Molech, nor shall you profane the name of your God: I *am* the LORD.

a. **You shall not let any of your descendants pass through the fire to Molech**: The horrific worship of the pagan idol **Molech** began by heating a metal statue representing the god until it was red hot. Then a living infant was placed on the outstretched hands of the statue while beating drums drowned out the screams of the child until it burned to death.

i. No wonder that the Bible identifies **Molech** with the demonic: *They even sacrificed their sons and their daughters to demons* (Psalm 106:37). In Leviticus 20:1-5, God pronounced the death sentence against all who worshipped Molech. Sometimes they worshipped that pagan idol by actually sacrificing their children in fire (Jeremiah 7:31).

ii. Despite this strong and clear command, even a man as great as Solomon at least sanctioned the worship of Molech and built a temple to this idol (1 Kings 11:7). One of the great crimes of the northern tribes of Israel was their worship of Molech, leading to the Assyrian captivity (2 Kings 17:17). King Manasseh of Judah gave his son to Molech (2 Kings 21:6). Up to the days of King Josiah of Judah, Molech worship continued, because he destroyed a place of worship to that idol (2 Kings 23:10).

iii. "Noting that the context deals with sexual activity, many scholars have advocated a position reflected in Jewish tradition that what is involved here is Jewish parents offering their children to Molech to grow up as temple prostitutes. This may be an attempt, however, to avoid the utter horror of what seems to be the face value reading of the text, since it is well known that the worship of Molech involved human sacrifice." (Rooker)

b. **Nor shall you profane the name of your God**: It is obvious God would condemn such an abomination. But this command is here in the context of sexual sins because often, Molech worship was a method of infanticide to eliminate children born outside of marriage, the result of the sexual acts God had commanded against.

i. Molech worship can be seen as an ancient version of birth control by infanticide, as even today sometimes abortion is used as birth control after the conception of the child.

ii. **Molech**: "The word itself is said to have made Hebrew speakers think of two things: (1) the word for 'king,' which has the same consonants, and (2) the word for 'shame,' which has the same vowels.

This information would suggest something like 'the King of Shame.'" (Peter-Contesse)

4. (22) Command against homosexual sex.

You shall not lie with a male as with a woman. It *is* an abomination.

a. **You shall not lie with a male as with a woman**: This is a simple and clear command against same-sex sexual acts. God's intention for sexual expression is within a marriage covenant between one man and one woman (Genesis 2:18-25, Matthew 19:4-6). Sexual acts between those of the same sex do not fulfill this intention. They go against God's design and the ultimate benefit of humanity, both collectively and individually.

i. This command – and similar commands through the Scriptures, such as in Romans 1:24-32 – are controversial and even considered offensive to many in modern western culture. Nevertheless, it is important to clearly understand and state what the Bible teaches on these matters because it is part of God's design and intention for humanity's ultimate good.

b. **It is an abomination**: This is one of the strongest words of condemnation in the vocabulary of Biblical Hebrew. Several other Bible passages prohibit homosexual acts, as Leviticus 20:13, 1 Corinthians 6:9, Revelation 22:15, and Romans 1:24-32 (which specifically speaks against lesbianism). The sin of homosexuality is described in passages such as Genesis 19:5 and Judges 19:22-25. Additionally, homosexuality was part of the idolatrous perversions which were allowed in Israel at its times of backsliding (1 Kings 14:24, 15:12, and 22:46).

i. "An abomination, a term especially frequent in the Book of Deuteronomy, refers to an act that is abhorrent or repugnant, such as idolatry and inappropriate worship of God." (Rooker)

c. **It is an abomination**: Specifically, what is condemned is the practice of male homosexuality. This prohibition is widely rejected and despised by many in modern western culture, and even considered hateful.

i. One reason this is considered hateful is because of a radical shift in thinking regarding homosexuality over the last few generations. For centuries, homosexuality was thought of as something that people *did* or *practiced*. In the last few generations, western culture in general sees homosexuality as defining one's *identity*.

ii. Christians must take great care to not *hate* people because they regard their sins as especially ugly – no matter what the sin is. Nevertheless, Christians must also take equal care not to *love* or *approve* of sins because they regard those who practice those sins as especially good.

There is great truth in the familiar saying, "love the sinner and hate the sin."

iii. If homosexual behavior is regarded as **an abomination** (as God clearly regards it), then that behavior cannot be approved of on the basis of *love*. The issue isn't love; the issue is of sexual conduct. Of course, the Bible in no way condemns love between people of the same sex, but it does say that *sexual conduct* between those people is sin.

iv. If homosexual behavior is regarded as **an abomination** (as God clearly regards it), then that behavior cannot be approved of on the basis of *inborn nature*. To the time of this writing there is no definitive scientific answer as to whether homosexual desire exists because of genetics, family dynamics in child-raising, early abuse, learned behavior, or other factors or a combination of factors. In some ways the answer to that question is irrelevant. The Bible says we are all born sinners, and our sinful desires may be expressed in different ways from person to person.

v. However, the percentage of those who say they are sexually attracted to those of their same-sex is much lower than commonly supposed. According to 2018 data from the United States National Information Survey, 97.6% of adults identified as straight (heterosexual), 1.6% identified as gay or lesbian, and 0.8% identified as bisexual. From a Christian perspective, the *sexual behavior* of the 2% to 3% of the population that identifies as homosexual or bisexual should not be approved of and should be regarded as a sin – even **an abomination**. Yet undeniably, those individuals deserve the respect and compassion that is due to everyone made in the image of God.

5. (23) The command against bestiality – sexual relations with animals.

Nor shall you mate with any animal, to defile yourself with it. Nor shall any woman stand before an animal to mate with it. It *is* perversion.

a. **Nor shall you mate with any animal**: This is a simple and clear command against sexual acts with animals. God's intention for sexual expression is within a marriage covenant between one man and one woman (Genesis 2:18-25, Matthew 19:4-6). Sexual acts with animals do not fulfill this intention. They go against God's design and the ultimate benefit of humanity, both collectively and individually.

i. "In contrast, the gods of Ugarit, by their example, led their devotees in this sin." (Harris)

ii. "That this was often done in Egypt there can be no doubt; and we have already seen, from the testimony of *Herodotus*, that an act of this kind actually took place while he was in Egypt." (Clarke)

b. **It is perversion**: To practice this was to **defile yourself**; to make yourself unclean and impure. It was rightly regarded as **perversion**, an ungodly combining of what should not be brought together when it comes to sexual behavior.

i. **Perversion**: "The term *tebel* is from the root *bll*, which means 'to mix' and indicates that this sexual practice involves an improper mixing together of the different species, stepping over the boundaries God has established (Genesis 1:1–2:3)." (Rooker)

ii. "This offensive sex act apparently was prevalent among the Canaanites." (Kaiser, commentary on Exodus)

iii. "Bestiality was not only an obvious perversion: it figured so often in the Canaanite cycle 'Tales of Baal' that it probably had a religious significance for the Canaanites." (Cole, commentary on Exodus)

iv. It is surprising to some that bestiality is legal in some European nations, and a subculture practices and promotes it. Yet there should be no surprise; if God's standard is rejected in one area of sexual morality, then the standards are often left up to the individual to decide. It is Christian civilization and morality that has discouraged and condemned fornication, adultery, pedophilia, polygamy, prostitution, homosexuality, gender confusion and the like. As Christian civilization and morality are increasingly mocked and rejected, it is no surprise that *all* of these sexual practices are increasingly practiced, supported, and encouraged.

6. (24-30) Summation: The urgency to obey God's command for sexual morality.

'Do not defile yourselves with any of these things; for by all these the nations are defiled, which I am casting out before you. For the land is defiled; therefore I visit the punishment of its iniquity upon it, and the land vomits out its inhabitants. You shall therefore keep My statutes and My judgments, and shall not commit *any* of these abominations, *either* any of your own nation or any stranger who dwells among you (for all these abominations the men of the land have done, who *were* before you, and thus the land is defiled), lest the land vomit you out also when you defile it, as it vomited out the nations that *were* before you. For whoever commits any of these abominations, the persons who commit *them* shall be cut off from among their people. 'Therefore you shall

keep My ordinance, so that *you* do not commit *any* of these abominable customs which were committed before you, and that you do not defile yourselves by them: I *am* the LORD your God.'"

a. **Do not defile yourselves**: Our modern culture often refuses to see any aspect of sexual conduct as *defiling*. The only measure is immediate pleasure, not right or wrong. But sexual sin *does* **defile** us, and it *does* harm us. God's laws are given for our best, not in an attempt to merely test us or boss us around.

 i. Statistically speaking, married couples live longer, get more enjoyment out of sex, have more sex, and are happier than those who are not married – obviously, trends that show God's way is the best way.

b. **For the land is defiled**: One of the reasons God brought Israel to defeat and displace the Canaanites was as a judgment against their sexual perversions. If Israel practiced the same sins to the same degree, they could also expect to be cast out of the land. In nations that celebrate and promote similar sins today, we should expect that the judgment of God would eventually come, and the land will **vomit** out its inhabitants.

 i. "Since the chapter opened with the statement that the Israelites are soon to enter the land of Canaan (18:3), it is clear that the iniquity of the Amorite/Canaanite is now complete (Genesis 15:16)." (Rooker)

c. **The persons who commit them shall be cut off from among their people**: God commanded that in Israel, there should be a strong sense of social disapproval – amounting to exile – towards those who broke these laws of sexual morality. These are family-killing sins and therefore civilization-killing sins.

 i. Rooker cites Kellogg: "Where there is incest or adultery, we may truly say the family is murdered; what murder is to the individual, that, precisely, are crimes of this class to the family."

 ii. It was not that these things were never done in Israel; it was simply that it was clear that society said those things were wrong and should never be approved. More and more, modern culture refuses to call almost any kind of sexual activity sin.

 iii. **Therefore you shall keep My ordinance**: "Let us remember the imperative tone of these words, and ask God to work in us to will and to do of His good pleasure." (Meyer)

Leviticus 19 – Many Various Laws

A. Laws regarding matters already covered.

1. (1-2) The general call to holiness.

And the LORD spoke to Moses, saying, "Speak to all the congregation of the children of Israel, and say to them: 'You shall be holy, for I the LORD your God *am* holy.

a. **You shall be holy**: The idea behind the word **holy** is "separate." As it is applied to God, it describes God's *apartness*. It means that God is different than man and from all others; different in His being and different in the greatness and majesty of His attributes. He has a righteousness unlike any other; a justice unlike any other; a purity unlike any other – and love, grace, and mercy unlike any other.

i. Part of this idea is that God is not merely a *super*-man; His being and character are divine, not human. The divine is a different order of being than the human.

b. **Be holy, for I the LORD your God am holy**: God is separate from man and from all creation. Yet because humans are made in the image of God, they can follow in His steps and also **be holy**. In this context, Israel was to be different; separate from the nations and the peoples around them.

i. To **be holy** means to be more like God, our separation unto Him and His truth – and naturally, separating ourselves from those things that are *not* like Him and *not* according to His truth.

ii. "A people created and governed by God are intended to represent Him and the truth concerning Him to other people." (Morgan)

iii. Matthew Poole understood this as God's declaration, **I the LORD your God am holy**, "both in my essence, and in all my laws, which are holy and just and good, and in all my actions; whereas the gods of the heathens are unholy both in their laws and institutions, whereby they allow and require filthy and abominable actions; and in their practices, some of them having given wicked examples to their worshippers."

2. (3) The law to respect parents.

'Every one of you shall revere his mother and his father, and keep My Sabbaths: I *am* the LORD your God.

a. **Every one of you shall revere his mother and his father**: This line essentially repeats the idea of the fifth commandment, found in Exodus 20:12. Honor for parents is an essential building block for the stability and health of all society. If the younger generations are constantly at war with older generations, the foundations of society will be destroyed.

i. "Respect for one's parents is a subject that receives a great amount of attention in the Book of Proverbs (1:8; 6:20; 10:1; 17:25; 23:22; 29:3)." (Rooker)

ii. "The *mother* is put first, partly because the practice of this duty begins there, mothers, by perpetual converse, being more and sooner known to their children than their fathers; and partly because this duty is most commonly neglected to the mother." (Poole)

b. **And keep My Sabbaths**: This line essentially repeats the fourth commandment, found in Exodus 20:8-11. Here, reverence for parents is linked to reverence for the LORD. Submitting to parental authority is a step to submitting to Divine authority.

i. "Reverencing parents is an act of piety towards God, since the parents are substitutes for the heavenly Father as far as their children are concerned." (Harrison)

ii. The command in Exodus 2:8-11 is specifically to *remember* the Sabbath. Here, the command is to **keep My Sabbaths** – to hold them as God commanded, as a day of rest.

iii. Like everything in the Bible, we understand this from the perspective of the whole Bible, not this single passage. With this understanding, we see that there is a real sense in which Jesus fulfilled the purpose and plan of the Sabbath *for* us and *in* us (Hebrews 4:9-11) – He is our rest, when we remember His finished work we **keep** God's **Sabbaths**, we *remember the rest.*

iv. Therefore, the whole of Scripture makes it clear that under the New Covenant, no one is under obligation to observe a Sabbath day (Colossians 2:16-17 and Galatians 4:9-11). Galatians 4:10 tells us that Christians are not bound to observe *days and months and seasons and years*. The rest we enter into as Christians is something to experience every day, not just one day a week - the rest of knowing we don't have to work to save ourselves, but our salvation is accomplished in Jesus (Hebrews 4:9-10).

v. Yet we dare not ignore the importance of a day of rest – God has built us so that we *need* one. Six days of work and one day of rest is good for us spiritually, mentally, and physically. Like an automobile that needs regular maintenance, we need regular rest – or we will not wear well. Some people are like high mileage automobiles that haven't been maintained well, and it shows.

3. (4) The law against idolatry.

'Do not turn to idols, nor make for yourselves molded gods: I *am* the LORD your God.

a. **Do not turn to idols**: This line essentially repeats the idea of the second commandment, found in Exodus 20:4-6. The word for **idols** literally means *nothings*. Idols represent gods that are not real and are really *nothings*.

i. "This word comes from a root meaning worthless, inadequate, or nothingness. It is frequently used in the Old Testament to refer to the gods of other groups of people. The Israelites did not consider them of any value." (Peter-Contesse)

b. **Nor make for yourselves molded gods**: Israel had significant trouble with the worship of idols until the Babylonian captivity (some 800 years from the time of Leviticus). The attraction was not so much to the **molded gods** themselves, as to what they represented – financial success, pleasure, and self-worship.

i. After the Babylonian captivity, Israel was cured of her gross idolatry of **molded gods** and began a more dangerous form of idolatry – idolatry of the nation itself, idolatry of the temple and its ceremonies, and an idolatry of tradition.

4. (5-8) Laws regarding offerings.

'And if you offer a sacrifice of a peace offering to the LORD, you shall offer it of your own free will. It shall be eaten the same day you offer *it*, and on the next day. And if any remains until the third day, it shall be burned in the fire. And if it is eaten at all on the third day, it *is* an abomination. It shall not be accepted. Therefore *everyone* who eats it shall bear his iniquity, because he has profaned the hallowed *offering* of the LORD; and that person shall be cut off from his people.

a. **If you offer a sacrifice of a peace offering**: A **peace offering** (for the enjoyment of **peace** with God and fellowship with Him) was always to be made of one's **own free will**. God did not want forced fellowship from His people.

b. **It shall be eaten the same day you offer it**: Nor did God want *stale* fellowship with His people. The meat of a peace offering was not to be eaten after two days.

> i. **He has profaned the hallowed offering of the LORD**: "To profane something is to treat it as if it were not sacred. The whole expression may be rendered 'has shown his spite for what belongs to the LORD' or 'has desecrated something the Lord considers sacred.'" (Peter-Contesse)

B. Other laws.

1. (9-10) Providing for the poor by leaving fields incompletely harvested.

'When you reap the harvest of your land, you shall not wholly reap the corners of your field, nor shall you gather the gleanings of your harvest. And you shall not glean your vineyard, nor shall you gather *every* grape of your vineyard; you shall leave them for the poor and the stranger: I *am* the LORD your God.

a. **You shall not wholly reap the corners of your field**: This was one of the public assistance programs in Israel. Farmers were not to *completely* harvest their fields, so the poor and needy could come and glean the remains for themselves. Grain was left at the **corners** of the **field**, and grapes were left on the vine. This shows God cares for the poor and wants them to have opportunities.

> i. This is exactly what Ruth was doing when Boaz noticed her (Ruth 2:2-3).

> ii. This was not the only care given to the poor in Israel. Deuteronomy 14:28-29 and 26:12-15 also command that every three years there be a special tithe collected for the relief of the poor.

b. **You shall leave them for the poor and the stranger**: This was a wonderful way to help the poor and the foreigner. It commanded the farmers to have a generous heart, and the poor to be active and to work for their food. It made a way for the poor to provide for their own needs with both work and dignity.

> i. "By gleaning the corners and the leftovers of the field, the poor were spared the embarrassment of asking for charity." (Rooker)

ii. "This is holiness according to the Divine standard, which ever has this element of compassion." (Morgan)

2. (11-13) Honest dealing.

'You shall not steal, nor deal falsely, nor lie to one another. And you shall not swear by My name falsely, nor shall you profane the name of your God: I *am* the LORD.

'You shall not cheat your neighbor, nor rob *him.* The wages of him who is hired shall not remain with you all night until morning.

a. **You shall not steal**: In essence, this repeats the eighth commandment (Exodus 20:15). This command is another important foundation for human society, establishing the right to personal property. God has clearly entrusted certain possessions to certain individuals, and other people or governments are not permitted to take that property without proper legal process.

i. Ephesians 4:28 gives the solution to stealing. *Let him who stole steal no longer, but rather let him labor, working with his hands what is good, that he may have something to give him who has need.*

b. **Nor deal falsely**: In the context of **you shall not steal**, this probably has reference to false dealing in order to steal from someone or take money from them deceptively.

c. **You shall not swear by My name falsely**: This is an aspect of what is forbidden under the third commandment (Exodus 20:7), against taking God's name in vain. Again, in context, it probably has the idea of swearing oaths to deceive others in taking money from them.

d. **You shall not cheat your neighbor**: To cheat – to take money from others with some form of deception – is the same as to **rob him**. Cheating is a form of robbery or stealing, and God commands against it.

e. **The wages of him who is hired shall not remain with you**: God commands the prompt payment of those who are **hired**. When people are hired and not paid, it is not only a sin against those hired – it is also a sin against God.

i. "For this plain reason, it is the support of the man's life and family, and they need to expend it as fast as it is earned." (Clarke)

3. (14) Basic human compassion commanded.

You shall not curse the deaf, nor put a stumbling block before the blind, but shall fear your God: I *am* the LORD.

a. **You shall not curse the deaf**: God commanded Israel to not mistreat those with physical disabilities. Cursing **the deaf** is cruel because they can't hear your curse, though others can. To **put a stumbling block before the blind** is just mean.

i. "He who is capable of doing this, must have a heart cased with cruelty." (Clarke)

ii. "Even if the deaf person were unable to hear the curse, people thought that a curse had its own power to cause harm. And the deaf man would be unable to do anything to counteract it." (Peter-Contesse)

iii. This law sought to command and build basic kindness among the people of Israel. An accurate and revealing measure of our humanity is how we treat the weak and unfortunate.

iv. This law also sought to correct bad theology. It was common then (and still exists today) for people to think that if someone had a physical disability (such as being **deaf** or **blind**), then that person was specially cursed by God. They thought it had to do with some special or specific sin from that person or their ancestors. They thought if God had so cursed them, then they could also curse them. With this command, God corrected that bad thinking.

b. **Nor put a stumbling block before the blind**: It would take a cruel, hard-hearted person to deliberately **put a stumbling block before the blind** – to deliberately trip a blind person. That this command was necessary shows us the kind of rough people the Israelites were after 400 years of slavery in Egypt. Their cruel environment made cruelty seem normal to them. This had to change.

i. These commands regarding kindness and generosity are in the midst of what is often called the *holiness code* of Israel. This reminds us of something often forgotten: generosity and kindness to those in need is an important aspect of holiness.

ii. "Under these two particulars are manifestly and especially forbidden all injuries done to such as are unable to right or defend themselves; of whom God here takes the more care." (Poole)

4. (15-16) Laws regarding justice and truthfulness.

'**You shall do no injustice in judgment. You shall not be partial to the poor, nor honor the person of the mighty. In righteousness you shall judge your neighbor. You shall not go about** *as* **a talebearer among your people; nor shall you take a stand against the life of your neighbor: I** *am* **the L**ORD**.**

a. **You shall do no injustice in judgment**: This was a command to judges and magistrates. Exodus 21-23 gives many principles to the judges of ancient Israel for making their legal decisions. Yet all was based on the fundamental responsibility to **do no injustice in judgment**.

i. Jesus repeated this foundational principle: *Do not judge according to appearance, but judge with righteous judgment.* (John 7:24)

b. **You shall not be partial to the poor, nor honor the person of the mighty**: To give preference to a person just because they are **poor**, or just because they are **mighty**, is to do **injustice in judgment**. It should not be done.

i. This specific command speaks against a popular philosophy in the modern western world. An aspect of what is sometimes known as "critical theory" basically divides everyone into one of two categories: the *oppressors* and their *victims*. Their idea is that all who are **mighty** are oppressors, and all who are **poor** are victims – and that preference should always be given to the **poor** whom they understand to be victims. This goes against what God commands; this is to do **injustice in judgment**.

ii. Certainly it is more common to **honor the person of the mighty** than it is to **be partial to the poor**. But they are both sins; they both are an **injustice**. Things should be judged according to truth and evidence of the truth, not according to class theories. As God says: **In righteousness you shall judge your neighbor**.

c. **You shall not go about as a talebearer among your people**: A **talebearer** is essentially a gossip, someone who cannot mind their own business (1 Thessalonians 4:11). They take great pleasure in talking about the lives of other people and spreading stories.

i. Adam Clarke described the **talebearer**: "The person who travels about dealing in scandal and calumny, getting the secrets of every person and family, and *retailing* them wherever he goes. A more despicable character exists not: such a person is a pest to society, and should be exiled from the habitations of men."

ii. **A talebearer**, "who makes it his business to go up and down from one to another, and divulge evil and false reports concerning others, which, though many times it proceeds only from levity and talkativeness, yet apparently tends to the great injury of our neighbor." (Poole)

d. **Nor shall you take a stand against the life of your neighbor**: God commands us to promote and protect the lives of those around us. We have no excuse to be indifferent to the loss of life.

i. "*Stand forth against the life of your neighbor*: literally, 'stand upon the blood of your neighbor.' The exact meaning of this expression is uncertain…. most commentators take it to mean that, whenever a person is in danger of losing his life as the result of a legal case, a witness should not fail to speak out." (Peter-Contesse)

5. (17-18) The command to love one's neighbor.

'You shall not hate your brother in your heart. You shall surely rebuke your neighbor, and not bear sin because of him. You shall not take vengeance, nor bear any grudge against the children of your people, but you shall love your neighbor as yourself: I *am* the LORD.

a. **You shall not hate your brother in your heart**: Love for one's brother is commanded, not only in action but also in **heart**. Yet if it is not present in the heart, then it should be in one's actions and the heart will follow. We should not stop at treating others well and having a heart of hatred towards them; God desires to change our hearts to love them.

b. **You shall surely rebuke**: Love will **rebuke** another when it is necessary. We all have blind spots where we think everything is fine, but it is evident to others that we need to be corrected.

c. **You shall not take vengeance**: Vengeance belongs to God (Romans 12:19) and there is a sense in which we can hold back God's work of vengeance upon others by seeking it ourselves.

i. Of course, this principle applies to interpersonal relationships, and not to the rightful functions of government in keeping the law. Criminals cannot be let free because vengeance belongs to God. God exercises His vengeance through the rightful use of government authority (Romans 13:1-7). It is appropriate to both *personally* forgive the criminal and testify against them in court.

d. **Nor bear any grudge**: This is very difficult for many people. It is easy to cherish a grudge against another, especially when it is deserved, but too much damage is done to the one holding the grudge.

e. **You shall love your neighbor as yourself**: Some are surprised to see this generous command in what they believe to be the harsh Old Testament, but even the Old Covenant clearly commands us to love others.

i. "The significance of the verse is also highlighted by the fact that Jesus and Paul both cited this verse as a summary of the duties one has to his fellow man (Matthew 22:39-40, Romans 13:9)." (Rooker)

ii. Unfortunately, many ancient Jews had a narrow definition of who their **neighbor** was and only considered their friends and countrymen their neighbors. Jesus commanded us to *love your enemies* (Luke 6:27), and showed our neighbor was the one in need, even if they might be regarded as a traditional enemy (Luke 10:25-37).

iii. The command to love your neighbor **as yourself** is simple yet commonly misunderstood. This doesn't mean that we must love ourselves *before* we can love anyone else; it means that in the same way we take care of ourselves and are concerned about our own interests, we should take care and have concern for the interests of others.

iv. We already love ourselves: *For no one ever hated his own flesh, but nourishes and cherishes it* (Ephesians 5:29). Paul warned that in the last days, *men will be lovers of themselves* (2 Timothy 3:2) – and not in a positive sense! In fact, our misery when things are going badly shows we love ourselves; we rejoice in the misery of those we hate. Our challenge is to show others the same love we show ourselves.

6. (19) Laws of purity in response to pagan practices.

'You shall keep My statutes. You shall not let your livestock breed with another kind. You shall not sow your field with mixed seed. Nor shall a garment of mixed linen and wool come upon you.

a. **You shall not sow your field with mixed seed**: The mixing of these things – different species of livestock, seeds, and fabrics – was usually seen by ancient pagans to be a source of magical power. God wanted Israel to have no association with these pagan customs.

i. "Partly, to teach the Israelites to avoid mixtures with other nations, either in marriage or in religion; which also may be signified by the following prohibitions." (Poole)

b. **Nor shall a garment of mixed linen and wool come upon you**: Since those pagan customs are no longer an issue in our day, we shouldn't worry about mixing wool, linen, or other fabrics. This law is a good example of something that is no longer binding upon Christians today because the pagan custom the law guarded against is no longer practiced.

i. However, in our modern age there are *important distinctions* that have become blurred and things Christians must not participate in. The present-day blurring of distinctions between genders should be resisted by Christians.

7. (20-22) The penalty for unlawful intercourse with a concubine.

'Whoever lies carnally with a woman who *is* betrothed to a man as a concubine, and who has not at all been redeemed nor given her freedom, for this there shall be scourging; *but* they shall not be put to death,

because she was not free. And he shall bring his trespass offering to the LORD, to the door of the tabernacle of meeting, a ram as a trespass offering. The priest shall make atonement for him with the ram of the trespass offering before the LORD for his sin which he has committed. And the sin which he has committed shall be forgiven him.

a. **Whoever lies carnally with a woman who is betrothed to a man as a concubine**: This deals with a woman who was a **concubine** in the sense she was a slave girl, who was eligible to be married.

i. This is the situation described: A slave girl is engaged to marry a free man, and then a different man has sex with her. Normally, the penalty was death; but because the woman was a slave and was presumed to be not free to resist (or guarded by a father), the penalty was not death. Yet, because of the rape, she was not marriable to her fiancée, so he must be reimbursed (the punishment mentioned). Then the moral guilt would be settled by sacrifice, and presumably the man who had sex with her would be obliged to marry her.

b. **And the sin which he has committed shall be forgiven him**: With the appropriate sacrifice, the sin could be **forgiven**.

i. "It is worth noting that only the man was considered blameworthy, not the female slave. Being a slave, the woman may have felt she had little recourse in resisting a male who was a free man and thus more powerful both in the social and economic spheres." (Rooker)

8. (23-25) Regarding the fruit in the land of Canaan.

'When you come into the land, and have planted all kinds of trees for food, then you shall count their fruit as uncircumcised. Three years it shall be as uncircumcised to you. *It* shall not be eaten. But in the fourth year all its fruit shall be holy, a praise to the LORD. And in the fifth year you may eat its fruit, that it may yield to you its increase: I *am* the LORD your God.

a. **When you come into the land**: God reminded Israel of their ultimate goal – the promised land, the land of Canaan – and told them not to eat of the fruit of the trees they plant there for three years. Then the fruit of the fourth year belonged to the LORD, and the fruit of the fifth year could be eaten.

b. **That it may yield to you its increase**: God knew that not harvesting the fruit for this period would be beneficial for both the trees and the surrounding ecology, resulting in ultimately more productive fruit trees.

i. "The reason for this law is not stated, but it does reinforce to the Israelites that the land is the Lord's and that he is giving it to them as a gift." (Rooker)

9. (26-31) Laws to insure separation from pagan practices.

'You shall not eat *anything* with the blood, nor shall you practice divination or soothsaying. You shall not shave around the sides of your head, nor shall you disfigure the edges of your beard. You shall not make any cuttings in your flesh for the dead, nor tattoo any marks on you: I *am* the LORD.

'Do not prostitute your daughter, to cause her to be a harlot, lest the land fall into harlotry, and the land become full of wickedness.

'You shall keep My Sabbaths and reverence My sanctuary: I *am* the LORD.

'Give no regard to mediums and familiar spirits; do not seek after them, to be defiled by them: I *am* the LORD your God.

a. **You shall not eat anything with the blood**: Eating blood was a practice in many pagan cultic ceremonies, as was **divination** and **soothsaying**. Therefore, both were directly forbidden.

i. Harrison on **soothsaying**: "The prognostication of favourable times for specific forms of action." This was predicting lucky days or favorable times as an astrologer or others might do.

ii. "Pagans often employed divination and sorcery to try to determine what events would soon transpire. Divination and sorcery were widespread in the ancient Near East, particularly in Mesopotamia and Egypt." (Rooker)

b. **You shall not shave around the sides of your head, nor shall you disfigure the edges of your beard**: To do this was to imitate pagan customs of that day. Today, Jewish orthodox men are noticeable by their untrimmed beards and the long, curly locks on the sides of their heads.

i. "This the Gentiles did, either for the worship of the devils or idols, to whom young men used to consecrate their hair, being cut off from their heads, as Homer, Plutarch, and many others write; or in funerals or immoderate mournings, as appears from Isaiah 15:2 Jeremiah 48:37." (Poole)

c. **Cuttings in the flesh for the dead, nor tattoo any marks on you**: These were also pagan practices God wanted Israel to be separate from. The trimming of the hair, the beard, cutting, and tattoos were all connected with pagan rites of mourning.

i. **Cuttings in the flesh for the dead**: "The reference here is to the practice of making deep gashes in the skin while mourning the death of a relative. This was done to provide life blood for the spirit of the dead person rather than to express sorrow." (Peter-Contesse)

ii. "The tattoo indicated that one was a slave to a particular deity." (Rooker)

iii. "Ancient writers abound with accounts of marks made on the face, arms, etc., in honour of different idols; and to this the inspired penman alludes." (Clarke)

iv. Part of this message to us today is that what our culture thinks and how they perceive things is important. If some clothing or jewelry or body decoration would associate us with the pagan world, it should not be done. This is a difficult line to draw because the standards of culture are always changing. Some modern examples of changing standards are hair length and earrings for men.

v. In Paul's day, in the city of Corinth, only prostitutes went around without a head covering – so it was right for the Christian women of Corinth to wear veils, though not required to by the letter of the law (1 Corinthians 11:5-6).

d. **Do not prostitute your daughter, to cause her to be a harlot**: To **prostitute your daughter** in this context probably means to give her as a ritual prostitute at a pagan temple. This was of course forbidden, though in the eyes of the pagan culture, it was a religious thing to do.

i. "In some neighboring religions, people thought they were being pious by making their daughters participate in the cult of fertility. But such religious prostitution was not acceptable for the Israelites." (Peter-Contesse)

ii. "This was a very frequent custom, and with examples of it writers of antiquity abound. The Cyprian women, according to Justin, gained that portion which their husbands received with them at marriage by previous public prostitution." (Clarke)

e. **Mediums and familiar spirits**: These were ways the pagans sought to contact the dead or other spirits; this was a doorway into the occult, and strictly forbidden – those who **seek after** these things are **defiled** – "made dirty" by them.

i. The word for **familiar spirits** comes from a root meaning "to know"; "perhaps referring to the occultic information which the practitioner of necromancy purported to have." (Harrison)

ii. "To attempt to know what God has not thought proper to reveal, is a sin against his wisdom, providence, and goodness. In mercy, great mercy, God has hidden the knowledge of futurity from man, and given him *hope* – the *expectation of future good*, in its place." (Clarke)

iii. "In some Near Eastern societies such mediums would dig a small hole in the earth to symbolize a grave, and then put offerings in it to attract the attention of the person whom the medium desired to contact." (Harrison)

iv. "Not only all real dealers with familiar spirits, or necromantic or magical superstitions, are here forbidden, but also all *pretenders* to the knowledge of futurity, fortune-tellers, astrologers, and so forth." (Clarke)

10. (32-37) Further laws of kindness and justice.

'You shall rise before the gray headed and honor the presence of an old man, and fear your God: I *am* the LORD.

'And if a stranger dwells with you in your land, you shall not mistreat him. The stranger who dwells among you shall be to you as one born among you, and you shall love him as yourself; for you were strangers in the land of Egypt: I *am* the LORD your God.

'You shall do no injustice in judgment, in measurement of length, weight, or volume. You shall have honest scales, honest weights, an honest ephah, and an honest hin: I *am* the LORD your God, who brought you out of the land of Egypt.

'Therefore you shall observe all My statutes and all My judgments, and perform them: I *am* the LORD.'"

a. **You shall rise before the gray headed and honor the presence of an old man.... if a stranger dwells with you in your land, you shall not mistreat him**: These are all expositions on the principle of *you shall love your neighbor as yourself* (Leviticus 19:18). If we were the old man, or the stranger, or the consumer, we would want fair and kind treatment.

b. **You shall do no injustice in judgment, in measurement of length, weight, or volume**: God cares that we do business honestly. The surrounding culture may tell us that it doesn't matter how we make our money, but God tells us to use **honest** measurements in all our business. This idea is repeated in passages such as Proverbs 11:1, 16:11, and 20:23.

c. **I am the LORD**: 15 times in this chapter, God declared that He is the LORD – and the one with the right to tell us what to do. This is something that God expected ancient Israel to respect and expects His modern-day followers to also respect.

Leviticus 20 – Penalties for Laws Already Given

"Whereas Leviticus 18 addresses the would-be offender of a God-given decree, Leviticus 20 addresses the Israelite community, which was responsible for seeing that violations of Law receive their just reward." (Mark F. Rooker)

A. The penalty for sins of idolatry.

1. (1-5) Molech worship.

Then the LORD spoke to Moses, saying, "Again, you shall say to the children of Israel: 'Whoever of the children of Israel, or of the strangers who dwell in Israel, who gives *any* of his descendants to Molech, he shall surely be put to death. The people of the land shall stone him with stones. I will set My face against that man, and will cut him off from his people, because he has given *some* of his descendants to Molech, to defile My sanctuary and profane My holy name. And if the people of the land should in any way hide their eyes from the man, when he gives *some* of his descendants to Molech, and they do not kill him, then I will set My face against that man and against his family; and I will cut him off from his people, and all who prostitute themselves with him to commit harlotry with Molech.

a. **Who gives any of his descendants to Molech, he shall surely be put to death**: The worship of the horrific idol Molech was mentioned in Leviticus 18:21. Molech was worshipped by heating a metal statue representing the god until it was red hot, then by placing a living infant on the outstretched hands of the statue, while beating drums drowned out the screams of the child until it burned to death.

i. There are some who believe that in the worship of **Molech** infants were not burned to death; they were only passed through a fire in a ritual in honor to the idol. It is possible that this happened in some cases, but it seems certain that at least one aspect of the offering of infants to Molech was actual human sacrifice.

ii. **Shall surely be put to death**: "This is a very emphatic construction in Hebrew which may be translated literally, 'dying he shall die.'" (Peter-Contesse)

b. **The people of the land shall stone him with stones**: In the case of child sacrifice to Molech, God commanded that the execution be carried out by stoning, performed by the community (**the people of the land**). This was to show that this was, in a powerful way, a sin against the community and would be punished by the community.

c. **If the people of the land should in any way hide their eyes from the man**: To ignore great evil is in itself evil.

d. **I will set My face against that man and against his family**: The penalty for Molech worship was death and if the sentence was not carried out by Israel, God declared He would **set My face against that man and against his family**. God would prosecute if the legal system of Israel failed to.

2. (6-8) The penalty for involvement with the occult.

'And the person who turns to mediums and familiar spirits, to prostitute himself with them, I will set My face against that person and cut him off from his people. Consecrate yourselves therefore, and be holy, for I *am* the LORD your God. And you shall keep My statutes, and perform them: I *am* the LORD who sanctifies you.

a. **I will set My face against that person and cut them off from his people**: In this specific passage, God gave Israel nothing to do regarding the penalty. He simply said that *He* would execute the penalty. Involvement in such occult practices will always separate someone from God.

i. This was the driving force behind the Ephesian church's dramatic rejection of magic and occult materials (Acts 19:17-20). Their hearts were turned to God, so they automatically turned away from **mediums and familiar spirits**.

ii. Adam Clarke on **familiar spirits**: "A spirit or demon, which, by magical rites, is supposed to be bound to appear at the call of his employer."

iii. 1 John 4:2 makes it clear there are spirits who are not from God; such occult, Jesus-denying spirits must be rejected completely.

b. **Consecrate yourselves.... I am the LORD who sanctifies you**: These are two important aspects of our ongoing walk with God. In His normal way of dealing with His people, God will not *force* them to be separated unto Him. He does the work, but He does it in and through our own cooperating efforts and yielded will.

B. The penalties for sins of immorality.

1. (9) The penalty for the cursing of a parent.

'For everyone who curses his father or his mother shall surely be put to death. He has cursed his father or his mother. His blood *shall be* upon him.

a. **Everyone who curses his father or his mother**: Virtually all commentators agree this is not the outburst of a small child – or even an adolescent – against their parent, but the settled heart of an adult child against their parent. Such inter-generational warfare was not to be tolerated and was punishable by death. This was a crime against the family and the community.

i. "Unlike other ancient Near Eastern civilizations, in Israel crimes of a religious nature or against family life received the strongest punishment. This pattern contrasts with the cuneiform laws of the ancient Near East, where violations resulting in economic loss tended to be treated more severely." (Rooker)

ii. This command against cursing one's parents was quoted by Jesus as He spoke to the religious leaders (Mathew 15:4, Mark 7:10). Jesus observed that they used clever, hypocritical tricks to avoid fulfilling the spirit of this command.

b. **Curses his father or his mother**: This wasn't merely saying something bad about or to one's parents; it was likely the calling down of a death-curse on them.

i. "Elaborate curses, many of which appear to have the nature of magical spells, were current in the ancient Near East, and amongst superstitious people often worked with devastating effect since in the eastern mind the curse carried with itself its own power of execution." (Harrison)

c. **Shall surely be put to death**: Even considering that this law applied to an adult child who threatened their parent, this was still a severe law. Yet according to Deuteronomy 21:18-21, and as it was practiced in ancient Israel, it had a built-in protection for the rights of the child.

i. Deuteronomy 21:18-21 states that the parent did not have the right to carry out this punishment, but they had to bring the accused child before the elders and judges of the city. This meant that the parent –

against all customs of that time – did not have the absolute power of life and death over their children.

ii. As a practical matter, the judges of Israel rarely if ever administered the death penalty in such cases, yet the child was held accountable.

iii. **His blood shall be upon him**: "This expression indicates that the person who committed the act is alone responsible for his own death. The blame cannot be shared with anyone else." (Peter-Contesse)

2. (10) The penalty for adultery.

'The man who commits adultery with *another* man's wife, *he* who commits adultery with his neighbor's wife, the adulterer and the adulteress, shall surely be put to death.

a. **The adulterer and the adulteress, shall surely be put to death**: God commanded the death penalty for adultery in ancient Israel. As with previous laws and their penalties, this was because of the exceedingly great social consequences of this sin. **Adultery** murders marriages, and God commanded the ultimate penalty to discourage it.

b. **Shall surely be put to death**: As a practical matter, this death penalty was rarely carried out, as was the case in most of the situations in chapter 20 where capital punishment was commanded. This is because any capital crime required two or three witnesses, and the witnesses had to be so certain of what they saw that they were willing to "cast the first stone" – that is, initiate the execution (Deuteronomy 17:6-7).

i. So, particularly in a case of adultery (or other sexual sins) there would rarely be two eyewitnesses willing to initiate the execution – and so the death penalty would not be carried out.

ii. This also helps us to understand what Jesus did when He confronted the religious leaders who brought to Him the woman taken in adultery (John 8:1-12). By their presence and words, they claimed to have caught the woman in the act of adultery – but they did not *also* bring the guilty man. No one was willing to identify themselves as a witness and start the execution of the woman (to cast the first stone).

c. **Shall surely be put to death**: Even though the death penalty was carried out so rarely in ancient Israel (especially for these crimes), it still did good for Israel to have it. This penalty in the law of Israel clearly communicated an *ideal* that Israel was to reach for. It made people regard their sin much more seriously.

i. In ancient Israel, this was the strongest way to simply say: *Adultery is wrong, cursing your parents is wrong, incest is wrong*. Even if those who commit these sins escape the penalty, God regarded it as wrong, and the community of Israel regarded it as wrong.

ii. "As moral laws the sexual offenses are still applicable during the age of the church, though like the crime of cursing of parents the capital punishments for these offenses were limited to the time when God's people constituted a redeemed theocratic nation (John 8:1-11). Thus the capital punishments for these sexual offenses were not intended to be executed beyond Israel." (Rooker)

3. (11-12) The penalty for sins of incest.

The man who lies with his father's wife has uncovered his father's nakedness; both of them shall surely be put to death. Their blood *shall be* upon them. If a man lies with his daughter-in-law, both of them shall surely be put to death. They have committed perversion. Their blood *shall be* upon them.

a. **The man who lies with his father's wife**: The specific laws against incest were more completely explained in Leviticus 18:6-18.

i. **Perversion**: "It carries the idea of 'confusion' or of something that is out of harmony with the normal order of creation. In view of the context it may be legitimately translated *incest* here." (Peter-Contesse)

b. **Both of them shall surely be put to death**: In Leviticus 18 the penalty for the crime of incest was not explained. Here, God declared that in ancient Israel it should be punished by **death**. Incest is a sin that murders families and was not to be permitted.

4. (13) The penalty for homosexual sin.

If a man lies with a male as he lies with a woman, both of them have committed an abomination. They shall surely be put to death. Their blood *shall be* upon them.

a. **If a man lies with a male as he lies with a woman, both of them have committed an abomination. They shall surely be put to death**: The specific law against homosexuality was previously mentioned in Leviticus 18:22.

b. **They shall surely be put to death**: Though God here commanded the death penalty (under the guidelines of Deuteronomy 17:6-7) for the practice of homosexual sex acts, we should note this was the same punishment as for adultery or incest. Homosexual practices were regarded as these other family-killing sins.

5. (14) The penalty for marrying both a woman and her mother.

If a man marries a woman and her mother, it *is* wickedness. They shall be burned with fire, both he and they, that there may be no wickedness among you.

a. **If a man marries a woman and her mother**: This was spoken against previously in Leviticus 18:17.

b. **They shall be burned with fire**: The death penalty was also commanded for this sin in ancient Israel.

i. Adam Clarke believed the phrase **shall be burned with fire** did not refer to execution. "It is very likely that the crime mentioned in this verse was not punished by *burning alive*, but by some kind of *branding*, by which they were ever after rendered infamous.... *Branding* with a hot iron would certainly accomplish every desirable end both for punishment and prevention."

6. (15-16) The penalty for bestiality.

If a man mates with an animal, he shall surely be put to death, and you shall kill the animal. If a woman approaches any animal and mates with it, you shall kill the woman and the animal. They shall surely be put to death. Their blood *is* upon them.

a. **If a man mates with an animal**: The sin of bestiality was spoken against previously in Leviticus 18:23.

b. **Their blood is upon them**: God commanded the death penalty in ancient Israel for such perverse sexual expressions. Those who committed such acts were responsible for their own death.

i. **And the animal**: "Lest the sight of such a beast should bring that loathsome sin to remembrance." (Trapp)

7. (17-21) Penalties for other sexual sins.

'If a man takes his sister, his father's daughter or his mother's daughter, and sees her nakedness and she sees his nakedness, it *is* a wicked thing. And they shall be cut off in the sight of their people. He has uncovered his sister's nakedness. He shall bear his guilt. If a man lies with a woman during her sickness and uncovers her nakedness, he has exposed her flow, and she has uncovered the flow of her blood. Both of them shall be cut off from their people. 'You shall not uncover the nakedness of your mother's sister nor of your father's sister, for that would uncover his near of kin. They shall bear their guilt. If a man lies with his uncle's wife, he has uncovered his uncle's nakedness. They shall bear their sin; they shall die childless. If a man takes his brother's wife, it *is* an

unclean thing. He has uncovered his brother's nakedness. They shall be childless.

a. **If a man takes his sister, his father's daughter or his mother's daughter**: The specific laws against incest were more completely explained in Leviticus 18:6-18. Here, penalties against these sins are stated.

b. **They shall be cut off in the sight of their people**: The penalty for these sins was not death, as in most of the sexual sins previously mentioned in this chapter. Rather, the penalty for these sins was that the offending parties would be **cut off** – that is, driven out. They were exiled from Israel or excluded from the community within Israel until the sin was repented of, atoned for, or cleansed through a ceremonial cleansing.

c. **They shall bear their sin; they shall die childless**: The last two sins in this section (sexual activity with an aunt or adultery) bear penalties that seem to belong to God alone – **they shall be childless**.

i. "Dying childless was regarded as a tragedy in biblical times…. In a sense dying childless was a form of death because the guilty party's name became extinct." (Rooker)

ii. Peter-Contesse suggested another idea on the word **childless**: "The root word here means 'stripped,' but it has traditionally been understood to mean 'deprived of children.' It is so translated in Genesis 15:2 to describe Abram. But in this context it is more likely that it means 'stripped of posterity,' indicating not only that the guilty parties would not bear any children, but also that any offspring that they already had (separately) would be taken from them."

iii. Matthew Poole offered one more suggestion: "Or shall not be reputed their genuine children, but bastards, and therefore excluded from the congregation of the Lord, Deuteronomy 23:2."

8. (22-26) Summation: Why God called Israel to such holiness.

'You shall therefore keep all My statutes and all My judgments, and perform them, that the land where I am bringing you to dwell may not vomit you out. And you shall not walk in the statutes of the nation which I am casting out before you; for they commit all these things, and therefore I abhor them. But I have said to you, "You shall inherit their land, and I will give it to you to possess, a land flowing with milk and honey." I *am* the LORD your God, who has separated you from the peoples. You shall therefore distinguish between clean animals and unclean, between unclean birds and clean, and you shall not make yourselves abominable by beast or by bird, or by any kind of living thing that creeps on the ground, which I have separated from you as

unclean. And you shall be holy to Me, for I the LORD *am* holy, and have separated you from the peoples, that you should be Mine.

a. **You shall not walk in the statutes of the nation which I am casting out before you**: The Canaanites who presently lived in the Promised Land were deeply involved in these sins, and because of that, God would use Israel to judge them and drive them out.

b. **That the land where I am bringing you to dwell may not vomit you out**: God pleaded with Israel to obey Him, that the same fate would not befall Israel. Unfortunately, eventually it did – and the land did cast out Israel, resulting in the exile both for the northern nation of Israel and the southern nation of Judah.

i. **May not vomit you out**: "The very land referred to in this word of the law of God, stands today at the centre of the earth, a standing witness to the truth. There it has been for ages, fruitless and barren, and yet naturally there is no land more fertile. Men corrupted it, and it vomited them out." (Morgan)

ii. "The principle is of the widest application. Whatever the territory man reigns over, it is affected by his character. If he be polluted and corrupt, then all that is under his sway becomes polluted and corrupt." (Morgan)

c. **I am the LORD your God, who has separated you from the peoples**: One reason for many of these laws (and the strong punishments supporting the laws) was the fact that Israel was God's chosen nation, **separated... from the peoples**. This is an important reason why God wanted them to **distinguish between clean animals and unclean** and other aspects of this holiness code.

i. Israel was chosen – **separated...from the peoples** – because they had and have an important role in God's unfolding plan of the ages. They were chosen to receive the covenants, chosen to receive God's revealed word, and chosen to be the lineage of the Messiah. They were not chosen for eternal salvation, as if being of Israel guaranteed their salvation.

ii. Paul and Barnabas were separated by the Holy Spirit for the special work He had them to do (Acts 13:1-2). There is a sense in which every believer is separated unto God for His purpose and plan. "What an honour is this! To be for God Himself: to do His errands, to fulfil His behests and give Him pleasure! Rejoice greatly when God says, 'Thou art Mine.'" (Meyer)

d. **That you should be Mine**: These laws were not only given so that Israel could possess the land; they were also so God could possess Israel – so they would be **holy to Me, for I the LORD am holy...that you should be Mine**.

i. This demonstrates that God wants more than robotic obedience from His people. God wants relationship with His people, and their loyalty within that relationship (**that you should be Mine**). Both relationship and obedience are important, but God doesn't want our obedience to Him apart from relationship.

9. (27) Penalty for being a medium or practitioner of the occult.

'A man or a woman who is a medium, or who has familiar spirits, shall surely be put to death; they shall stone them with stones. Their blood *shall be* upon them.'"

a. **A man or a woman who is a medium, or who has familiar spirits, shall surely be put to death**: In ancient Israel, if one consulted a medium, they were to be *cut off* – excluded from the community of Israel (Leviticus 19:31, 20:6). But if someone was the actual practitioner of these occult arts, they were to be **put to death** under the law of Israel.

b. **Their blood shall be upon them**: The **medium** or the one who dealt with **familiar spirits** in ancient Israel bore the responsibility for their own death. They were guilty before God and the community.

i. The **medium** or the one who dealt with **familiar spirits** in ancient Israel led others into sin. It is a much more serious thing to lead others into sin than to sin ourselves – and so the penalty is greater, even as Jesus said: *But whoever causes one of these little ones who believe in Me to sin, it would be better for him if a millstone were hung around his neck, and he were drowned in the depth of the sea.* (Matthew 18:6)

Leviticus 21 – Specific Instructions for the Priests

A. Laws for priests in general.

1. (1-4) Priests are forbidden from touching dead bodies.

And the LORD said to Moses, "Speak to the priests, the sons of Aaron, and say to them: 'None shall defile himself for the dead among his people, except for his relatives who are nearest to him: his mother, his father, his son, his daughter, and his brother; also his virgin sister who is near to him, who has had no husband, for her he may defile himself. *Otherwise* he shall not defile himself, *being* a chief man among his people, to profane himself.

a. **Speak to the priests, the sons of Aaron**: The priests came from a particular family of the tribe of Levi – the family of Aaron, the brother of Moses. The priests had a special responsibility to represent God before the people and the people before God. Therefore, they had a special call to holiness and ritualistic purity.

i. The purpose of these laws was to illustrate the purity and separation from sin that was to characterize the priest. A dead body is a picture of sin's result in this world, especially in the way the body quickly rots.

ii. "Any contact with a dead body was thought to make a person ritually unclean. See Numbers 19." (Peter-Contesse)

b. **None shall defile himself for the dead among his people**: This was not only about touching a dead body but even being in the same room as a dead body or walking over a grave or touching a tomb. To come close to **the dead** was to **defile** the priest, making him ceremonially unclean.

i. Therefore, in contrast to most of the pagan religious systems of Israel's neighbors, the priests did not prepare dead bodies for burial. Holiness gives *life*; God did not want His holy priests to be too closely associated with *death*. God did not want His priests and His worship to be dominated by death, but by life. God also did not want His priests anywhere near the death cults of the pagans.

ii. "By touching of the dead body, or abiding in the same house with it, or assisting at his funerals, or eating of the funeral feast." (Poole)

c. **Except for his relatives who are nearest to him**: A priest could participate in the burial rites for an immediate family member, but for no one else. Verse 3 makes no mention of the wife, but many think it is implied. The priest Ezekiel mourned the death of his wife, even though he did so in silence (Ezekiel 24:16-17).

2. (5) Priests must not imitate the mourning practices of the pagans.

'They shall not make any bald *place* on their heads, nor shall they shave the edges of their beards nor make any cuttings in their flesh.

a. **They shall not make any bald place on their heads**: The same law was given to Israel in general in Leviticus 19:27-28. There, the command was connected to pagan rites for burial and mourning. The idea is the same here.

i. "This has nothing to do with natural baldness (as in chapter 13) but involves the intentional shaving of a part of the head to make a bald spot. This was done by some to mourn the dead." (Peter-Contesse)

ii. "This appears to have been a general custom among the heathen. In the book of Baruch, chapter 6:31, the priests of Babylon are represented *sitting in their temples, with their clothes rent, and their heads and beards shaven, and having nothing upon their heads.*" (Clarke)

b. **Nor make any cuttings in their flesh**: The prophets of Baal cut themselves to impress their false god (1 Kings 18:28). The priests who served Yahweh, the God of Israel, were prohibited from doing this in mourning rites or any other context.

3. (6-9) The marriage practices of priests.

They shall be holy to their God and not profane the name of their God, for they offer the offerings of the LORD made by fire, *and* the bread of their God; therefore they shall be holy. They shall not take a wife *who is* a harlot or a defiled woman, nor shall they take a woman divorced from her husband; for *the priest* is holy to his God. Therefore you shall consecrate him, for he offers the bread of your God. He shall be holy to you, for I the LORD, who sanctify you, *am* holy. The daughter of any priest, if she profanes herself by playing the harlot, she profanes her father. She shall be burned with fire.

a. **They shall be holy to their God and not profane the name of their God**: This summarizes the *reason* for the commands to the priests in this chapter. God wanted them to be holy and to display that holiness to the people. To be **profane** is the opposite of being **holy**.

i. **Profane**: "One may also say 'to dishonor,' or 'bring disgrace on,' or 'bring shame to.'" (Peter-Contesse)

b. **For they offer the offerings of the LORD made by fire, and the bread of their God**: This holiness was important for the priests because they performed the sacrifices burnt on the altar (**made by fire**). They also daily brought the new bread into the tabernacle, the bread that pictured Israel's fellowship with God (**the bread of their God**). Only the priests could do these things, and their special privileges meant they also had special responsibilities.

i. The role of the priest in offering the **bread of their God** was so important that the phrase is repeated again in verse 8. This emphasized the connection between holiness and fellowship with God (because the **bread of their God** was a picture of fellowship, as if God and His people shared bread together). The connection between holiness and fellowship is also clearly stated in the New Testament, in passages such as 1 John 1:5-6.

ii. Actually, the term **bread of their God** included the showbread, but also all the sacrificial food portions that belonged to the priests. "The shew-bread; or rather, all the other offerings besides burnt offerings; which are called bread…because bread is commonly put for all food, as below, Leviticus 21:17, 21." (Poole)

c. **They shall not take a wife who is a harlot or a defiled woman**: Priests were only to take virgins for wives. This meant they could not marry a woman who was **a harlot**, a woman who was **defiled** in some way, or a woman who was **divorced**. It is unclear if marriage to a widow was allowed.

i. This was another way to illustrate the commitment and purity that was required of priests. A priest – under the Old or New Covenant – was to only set their affection on that which is pure.

ii. "The mention of a *harlot* is intended to remind the Israelites that cultic prostitution of the Canaanite variety had no place whatever in the life of the covenant community, since such behaviour would profane God's holy name." (Harrison)

iii. It is possible that the word **defiled** in verse 7 is just a further explanation of the word **harlot** – someone who is defiled through ritual prostitution connected with pagan idols. Or, the **defiled** one "may simply be one who has been seduced or violated and therefore lost her virginity." (Peter-Contesse)

iv. **Divorced**: The fact that priests were specifically prohibited from marrying divorced women means that it *was* allowed for the Israelite who was not a priest.

d. **The daughter of any priest**: The holiness expected of a priest also extended to his household, his immediate family. Therefore, the daughter of a priest had a special responsibility to be pure. It would not be tolerated for her to be a **harlot**, and this probably especially has the sense of prostitution connected to pagan rituals and gods.

i. This was prohibited under the general laws of Israel, but special mention is made of it here to emphasize the holiness of the priest and his family. "A priest who would allow a prostitute to reside under his roof would not be qualified to render decisions on behalf of the covenant community." (Rooker)

ii. The idea that a leader among God's people must lead his household well is repeated in the New Testament (1 Timothy 3:4-5, Titus 1:6).

B. Requirements regarding the high priest and the selection of priests.

1. (10-15) The responsibility of the high priest.

'**He who is the high priest among his brethren, on whose head the anointing oil was poured and who is consecrated to wear the garments, shall not uncover his head nor tear his clothes; nor shall he go near any dead body, nor defile himself for his father or his mother; nor shall he go out of the sanctuary, nor profane the sanctuary of his God; for the consecration of the anointing oil of his God *is* upon him: I *am* the LORD. And he shall take a wife in her virginity. A widow or a divorced woman or a defiled woman *or* a harlot—these he shall not marry; but he shall take a virgin of his own people as wife. Nor shall he profane his posterity among his people, for I the LORD sanctify him.'**

a. **He who is the high priest among his brethren**: The **high priest** had a special responsibility to honor and illustrate the holiness of God. He had a special **anointing** with oil and had special **garments** to wear (Exodus 28:1-30). The laws that applied to other priests applied to him, but are stated here for greater emphasis.

i. When we read of the **high priest** and his special **anointing** and **garments**, we consider Jesus. Jesus was a **high priest**, but not after the order of Aaron. Jesus was a **high priest** after the order of Melchizedek (Hebrews 5:1-11).

ii. "This is the first place [in the Bible] where this title is introduced; the title is very emphatic, *haccohen haggadol, that priest, the great one.*" (Clarke)

b. **Shall not uncover his head nor tear his clothes**: The common priests were commanded to not defile themselves for the dead, not coming near a dead body (verse 1). An exception was made for certain close relatives (verses 2-4). However, the **high priest** was prohibited from mourning or coming into contact with **any dead body**, even **his father or his mother**.

i. Israel as a nation was called to holiness (Leviticus 19:2). Yet, the priests were called to greater holiness (21:1-9). In turn, the high priest was called to greater holiness than even the common priests.

ii. "The threefold degree of holiness among the Israelites – the people, the priests, and the high priest – corresponds to the graduation of holiness in the tabernacle – the outer court, the Holy Place, the Most Holy Place." (Rooker)

iii. To **uncover** the **head** or to **tear** the **clothes** were dramatic signs of horror or mourning for the dead. The high priest who sat at the trial of Jesus tore his clothes (Matthew 26:65), in a dramatic display of horror that Jesus claimed to be God.

iv. "It is, of course, implied that if this is not done for the high priest's own parents, it must certainly not be done for any of the other relatives mentioned in verses 2 and 3." (Peter-Contesse)

c. **And he shall take a wife in her virginity**: The common priests were also commanded (verse 7) to not take a wife of a **divorced woman** or a **harlot** or a **defiled woman**. For the **high priest**, the standard was even higher. He could not marry a **widow**; his wife had to be **a virgin of his own people**.

d. **Nor shall he profane his posterity**: The high priest also had to raise his children before the LORD, and not **profane** them by any dedication or service to the pagan gods of the surrounding nations.

2. (16-24) Ministering priests must be free from physical defects.

And the LORD spoke to Moses, saying, "Speak to Aaron, saying: 'No man of your descendants in *succeeding* generations, who has *any* defect, may approach to offer the bread of his God. For any man who has a defect shall not approach: a man blind or lame, who has a marred *face* or any *limb* too long, a man who has a broken foot or broken hand, or is a hunchback or a dwarf, or *a man* who has a defect in his eye, or eczema or scab, or is a eunuch. No man of the descendants of Aaron the priest, who has a defect, shall come near to offer the offerings made by fire to the LORD. He has a defect; he shall not come near to offer the bread of

his God. He may eat the bread of his God, *both* the most holy and the holy; only he shall not go near the veil or approach the altar, because he has a defect, lest he profane My sanctuaries; for I the LORD sanctify them.'" And Moses told *it* to Aaron and his sons, and to all the children of Israel.

a. **No man of your descendants in succeeding generations, who has any defect, may approach to offer the bread of his God**: This shows God's standard for those who would come before Him in service as priests. The command against the priestly service of those with physical defects was meant to point to the even more obvious need to be free from spiritual defects when coming to God.

i. Every animal brought for sacrifice to the LORD had to be without blemish (Leviticus 1:3, 3:1). Here we see that the priest who offered the sacrifice also had to be without blemish (**defect**). Yet, the "perfection" in both the sacrifice and the priest was not true perfection; it was only in comparison to others. The combination of the perfect offering (1 Peter 1:19) and the perfect offerer (Hebrews 7:26) was fulfilled in Jesus Christ.

ii. "The twelve physical abnormalities listed may be representative, although this passage comprises the most comprehensive discussion on the subject of defects in the Bible." (Rooker)

iii. **A dwarf**: "It may be understood here either as an abnormally short person (*dwarf*) or as a person who is abnormally thin and sickly." (Peter-Contesse)

iv. **Only he shall not go near the veil**: "The expression *come near the veil*, then, means to go into the first part of the sanctuary to put bread on the table, to light the lamps, and to burn the incense to God." (Peter-Contesse)

v. "In intertestamental days Antigonus had the ears of the high priest Hyracanus II (ca. 40 B.C.) cut off so that (because of this law) he would forever be disqualified from being high priest again." (Rooker)

b. **He may eat the bread of his God**: This indicates that those in priestly families could be supported by the priesthood. One with a physical defect could not serve as a priest, but they could **eat the bread of his God**, enjoying his relationship with Israel's covenant God.

i. It says of the one with the defect, "**his God**." This means that Yahweh was still the God of that one, and did not exclude them from relationship, only from specific priestly service. "Our involuntary weaknesses shall not debar us from benefit by Christ." (Trapp)

Leviticus 22 – More Specific Instructions for Priests

A. Things that might defile a priest.

1. (1-3) The need for ceremonial purity.

Then the LORD spoke to Moses, saying, "Speak to Aaron and his sons, that they separate themselves from the holy things of the children of Israel, and that they do not profane My holy name *by* what they dedicate to Me: I *am* the LORD. Say to them: 'Whoever of all your descendants throughout your generations, who goes near the holy things which the children of Israel dedicate to the LORD, while he has uncleanness upon him, that person shall be cut off from My presence: I *am* the LORD.

a. **That they separate themselves from the holy things of the children of Israel**: The priests of Israel often dealt with things that had been declared holy. The altar, the table of showbread, the golden lampstand, and the altar of incense were all **holy things**. They did not belong to the priests. They belonged to the LORD, so there was a sense of separation from the **holy things** that the priest had to observe. To fail to do so was to **profane** God's **holy name**.

i. The phrase **that they separate themselves** is difficult to translate. "A wide range of different translations…agree with TEV [Today's English Version] that the meaning of the verb here is '*treat with respect*,' 'be careful with,' or 'be scrupulous about.'" (Peter-Contesse)

ii. "The word translated [**separate themselves from**] (*nzr*) is cognate to the noun from which we get the word 'Nazirite,' thus the connotation 'to put away for separate use' or 'treat as distinct.'" (Rooker)

iii. In the context of this chapter, **holy things** also refers to the sacrificial meat and produce that were made sacred because they were offered to the LORD.

b. **Who goes near the holy things which the children of Israel dedicate to the LORD, while he has uncleanness upon him, that person shall be cut off**: Therefore, the service of the temple had to be performed when the priest was ritually pure. The priest's portion of what was dedicated to the LORD in sacrifice had to be eaten when ritually clean. If a priest (or their family, or anyone else) even went **near the holy things** in ritual **uncleanness**, they were to be **cut off** from God's **presence**.

> i. **Cut off from My presence**: "The meaning of this expression is clarified by another that is frequently used in the Old Testament, 'to stand before someone' (see Deuteronomy 10:8, for example), which means 'to serve someone.' So the words 'to be cut off from before someone' mean to be no longer allowed to serve that person." (Peter-Contesse)

> ii. All the ceremonies and rituals of the Old Covenant pointed towards a perfect fulfillment by Jesus the Messiah under the New Covenant (Colossians 2:16-17; Hebrews 8:4-5; 10:1). Therefore, the idea that a priest could not serve in a ceremonially defiled (unclean) condition was important. Fellowship with God had to be done on the basis of being declared clean and righteous by God.

2. (4-8) Examples of things that might defile a priest.

'Whatever man of the descendants of Aaron, who *is* a leper or has a discharge, shall not eat the holy offerings until he is clean. And whoever touches anything made unclean *by* a corpse, or a man who has had an emission of semen, or whoever touches any creeping thing by which he would be made unclean, or any person by whom he would become unclean, whatever his uncleanness may be—the person who has touched any such thing shall be unclean until evening, and shall not eat the holy *offerings* unless he washes his body with water. And when the sun goes down he shall be clean; and afterward he may eat the holy *offerings*, because it *is* his food. Whatever dies *naturally* or is torn *by beasts* he shall not eat, to defile himself with it: I *am* the LORD.

a. **Whatever man of the descendants of Aaron**: This was another way to refer to the priests and their families. All the priests came from the family of Aaron.

b. **Who is a leper or has a discharge, shall not eat the holy offerings until he is clean**: In verse 3 it is commanded that no one can come near the holy things while ritually impure. Here are some specific things that could make a person ritually impure **until evening**.

- It could be by disease or evidence of illness (**a leper or has a discharge**).
- It could be something connected with death (**unclean by a corpse**).
- It could be a normal function that made one temporarily unclean (**an emission of semen**).
- It could be by contact with something unclean (**whoever touches any creeping thing**).

    i. Violations of these examples would not ruin a man's career as a priest. A violation would make the priest ceremonially unclean until evening. Once ceremonial cleanliness was restored, they could be restored to their priestly service as before.

c. **Shall not eat the holy offerings unless he washes his body with water**: Becoming ritually unclean did not end a man's service as a priest or forever prevent him from eating the portion of the sacrifices that went to the priests. If the priest became unclean, he would perform a ceremonial washing and remain ritually impure **until evening**.

d. **And when the sun goes down he shall be clean**: The Jewish people start their days at sundown, not sunrise or midnight. With this description, God indicates that one can start the new day clean and pure to the LORD. No matter how we might have failed the day before, we can begin each new day pure and close to the LORD. His mercies are new every morning (Lamentations 3:23).

e. **Whatever dies naturally or is torn by beasts he shall not eat**: This was already written as a law for Israel in general (Leviticus 17:15-16). Here the law is restated with emphasis for the priests.

3. (9) Summary of the command for ritual purity among the priests.

'They shall therefore keep My ordinance, lest they bear sin for it and die thereby, if they profane it: I the LORD sanctify them.

a. **Lest they bear sin for it and die thereby**: This more severe punishment for the willful ritual uncleanness of the priests was appropriate considering their greater knowledge of the things of God and their greater responsibility.

    i. **Keep My ordinance**: "This is a somewhat technical word referring to the ceremonial duties required of the priests and Levites." (Peter-Contesse)

b. **I the LORD sanctify them**: God set the priests apart for His own pleasure and purpose. This great blessing carried with it a great responsibility. He who is given more will be accountable for more (Luke 12:47-48).

4. (10-13) Only the priest and his household could eat of the offerings.

'No outsider shall eat the holy *offering;* one who dwells with the priest, or a hired servant, shall not eat the holy thing. But if the priest buys a person with his money, he may eat it; and one who is born in his house may eat his food. If the priest's daughter is married to an outsider, she may not eat of the holy offerings. But if the priest's daughter is a widow or divorced, and has no child, and has returned to her father's house as in her youth, she may eat her father's food; but no outsider shall eat it.

a. **No outsider shall eat the holy offering**: The meat and produce that came from the priest's portion of sacrifices made to the LORD was reserved for the priest's extended household alone. A mere visitor (**one who dwells**) or **hired** person could not **eat the holy thing**. A slave in the priest's household could eat of it (**if the priest buys a person**), as could an adult daughter who came back into the father's home.

i. The command against giving the priest's portion to a visitor in the priest's home went somewhat against the strong custom of hospitality in that culture, which normally insisted on giving guests the very best the home had to offer.

ii. **Outsider**: "The word was also used, however, of those who do not belong to the priesthood (Exodus 29:33; Numbers 3:10, 38; 18:4, 7). It may therefore be rendered 'layman.'" (Rooker)

iii. **If the priest's daughter...has returned to her father's house in her youth**: "The daughter would have the legal status she had before marriage, living under her father's roof and dependent on her father for her livelihood." (Rooker)

iv. "The daughter's change of status indicated that the holiness of a priest extended throughout his household. A New Testament parallel pertains to those who reside in the home of believer priests (1 Corinthians 7:14)." (Rooker)

b. **If the priest buys a person with his money, he may eat it**: A **hired servant** (a temporary worker) was not considered part of the priest's household. But a slave or the child of a slave born in the priest's home was considered part of his family and therefore could eat of the sacred offering.

i. This shows that a slave was considered part of the priest's household or family and entitled to **eat the holy offering**. In ancient Israel, slaves were normally regarded as a part of the family.

ii. The issue of slavery will be dealt with in greater detail in chapter 25. Yet, Adam Clarke's comments are helpful: "We see that it was lawful, under the Mosaic economy, to have *slaves* under certain restrictions;

but these were taken from among the heathen, and instructed in the true religion; hence we find, as in the above case, that they were reckoned as a *part of the priest's own family*, and *treated as such*. They certainly have privileges which did not extend either to *sojourners* or to *hired servants*."

iii. "Therefore their situation was incomparably better than the situation of the slaves under different European governments, of whose souls their pitiless possessors in general take no care, while they themselves venture to profess the Christian religion, and quote the Mosaic law in vindication of their system of slavery. How preposterous is such conduct! And how intolerable!" (Clarke)

5. (14-16) Restitution for the accidental eating of **the holy offering**.

'And if a man eats the holy *offering* unintentionally, then he shall restore a holy *offering* to the priest, and add one-fifth to it. They shall not profane the holy *offerings* of the children of Israel, which they offer to the LORD, or allow them to bear the guilt of trespass when they eat their holy *offerings*; for I the LORD sanctify them.'"

a. **If a man eats the holy offering unintentionally**: It was possible for someone considered an outsider to eat the portion reserved for the priest and his family. When that happened, they were commanded to make the common restitution required in regard to holy things: to **restore**, and then **add one fifth to it** (Leviticus 5:16, 6:5, 27:13-15).

i. **A man**: "It is implied that the man in question is also an 'outsider,' or one who is not permitted to eat food that was designated for the priestly family." (Peter-Contesse)

ii. The need to make restitution reminds us: "All the water in Jordan, and the ceremonies in Leviticus, cannot cleanse a man so long as the polluted thing remains in his hand." (Trapp)

b. **For I the LORD sanctify them**: This shows why the offerings had to be regarded with special care. These offerings were sanctified by the LORD Himself.

B. Examples of unacceptable sacrifices.

1. (17-21) The principle – offerings must be made without blemish or defect.

And the LORD spoke to Moses, saying, "Speak to Aaron and his sons, and to all the children of Israel, and say to them: 'Whatever man of the house of Israel, or of the strangers in Israel, who offers his sacrifice for any of his vows or for any of his freewill offerings, which they offer to the LORD as a burnt offering—*you shall offer* of your own free will a

male without blemish from the cattle, from the sheep, or from the goats. Whatever has a defect, you shall not offer, for it shall not be acceptable on your behalf. And whoever offers a sacrifice of a peace offering to the LORD, to fulfill *his* **vow, or a freewill offering from the cattle or the sheep, it must be perfect to be accepted; there shall be no defect in it.**

a. **A male without blemish from the cattle**: In several places before this, God declared that blemished, defective, or deformed animals were unacceptable for sacrifice to the LORD (Exodus 12:5, 29:1; Leviticus 1:3, 3:1). The priests were responsible to make certain that an animal brought for sacrifice did not have an observable **blemish** or **defect**.

i. God didn't want the cast-offs as sacrifices from the people. He had the right to receive the best they could offer. Deuteronomy 17:1 says, *You shall not sacrifice to the LORD your God a bull or sheep which has any blemish or defect, for that is an abomination to the LORD your God.*

ii. "To bring a defective gift to a superior would not only be ludicrous but insulting." (Rooker)

iii. "In the service of God, according to the law, neither an imperfect *offering* nor an imperfect *offerer* could be admitted." (Clarke)

iv. Unfortunately, this law was abused in the days of Jesus, where priests sometimes disqualified an animal for an insignificant reason. Then, the corrupt priest might require the purchase of an approved sacrificial animal at a dishonest high price (Matthew 21:12-13).

v. **A male without blemish**: "A male for a burnt-offering, which was always of that kind; but the females were accepted in peace-offerings, Leviticus 3:1, and sin-offerings, Leviticus 4:32 5:6." (Poole)

b. **Whatever has a defect, you shall not offer, for it shall not be acceptable on your behalf**: The prophet Malachi spoke out against those who brought God blemished, defective animals: *You offer defiled food on My altar. But say, 'In what way have we defiled You?' By saying, 'The table of the LORD is contemptible.' And when you offer the blind as a sacrifice, Is it not evil? And when you offer the lame and sick, Is it not evil? Offer it then to your governor! Would he be pleased with you? Would he accept you favorably?" Says the LORD of hosts.* (Malachi 1:7-8)

c. **It must be perfect**: This is a strong statement concerning what God regarded as an acceptable sacrifice. It does not say, "you must be mostly good." It does not say, "you must be sincere in trying to be good." It does not say, "you need to be getting better and better." It says, "perfect." Practically speaking, this was on a relative measure, but God put the standard this high for a reason.

i. **It must be perfect**: "The Hebrew word used here really means 'complete, whole, sound, unimpaired.' In this context it is the opposite of 'defective.'" (Peter-Contesse)

ii. This also was a picture of the Messiah to come, and the sacrifice He would offer and be – a **perfect** sacrifice.

- Jesus was perfect in His nature as both God and man.
- Jesus was perfect in His motives.
- Jesus was perfect in His attitude.
- Jesus was perfect in His obedience.
- Jesus was perfect in His sacrifice for sin on our behalf.

2. (22-23) Specific blemishes from a birth defect or disease to be rejected.

Those *that are* blind or broken or maimed, or have an ulcer or eczema or scabs, you shall not offer to the LORD, nor make an offering by fire of them on the altar to the LORD. Either a bull or a lamb that has any limb too long or too short you may offer *as* a freewill offering, but for a vow it shall not be accepted.

a. **Those that are blind or broken or maimed**: These are blemishes that might be caused by a birth defect, such as an animal that came out **maimed** in some manner. Animals diseased with **an ulcer or eczema or scabs** were also not acceptable for sacrifice.

i. "This verse lists six defects that make an animal unacceptable as a sacrifice. However, it is not easy to identify the meaning of each of these with certainty.... but this has little effect on the actual translation." (Peter-Contesse)

ii. The Bible says we should offer ourselves to God as a living sacrifice (Romans 12:1-2). This passage reminds us of what kind of sacrifice we should be.

- Our living sacrifice should not be blind; it should be with eyes wide open to the goodness and glory of God.
- Our living sacrifice should not be broken; it should be whole and complete to God.
- Our living sacrifice should not be deformed or maimed; it should not be with an inactive arm or leg, but instead be ready to serve.
- Our living sacrifice should not be with ulcers or scabs, with diseased and troubled flesh evident for all to see.

iii. "Would God that the best of our lives, the best hours of the morning, the best skill of our hands, the best thoughts of our minds, the very cream of our being, were given to our God!" (Spurgeon)

b. **A bull or a lamb that has any limb too long or too short you may offer as a freewill offering**: Certain defects were acceptable for an offering that was *not* to atone for sin, or that was not to fulfill a **vow**.

i. **A bull**: The "word used here is not restricted in meaning to the male of the species, but may also include females." (Peter-Contesse)

3. (24-25) Blemishes from castration to be rejected.

'You shall not offer to the LORD what is bruised or crushed, or torn or cut; nor shall you make *any offering of them* in your land. Nor from a foreigner's hand shall you offer any of these as the bread of your God, because their corruption *is* in them, *and* defects *are* in them. They shall not be accepted on your behalf.'"

a. **You shall not offer to the LORD that which is bruised or crushed**: If an animal was castrated in some way (**bruised or crushed, or torn or cut**) it was not acceptable for sacrifice. It didn't matter if the castration happened accidentally or on purpose.

i. The idea of castration is not clear in the New King James translation but is in many others. The New American Standard Bible (1995) reads: *Also anything with its testicles bruised or crushed or torn or cut, you shall not offer to the LORD, or sacrifice in your land*. Most modern translations agree with this rendering.

b. **Nor from a foreigner's hand shall you offer any of these**: God would not accept such defective sacrifices from an Israelite or from a **foreigner**. If an Israelite bought a castrated animal from a **foreigner's hand** they could not offer it.

4. (26-30) When animals may be offered as sacrifices.

And the LORD spoke to Moses, saying: "When a bull or a sheep or a goat is born, it shall be seven days with its mother; and from the eighth day and thereafter it shall be accepted as an offering made by fire to the LORD. *Whether it is* a cow or ewe, do not kill both her and her young on the same day. And when you offer a sacrifice of thanksgiving to the LORD, offer *it* of your own free will. On the same day it shall be eaten; you shall leave none of it until morning: I *am* the LORD.

a. **From the eighth day and thereafter it shall be accepted as an offering**: It was also prohibited to offer an animal less than eight days old. This was unnecessary cruelty to a newborn animal, and the practice was probably performed in pagan sacrifices to idols.

b. **Do not kill both her and her young on the same day**: To sacrifice a newborn or young animal and the mother of the animal **on the same day** was to imitate a Canaanite fertility ritual. This was forbidden to Israel.

> i. "These laws may have had a polemical function against pagan practices or they may merely promote sensitivities and high regard for life." (Rooker)

> ii. "The precept was certainly intended to inculcate mercy and tenderness of heart; and so the Jews understood it. When it is necessary to take away the lives of innocent animals for the support of our own, we should do it in such a way as not to blunt our moral feelings; and deplore the necessity, while we feel an express gratitude to God for permission, to do it." (Clarke)

> iii. **Ewe**: "The word used here may actually refer to a sheep or a goat." (Peter-Contesse)

c. **When you offer a sacrifice of thanksgiving to the LORD, offer it of your own free will**: When it came to an offering meant to show **thanksgiving**, God only wanted sincere gratitude. It had to come from the **free will** of the offerer.

d. **On the same day it shall be eaten**: When a **sacrifice of thanksgiving** was made, part of the animal was for the LORD and burned upon the altar. Part of it was for the priest, and given to him. The remaining meat from the animal was for the one who brought the offering, and they celebrated a meal with their household. This remaining meat had to be **eaten** on the **same day** the sacrifice was offered.

5. (31-33) Summary.

"Therefore you shall keep My commandments, and perform them: I *am* the LORD. You shall not profane My holy name, but I will be hallowed among the children of Israel. I *am* the LORD who sanctifies you, who brought you out of the land of Egypt, to be your God: I *am* the LORD."

a. **Therefore you shall keep My commandments, and perform them**: Here God gave Israel – especially the priests – four reasons to keep His **commandments** and to honor His name.

- Because of *who* God is (**I am the LORD**).
- Because of *what* He is (**My holy name**).
- Because of what He *is doing* (**I am the LORD who sanctifies you**).

- Because of what He *has done* (**who brought you out of the land of Egypt**).

    i. "Neither shall ye profane my holy name; either by despising me and my command yourselves, or by giving others occasion to profane them." (Poole)

b. **To be your God; I am the** LORD: Because Yahweh (**the** LORD) was the **God** of Israel, and because of all He had done for them, their obedience to Him was proper. These same reasons remain true for every believer today.

    i. "Jehovah is the God of holiness because He is essentially the God of love." (Morgan)

Leviticus 23 – The Feasts of the LORD

A. The Sabbath.

1. (1-2) Introduction to the feasts of the LORD.

And the LORD spoke to Moses, saying, "Speak to the children of Israel, and say to them: 'The feasts of the LORD, which you shall proclaim *to be* holy convocations, these *are* My feasts.

a. **Speak to the children of Israel**: This chapter commands and describes seven annual feasts that the people of Israel were commanded to observe and celebrate. There are many things for those who are not of the **children of Israel** to learn from the feasts, but they were originally given only to Israel and not to the nations.

b. **The feasts of the LORD**: These feasts, which are rich with symbolic and prophetic significance, were properly called the **feasts of the LORD**. They fundamentally belonged to God, and He gave them to Israel as **holy convocations**, sacred gatherings.

i. The major theme in all these feasts is *gratitude*, for what God has done and what God continues to give. Special "displays of the mercy, kindness, and providential care of God should be particularly remembered. When we recollect that we deserve nothing at his hands, and that the debt of gratitude is all the debt we can pay, in it we should be cheerful, fervent, and frequent. An ungrateful heart is an unfeeling, unloving, unbelieving, and disobedient heart. Reader, pray to God that he may deliver thee from its influence and its curse." (Clarke)

ii. **Holy convocations**: "Days for your assembling together to my worship and service in a special manner." (Poole)

iii. "The Feasts of Purim and Hanukkah are not addressed in this chapter since these feasts celebrate events that occurred after Moses' time." (Rooker)

208

2. (3) The **Sabbath**.

'Six days shall work be done, but the seventh day *is* a Sabbath of solemn rest, a holy convocation. You shall do no work *on it;* it *is* the Sabbath of the LORD in all your dwellings.

a. **The seventh day is a Sabbath of solemn rest**: The Sabbath was not properly a feast like the seven feasts to follow in this chapter. It was, however, **a holy convocation** – a day set apart not only for **solemn rest**, but also for the sacred gathering of the people of God.

i. Centuries after this, when the Jewish people were scattered in exile, they started to meet in synagogues on the morning of the **Sabbath**. The only appointed place for *sacrifice* was the altar at the tabernacle (or temple). Yet it may be that even before the establishment of the synagogue in exile, Israelites gathered on the Sabbath in a **holy convocation**, meeting to pray together and hear from the teaching Levites spread around the land of Israel.

ii. When Christians today gather on an appointed day of the week (often Sunday, as in John 20:19, Acts 20:7, and 1 Corinthians 16:2), they gather as **a holy convocation** – a sacred gathering before the LORD.

iii. "The whole phrase seems to emphasize that the day must be set aside for religious observance, and that the ordinary daily occupations were to be avoided." (Peter-Contesse)

iv. "The words translated *sabbath* and *rest* have the same root in Hebrew, and the word for *seventh* is also very similar." (Peter-Contesse)

b. **Six days work shall be done**: In a shortened form, this repeats the fourth of the Ten Commandments (Exodus 20:8-11). It commands not only a **seventh day** of Sabbath rest but also **six days** of work.

i. "He who idles his time away in the six days is equally culpable in the sight of God as he who works on the seventh." (Adam Clarke, commentary on Exodus)

ii. Like everything in the Bible, we understand the **Sabbath of solemn rest** from the perspective of the whole Bible, not only this single passage. With this understanding, we see that there is a real sense in which Jesus fulfilled the purpose and plan of the Sabbath for us and in us (Hebrews 4:9-11). Jesus is our rest. When we remember His finished work, we remember the Sabbath, and we remember the rest.

iii. Therefore, the whole of Scripture makes it clear that under the New Covenant, no one is under obligation to observe a Sabbath day

(Colossians 2:16-17 and Galatians 4:9-11). Galatians 4:10 tells us that Christians are not bound to observe days and months and seasons and years. The rest we enter into as Christians is something to experience every day, not just one day a week. This is the rest of knowing we don't have to work to save ourselves, but our salvation is accomplished in Jesus Christ (Hebrews 4:9-10).

iv. The Sabbath commanded here, and observed by Israel, was a *shadow of things to come, but the substance is of Christ* (Colossians 2:16-17). In the New Covenant the idea isn't that there is no Sabbath, but that every day is a day of Sabbath rest in the finished work of God. Since the shadow of the Sabbath is fulfilled in Jesus, we are free to keep any particular day – or no day – as a Sabbath after the custom of ancient Israel.

B. The first four feasts, celebrated in the spring.

1. (4-5) The first feast: **Passover**.

'These *are* the feasts of the LORD, holy convocations which you shall proclaim at their appointed times. On the fourteenth *day* of the first month at twilight *is* the LORD's Passover.

a. **These are the feasts of the LORD**: After the reminder of the Sabbath in the previous verses, this begins the list of the seven **feasts of the LORD** Israel was commanded to observe and celebrate, and to do so **at their appointed times**.

b. **On the fourteenth day of the first month**: On the Jewish ceremonial calendar, the **first month** was known as Nisan. **Passover** was held on the fourteenth of Nisan each year. **Twilight** was the end of one day and the beginning of the new day.

c. **The LORD's Passover**: The account of the first Passover is told in Exodus 12. When Israel was a slave people in Egypt, through Moses God sent a series of plagues upon Egypt to convince Pharaoh to set the Hebrews free and allow them to go to Canaan. When the plagues did not convince Pharaoh, God sent one final plague: the death of the firstborn in every household across the land of Egypt. The households of the people of Israel were spared this terrible judgment, *if* they followed God's command to sacrifice a lamb and apply its blood to the top and sides of the doorway to their home. When the angel of judgment came to take the life of the firstborn of the households across the land of Egypt, the angel would *pass over* the homes that were under the blood of the lamb.

i. This command to recognize **the LORD's Passover** came before Israel had celebrated a second Passover (Numbers 9:1-14). The memory of the first Passover was still fresh in their minds, and God wanted it to remain fresh. From that time, God commanded Israel to observe the feast of Passover, to commemorate not only their deliverance from Egypt but also the escape from God's judgment as they applied and trusted in the blood of the lamb.

ii. In the New Testament, Jesus is clearly identified as our Passover lamb (1 Corinthians 5:7). The death of Jesus was at Passover (John 18:28). He is the Lamb of God (John 1:29, 1:36), and it is His blood that makes the judgment of God *pass over* each of us.

2. (6-8) The second feast: **The Feast of Unleavened Bread.**

And on the fifteenth day of the same month *is* the Feast of Unleavened Bread to the LORD; seven days you must eat unleavened bread. On the first day you shall have a holy convocation; you shall do no customary work on it. But you shall offer an offering made by fire to the LORD for seven days. The seventh day *shall be* a holy convocation; you shall do no customary work *on it.*'"

a. **The Feast of Unleavened Bread to the LORD**: The **Feast of Unleavened Bread** was originally established at the first Passover (Exodus 12:14-20). In some ways it was the second part of Passover, lasting from Nisan 15 to Nisan 21. This was one of the three feasts at which God commanded all the men of Israel to gather before Him yearly (Exodus 23:17).

i. "The celebration of Passover and Unleavened Bread marks the commencement of Israel's national existence; thus it corresponds to the celebration of Independence Day in the United States." (Rooker)

b. **Seven days you must eat unleavened bread**: For the first Passover, the unleavened bread following was a practical necessity – they left Egypt in such a hurry there was no time to allow for the bread dough to ferment with leaven (yeast) and rise. After the first Passover, the **Feast of Unleavened Bread** was a *testimony throughout your generations* (Exodus 12:14).

i. Spiritually speaking, this feast was an illustration of the purity God wanted Israel to live out after the blood-deliverance of Passover. Leaven (yeast) is a picture of sin and corruption, because of the way a little leaven influences a whole lump of bread dough, and also because of the way leaven "puffs up" the lump – even as pride and sin makes us "puffed up."

ii. The **Feast of Unleavened Bread** means all this and more to Christians: *Therefore purge out the old leaven, that you may be a new* *lump, since you truly are unleavened. For indeed Christ, our Passover, was sacrificed for us. Therefore let us keep the feast, not with old leaven, nor with the leaven of malice and wickedness, but with the unleavened bread of sincerity and truth.* (1 Corinthians 5:7-8)

iii. For ancient Israel, there may also have been a practical, sanitary reason in removing all the leaven from the bread dough once a year. Leaven was put in bread dough by taking a small piece of leavened bread dough from a previous batch. As this was passed on from one day's lump of bread dough to the next day's, all through a year, it was possible for harmful bacteria to develop in the dough. Once a year, it was good to remove all leaven and start all over with newly fermented leaven as a "starter."

c. **On the first day…. The seventh day**: On both the first and last day of the week-long **Feast of Unleavened Bread**, Israel was to gather in sacred assemblies (**a holy convocation**). They were also to regard those days as additional Sabbath days (**you shall do no customary work on it**).

i. A consistent message through the feasts is *the rest God has for His people is greater than the Sabbath.* That greater rest is fulfilled in the finished work of Jesus Christ.

3. (9-14) The third feast: **firstfruits**.

And the LORD spoke to Moses, saying, "Speak to the children of Israel, and say to them: 'When you come into the land which I give to you, and reap its harvest, then you shall bring a sheaf of the firstfruits of your harvest to the priest. He shall wave the sheaf before the LORD, to be accepted on your behalf; on the day after the Sabbath the priest shall wave it. And you shall offer on that day, when you wave the sheaf, a male lamb of the first year, without blemish, as a burnt offering to the LORD. Its grain offering *shall be* two-tenths *of an ephah* of fine flour mixed with oil, an offering made by fire to the LORD, for a sweet aroma; and its drink offering *shall be* of wine, one-fourth of a hin. You shall eat neither bread nor parched grain nor fresh grain until the same day that you have brought an offering to your God; *it shall be* a statute forever throughout your generations in all your dwellings.

a. **When you come into the land which I give you**: The feast of **firstfruits** was also called *The Feast of Harvest* in Exodus 23:16. It was not to be observed until Israel came into the land of Canaan. That God gave them the command for the feast was a promise that they would in fact come into the land and possess it. God said, **when you come into the land**, and not "*if* you come into the land."

i. This was one of the three feasts at which God commanded all the men of Israel to gather before Him yearly (Exodus 23:17).

b. **Then you shall bring a sheaf of the firstfruits of your harvest to the priest**: This was a celebration of the coming harvest and a giving of thanks for the harvest. The idea was to dedicate the first ripened stalks of grain to God, in anticipation of a greater harvest to come. A **sheaf** is a bundle of grain stalks, tied together.

i. "The firstfruits at Passover would be barley, which ripens in the warmer areas as early as March." (Harris)

ii. **On the day after the Sabbath**: This would be Sunday. "Here the Lord's day was prefigured, saith one, therefore prescribed, and instituted of God." (Trapp)

c. **Wave the sheaf before the LORD**: The sheaf was given to the priest, who waved it in thanks and honor to God. Then there was an offering of a year-old **male lamb** together with a **grain offering** and a **drink offering**.

i. By most accounts, the **grain offering** was made with **two-tenths of an ephah** – about four pounds (2 kilograms) of **fine flour mixed with oil**.

ii. The **drink offering** was required to be **a fourth of a hin** of wine, which most estimate to be about one quart or one liter. "It is quite common in Middle Eastern cultures. In the case of the Jews, it was poured out at the base of the altar of sacrifice or on the ground." (Peter-Contesse)

d. **On the day after the Sabbath the priest shall wave it**: The offering of **firstfruits** was to be celebrated on the day after the Sabbath that ended Passover and began the Feast of Unleavened Bread. This means that the first three feasts on Israel's calendar (Passover, the Feast of Unleavened Bread, and firstfruits) all happened close together, over a period of nine days.

e. **You shall eat neither bread nor parched grain**: The grain from the new harvest was not eaten until thanks had been given, and offerings made, for the new harvest.

i. "*Parched ears* of corn and *green ears, fried*, still constitute a part, and not a disagreeable one, of the food of the Arabs now resident in the Holy Land." (Clarke)

4. (15-21) The fourth feast: The Feast of Weeks (also called Pentecost).

This feast is not called "The Feast of Weeks" in this chapter but is given that title in Exodus 34:22, Numbers 28:26, and Deuteronomy 16:9-10.

'And you shall count for yourselves from the day after the Sabbath, from the day that you brought the sheaf of the wave offering: seven Sabbaths shall be completed. Count fifty days to the day after the seventh Sabbath; then you shall offer a new grain offering to the LORD. You shall bring from your dwellings two wave *loaves* of two-tenths *of an ephah.* They shall be of fine flour; they shall be baked with leaven. *They are* the firstfruits to the LORD. And you shall offer with the bread seven lambs of the first year, without blemish, one young bull, and two rams. They shall be *as* a burnt offering to the LORD, with their grain offering and their drink offerings, an offering made by fire for a sweet aroma to the LORD. Then you shall sacrifice one kid of the goats as a sin offering, and two male lambs of the first year as a sacrifice of a peace offering. The priest shall wave them with the bread of the firstfruits *as* a wave offering before the LORD, with the two lambs. They shall be holy to the LORD for the priest. And you shall proclaim on the same day *that* it is a holy convocation to you. You shall do no customary work *on it. It shall be* a statute forever in all your dwellings throughout your generations.

a. **Count fifty days to the day after the seventh Sabbath; then you shall offer a new grain offering to the LORD:** Fifty days after the feast of firstfruits, at the completion of the wheat harvest, Israel was to celebrate the feast of weeks (also called *The Feast of Ingathering* in Exodus 23:16 and *Pentecost* in Acts 2:1 and 20:16) by bringing a **new grain offering to the LORD** and offering specific sacrifices.

i. The name "Pentecost" means "fiftieth day" in Greek. This name is used of this festival in the New Testament because the feast was celebrated **fifty days** after the Feast of Unleavened Bread.

ii. **Count fifty days**: "According to the Hebrew way of calculating, the beginning and ending days of any given period are counted." (Peter-Contesse)

b. **You shall bring from your dwellings two wave loaves**: In the national ritual celebrating the feast of weeks, two loaves of bread (something like a modern, large pita bread) were waved before the LORD. Remarkably, these two loaves were to **be baked with leaven**.

c. **Offer with the bread seven lambs...one young bull, and two rams**: After the loaves of leavened bread were waved before the LORD, they were offered on the altar along with animal sacrifices **as a burnt offering** along with a **grain offering** and **drink offerings**.

i. This was highly unusual. Generally speaking, Israel was forbidden from offering any kind of leaven or yeast with a blood offering (Exodus 23:18, 34:25). There was a special symbolic message from God in the command to wave two leavened loaves of bread before Him at the feast of weeks, and then to offer those loaves with the burnt offerings.

ii. **Two rams**: "In Numbers 28:11, 19 it is two young bullocks and one ram.... therefore it was left to their liberty to choose which they would offer." (Poole)

d. **It is a holy convocation to you**: When these sacrifices were made at the tabernacle (or temple), it was another day for a holy gathering for Israel, and a day of rest (**you shall do no customary work**). This was one of the three feasts at which God commanded all the men of Israel to gather before Him yearly (Exodus 23:17).

5. (22) A reminder to be generous to the poor and the stranger.

'When you reap the harvest of your land, you shall not wholly reap the corners of your field when you reap, nor shall you gather any gleaning from your harvest. You shall leave them for the poor and for the stranger: I *am* the LORD your God.'"

a. **When you reap the harvest of your land**: God gave this command to Israel while they were still at Mount Sinai and a long way from the **land** God promised to give them. This was a command made in faith, with full assurance that God would fulfill what He had promised.

b. **You shall not wholly reap the corners of your field when you reap**: This repeats the command of Leviticus 19:9-10. This was a law to provide a way for the poor and the stranger to eat by working for themselves and gathering what was left behind from the harvest. This was an appropriate reminder right after the law concerning the harvest feast of Pentecost.

C. The last three feasts, celebrated in the fall.

1. (23-25) The fifth feast: The Feast of Trumpets (Rosh Hashanah).

Then the LORD spoke to Moses, saying, "Speak to the children of Israel, saying: 'In the seventh month, on the first *day* of the month, you shall have a sabbath-*rest,* a memorial of blowing of trumpets, a holy convocation. You shall do no customary work *on it;* and you shall offer an offering made by fire to the LORD.'"

a. **In the seventh month, on the first day of the month**: On the first day of the month of Tishri on the Jewish ceremonial calendar, God called for a special day of **sabbath-rest** and a ceremonial blowing of trumpets. This is the first mention of this feast in the Bible.

i. "The fall festivals of Trumpets, Day of Atonement, and Tabernacles during the seventh month (September/October) were celebrated in conjunction with the harvest of grapes, figs, and olives." (Rooker)

b. **A memorial of blowing of trumpets, a holy convocation**: On this day of special rest, **trumpets** were blown to gather together God's people for a **holy convocation**. There was also **an offering made by fire to the LORD**.

i. "The Trumpets called them to cease from servile work in order to worship." (Morgan)

2. (26-32) The sixth feast: The **Day of Atonement** (Yom Kippur).

And the LORD spoke to Moses, saying: "Also the tenth *day* of this seventh month *shall be* the Day of Atonement. It shall be a holy convocation for you; you shall afflict your souls, and offer an offering made by fire to the LORD. And you shall do no work on that same day, for it *is* the Day of Atonement, to make atonement for you before the LORD your God. For any person who is not afflicted *in soul* on that same day shall be cut off from his people. And any person who does any work on that same day, that person I will destroy from among his people. You shall do no manner of work; *it shall be* a statute forever throughout your generations in all your dwellings. It *shall be* to you a sabbath of *solemn* rest, and you shall afflict your souls; on the ninth *day* of the month at evening, from evening to evening, you shall celebrate your sabbath."

a. **Also the tenth day of this seventh month shall be the Day of Atonement**: On the tenth of Tishri, the people gathered again for a **holy convocation**. But this was not a celebration feast, but a day to **afflict your souls** in humble recognition of sin and the need for atonement.

b. **An offering made by fire to the LORD**: The priestly sacrifices and ceremonies for the **Day of Atonement** were described in Leviticus 16. Here, the emphasis is on what the individual Israelite did on that day.

c. **And you shall afflict your souls**: This command was first made in Leviticus 16:29, and both there and here we have no specific description of what it meant to **afflict your souls**. This has been interpreted as fasting for the entire day, and to make it a day of solemn reflection over one's sins and life the previous year. It was also a day of rest: **you shall do no work on that same day**.

d. **Any person who is not afflicted in soul on that same day shall be cut off from his people**: This strong statement of the command and punishment for disobedience is unique among these instructions for the feasts. In the strongest terms, God wanted His people to use this as a day of humble repentance, and to cease from their own work – while the high priest worked hard to make the sacrifice that would bring atonement to the people of God (Leviticus 16).

i. "*Cut off from his people*: the common expression for excommunication from the people of Israel." (Peter-Contesse)

3. (33-44) The seventh feast: The **Feast of Tabernacles** (Succoth).

Then the LORD spoke to Moses, saying, "Speak to the children of Israel, saying: 'The fifteenth day of this seventh month *shall be* the Feast of Tabernacles *for* seven days to the LORD. On the first day *there shall be* a holy convocation. You shall do no customary work *on it*. For seven days you shall offer an offering made by fire to the LORD. On the eighth day you shall have a holy convocation, and you shall offer an offering made by fire to the LORD. It *is* a sacred assembly, *and* you shall do no customary work *on it*. These *are* the feasts of the LORD which you shall proclaim *to be* holy convocations, to offer an offering made by fire to the LORD, a burnt offering and a grain offering, a sacrifice and drink offerings, everything on its day; besides the Sabbaths of the LORD, besides your gifts, besides all your vows, and besides all your freewill offerings which you give to the LORD. Also on the fifteenth day of the seventh month, when you have gathered in the fruit of the land, you shall keep the feast of the LORD *for* seven days; on the first day *there shall be* a sabbath-*rest*, and on the eighth day a sabbath-*rest*. And you shall take for yourselves on the first day the fruit of beautiful trees, branches of palm trees, the boughs of leafy trees, and willows of the brook; and you shall rejoice before the LORD your God for seven days. You shall keep it as a feast to the LORD for seven days in the year. *It shall be* a statute forever in your generations. You shall celebrate it in the seventh month. You shall dwell in booths for seven days. All who are native Israelites shall dwell in booths, that your generations may know that I made the children of Israel dwell in booths when I brought them out of the land of Egypt: I *am* the LORD your God.'" So Moses declared to the children of Israel the feasts of the LORD.

a. **The fifteenth day of this seventh month shall be the Feast of Tabernacles**: On the fifteenth day of the Jewish month, Tishri (on the Jewish ceremonial calendar), was the **Feast of Tabernacles**. It lasted **for seven days** and one additional day. This is the first mention of this feast in the Bible.

b. **On the first day…. On the eighth day**: The **Feast of Tabernacles** began and ended with **a holy convocation**, each of those days was a day of rest. Sacrifices were held throughout the week, including a **burnt offering**, a **grain offering**, and **drink offerings**.

c. **Besides your gifts, besides all your vows**: The week was also an appropriate time for people to bring their personal **gifts**, **vows**, and **freewill offerings** to the LORD.

> i. Alexander Maclaren noted that the Jewish Talmud says that on each of the seven days of the **Feast of Tabernacles** (and according to one Rabbi, also on the **eighth day**), a priest went down to the Pool of Siloam and drew water in a golden pitcher, which he brought back to the altar, pouring the water into a silver basin as the worshippers sang psalms from the "Great Hallel" collection of Psalms 113-118. This celebrated the water God miraculously provided for Israel in the wilderness. Then, *On the last day, that great day of the feast, Jesus stood and cried out, saying, "If anyone thirsts, let him come to Me and drink. He who believes in Me, as the Scripture has said, out of his heart will flow rivers of living water."* (John 7:37-38)

d. **You shall rejoice before the LORD your God for seven days**: This was the only feast of the seven in which rejoicing was commanded. This was to be a happy celebration of God's goodness and provision.

> i. "The feast of tabernacles was the consecration of joy. Other religions have had their festivals, in which wild tumult and foul orgies have debased the worshippers to the level of their gods. How different the pure gladness of this feast 'before the Lord'!" (Maclaren)

> ii. Remarkably, Zechariah 14:16-19 tells us that the Feast of Tabernacles will be celebrated by all the nations under the universal kingdom of the Messiah.

> iii. "The mandatory reading of the Law every seven years to the congregation was a distinctive of the Feast of Tabernacles (Deuteronomy 31:10-13)." (Rooker)

e. **You shall dwell in booths for seven days**: During the **Feast of Tabernacles**, Israelite families were to camp out in shelters made with the **branches of palm trees, the boughs of leafy trees**. During the years of the Exodus, they lived this way all the time because they had to. When they eventually came into the promised land, they lived this way for a week to remind them of their hardships in those years, and God's good provision in the wilderness.

> i. "Although not specifically stated in the text, we should assume that the branches from these trees would be used for the making of wooden booths." (Rooker)

ii. "Booths were erected in their cities or towns, either in their streets or gardens, or the tops of their houses, Nehemiah 8:16, which were made flat, and therefore were proper and fit for that use." (Poole)

f. **On the first day there shall be a sabbath-rest, and on the eighth day a sabbath rest**: The Feast of Tabernacles began and ended in rest. It was a time of celebration, rest, and refreshment.

i. God intended great *social* good in appointing the Sabbath and these yearly feasts. In almost all other ancient cultures, there was no weekly day of rest and there were no holidays. For Israel, God *commanded* a weekly day of rest, special holidays, vacation days. All of these were centered on Him.

D. The prophetic significance of the feasts of Leviticus 23.

1. On Israel's calendar, the four spring feasts were grouped together, and the three fall feasts were also grouped. There was a separation of time between these two groups of feasts.

2. As a group, the first four feasts point to the work of Jesus in His first coming – His earthly ministry as recorded in the New Testament accounts.

a. The feast of *Passover* clearly points to Jesus as our Passover (1 Corinthians 5:7). He was the Lamb of God who was sacrificed, and whose blood was received and applied, so the wrath of God would pass us over.

b. The feast of *Unleavened Bread* points to the time of Jesus' burial, after His perfect, sinless sacrifice on the cross. In this time Jesus was received by God the Father as holy and complete (the *Holy One* who would not *see corruption*, Acts 2:27), perfectly accomplishing our salvation.

c. The feast of *Firstfruits* points to the resurrection of Jesus, who was the first human to receive resurrection, never to die again. He is the *firstborn from the dead* (Colossians 1:18) and *has become the firstfruits of those who have fallen asleep.... Christ the firstfruits, afterward those who are Christ's at His coming.* (1 Corinthians 15:20, 23)

d. The feast of *Pentecost* points to the birth of the Church and the harvest of souls that came from it (Acts 2). Significantly, in the ritual at the feast of Pentecost, two *leavened* loaves of bread were waved as a holy offering to God, speaking of the bringing of "leavened" Gentiles into the church.

3. Between the first set of four feasts and the second set of three feasts, there is a significant time gap – almost four months. This was a time of *harvest* in Israel, even as our current age is a time of harvest for the church, *until the fullness of the Gentiles has come in.* (Romans 11:25)

4. The second group of the last three feasts points to events associated with the second coming of Jesus.

a. The feast of *Trumpets* points to the ultimate holy convocation of God's people at the sound of a trumpet – the rapture of the Church (1 Thessalonians 4:16-17). It also points to God's gathering of Israel for His special purpose in the last days.

b. The *Day of Atonement* not only points to the ultimate, perfect atonement Jesus offered on our behalf, but also of the affliction – and salvation – Israel will see during the Great Tribulation.

i. It will truly be a time when the soul of Israel is afflicted, but for their ultimate salvation. Jeremiah 30:7 says regarding that period: *Alas! For that day is great, so that none is like it, and it is the time of Jacob's trouble, but he shall be saved out of it.*

c. The feast of *Tabernacles* points to the millennial rest and comfort of God for Israel and all of God's people. From its beginning to its end, it is all about peace and rest.

i. The Feast of Tabernacles is specifically said to be celebrated during the millennium (Zechariah 14:16-19).

5. There is at least some evidence that each of the four feasts pointing to the first coming of Jesus saw their prophetic fulfillment on the exact day of the feast.

a. Jesus was actually crucified on the Passover (John 19:14). It is probably best to regard the meal He shared with His disciples (Matthew 26:17-19) as the Passover meal, but eaten the day before the actual Passover.

b. The body of Jesus was buried, and His holy and pure sacrifice acknowledged by God the Father during the Feast of Unleavened Bread.

c. Jesus rose from the dead on the celebration of firstfruits, the day after Passover's Sabbath.

d. The church was founded on the actual day of Pentecost (Acts 2:1), and a great harvest of souls for God's kingdom followed, including a harvest of Gentiles.

6. For this reason, some suggest that it would be consistent for God to gather His people to Himself on the day of the feast of trumpets, the Jewish holiday of *Rosh Hashanah*. This event is described in 1 Thessalonians 4:16-17 and is commonly called the rapture of the church.

Leviticus 24 – The Law Put into Action

A. Care for the tabernacle.

1. (1-4) Care of the tabernacle lamps.

Then the LORD spoke to Moses, saying: "Command the children of Israel that they bring to you pure oil of pressed olives for the light, to make the lamps burn continually. Outside the veil of the Testimony, in the tabernacle of meeting, Aaron shall be in charge of it from evening until morning before the LORD continually; *it shall be* **a statute forever in your generations. He shall be in charge of the lamps on the pure** *gold* **lampstand before the LORD continually.**

> a. **Pure oil of pressed olives for the light, to make the lamps burn continually**: The lamps in the tabernacle – standing on the solid gold lampstand (Exodus 25:31-40) – were the only source of light for the tabernacle. These lamps had to be constantly cared for, supplied with pure olive oil and their wicks trimmed. This care made the **lamps burn continually**.

> > i. **Outside the veil of the Testimony**: "The 'testimony' was a technical term for the Ten Commandments placed in the Ark (Exodus 25:16; 40:20; Deuteronomy 10:2; 1 Kings 8:9; Hebrews 9:4)." (Rooker)

> > ii. **Shall be in charge of it**: "The verb has been understood in slightly different ways: Today's English Version *'keep them burning'*; New International Version 'tend the lamps'; New Jewish Version 'set them up'; New English Bible 'keep in trim.' But the basic idea is doing all that is necessary to assure that the lamps are burning at the proper time." (Peter-Contesse)

> > iii. The **pure gold lampstand** became one of the enduring images representing Israel and the Jewish people. The **lampstand** in the temple in the time of Jesus was captured by Roman soldiers under the

command of Titus when Jerusalem was destroyed in A.D. 70. An image of that **lampstand** was carved in the arch in the city of Rome made to celebrate that victory. The image of the **lampstand** is also found in other ancient carvings and coins.

b. **From evening until morning before the LORD continually**: It was important that the light from the oil lamps shined **continually**. God did not want His tabernacle to be left in darkness.

i. The continual light of the tabernacle pointed to the coming Messiah. Jesus never stopped being the *light of the world* (John 8:12).

ii. There is also a sense in which the continually shining light points to the people of God. In a sense, we also are the light of the world (Matthew 5:14). "As the candle in the hand of the housewife, who sweeps her house diligently; as a lamp in the hand of the virgin expecting the bridegroom; or as a lighthouse on a rocky coast." (Meyer)

2. (5-9) Care of the tabernacle bread.

"And you shall take fine flour and bake twelve cakes with it. Two-tenths *of an ephah* shall be in each cake. You shall set them in two rows, six in a row, on the pure *gold* table before the LORD. And you shall put pure frankincense on *each* row, that it may be on the bread for a memorial, an offering made by fire to the LORD. Every Sabbath he shall set it in order before the LORD continually, *being taken* from the children of Israel by an everlasting covenant. And it shall be for Aaron and his sons, and they shall eat it in a holy place; for it *is* most holy to him from the offerings of the LORD made by fire, by a perpetual statute."

a. **You shall take fine flour and bake twelve cakes with it**: The **twelve cakes** of bread were arranged in an orderly way on the table of showbread (Exodus 25:23-30), which stood opposite the golden lampstand in the tabernacle (Exodus 26:35). They were equally divided into **two rows**, representing the twelve tribes of Israel in the presence of the LORD, in His tabernacle.

i. "*Two rows*: the term used here is a general one for 'arrangements' and may be understood as *rows* (as in most versions), or some other kind of arrangement such as 'piles.'" (Peter-Contesse)

ii. This bread is called *showbread* in Exodus 25:30, which literally means "bread of the face." This was bread associated with the presence of God. Eating bread together was a mark of friendship and fellowship. The **twelve cakes** of bread spoke of the relationship and fellowship the people of God had with their God.

b. **Set in order before the LORD continually**: The two aspects of this were a symbol of God's desired relationship with His people. God wants a proper, ordered relationship with His people (**set in order**). God also wants a continual, unbroken relationship with His people (**continually**).

> i. Ultimately, this was made possible by the person and work of Jesus the Messiah, who proclaimed Himself as the Bread of Life (John 6:35, 6:48).

> ii. God's people today are to have some of the nature of these **twelve cakes**. "The two rows of six cakes foreshadow the unity and order of the Church; the fine flour, its holy, equitable character; the pure frankincense, the fragrance of Christian love." (Meyer)

c. **They shall eat it in a holy place**: The bread was not only for display in a ritual. God wanted the people of God to actually receive, enjoy, and be nourished by the bread – which symbolized their relationship and fellowship with Him.

> i. Significantly, God wanted the fellowship fresh. The bread was to be replaced **every Sabbath**. He didn't want a stale communion with His people, but a continually fresh relationship.

B. The case of the Egyptian blasphemer.

1. (10-12) The crime of the Egyptian blasphemer.

Now the son of an Israelite woman, whose father *was* an Egyptian, went out among the children of Israel; and this Israelite *woman's* son and a man of Israel fought each other in the camp. And the Israelite woman's son blasphemed the name *of the LORD* and cursed; and so they brought him to Moses. (His mother's name *was* Shelomith the daughter of Dibri, of the tribe of Dan.) Then they put him in custody, that the mind of the LORD might be shown to them.

a. **Now the son of an Israelite woman, whose father was an Egyptian, went out among the children of Israel**: This man, half Egyptian and half Hebrew, was part of the mixed multitude (Exodus 12:38) that went with Israel out of Egypt.

> i. "Here also we have a fragment of history.... It may be that it was inserted here because of its occurrence during the period of the promulgation of the laws." (Morgan)

> ii. Adam Clarke wrote of Jewish legends regarding this man. "The rabbins, it is true, supply in their way this deficiency; they say he was the son of the Egyptian whom Moses slew, and that attempting to pitch his tent among those of the *tribe of Dan*, to which he belonged by

his mother's side, ver. 11, he was prevented by a person of that tribe as having no right to a station among them who were true Israelites both by father and mother. In consequence of this they say he blasphemed the name of the Lord."

b. **The Israelite woman's son blasphemed the name of the Lord and cursed**: The man committed the crime of *blasphemy*, which is to attack someone – especially God – with your words. It is somewhat like the modern idea of verbal abuse, but especially directed against God. The command against blaspheming God was given in Exodus 22:28.

i. "In the Near East the name of a person was bound up intimately with his character, so that in the case of God, blasphemy was in effect an act of repudiation." (Harrison)

ii. It seems that it was common for Egyptians to curse their many gods. The root of this man's sin was that he considered the God of Israel to be the same as the petty Egyptian gods.

c. **Then they put him in custody, that the mind of the Lord might be shown to them**: The people of Israel were wise in leaving this to the proper workings of justice and the **mind of the Lord**. This was not a mob working outside the process of law.

i. The issue was unclear because the man was a foreigner. The laws of Israel were not necessarily applied to foreigners as well as Israelites. The question was, "Does the law against blasphemy apply the same way against a foreigner in our midst?" The Law of Moses protected the foreigner (Exodus 23:9), but they needed guidance to understand to what extent the laws of Israel applied to foreigners among them.

2. (13-14) The penalty upon the Egyptian blasphemer.

And the Lord spoke to Moses, saying, "Take outside the camp him who has cursed; then let all who heard *him* lay their hands on his head, and let all the congregation stone him.

a. **Then let all who heard him lay their hands on his head**: This was done in accord with a principle later specifically stated in Deuteronomy 17:6-7. Two or three of the witnesses publicly laid **hands** on the accused, as a sure testimony to his guilt. This also meant that the guilty man knew his accusers and could not be condemned by secret accusers.

i. The accusation had to be established as true. Deuteronomy 19:16-19 says that a false witness was to suffer the same punishment that would be given to the one against whom he made the accusation.

ii. "By **laying their hands upon his head** they gave public testimony that they heard this person speak such words, and did in their own and in all the people's names desire and demand justice to be executed upon him." (Poole)

b. **And let all the congregation stone him**: God commanded execution by stoning for several reasons. First, stones were plentiful. More importantly, it was so that the community could participate in the execution. This was both a strong warning and a way of saying, "This man has not only sinned against God, he has also sinned against the community."

i. Therefore, the law applied to a foreigner. "It was a principle of justice and of mercy. Its first emphasis is upon the fact that those who enter the Kingdom of God, and enjoy its privileges, must be governed by its laws…. To enter that Kingdom is to renounce all other lordships, and to accept its laws." (Morgan)

3. (15-16) The principle for Israel to learn from the death of the blasphemer.

"Then you shall speak to the children of Israel, saying: 'Whoever curses his God shall bear his sin. And whoever blasphemes the name of the LORD shall surely be put to death. All the congregation shall certainly stone him, the stranger as well as him who is born in the land. When he blasphemes the name *of the LORD*, he shall be put to death.

a. **Whoever curses his God shall bear his sin**: This was a way to say, "the person who publicly curses God bears responsibility for the judgment against them."

b. **Whoever blasphemes the name of the LORD shall surely be put to death**: As the example of the Egyptian blasphemer proved, this was a severe judgment for what was considered a serious crime.

i. Adam Clarke on blasphemy in Matthew 9:3: "Whenever it is used in reference to GOD, it simply signifies, *to speak impiously* of his *nature*, or attributes, or works. *Injurious speaking* is its proper translation when referred to *man*."

ii. "If God required a foreigner to be executed for this offense, he would certainly not tolerate its violation among the Israelites, who were his people and hence were identified with his name." (Rooker)

iii. Taking great care to not blaspheme the name of the LORD, some Jewish people created traditions that took great care to avoid saying or writing the name of God. The thought was that if one never said (or wrote) the name of God, then one could never blaspheme God's name.

iv. By some accounts, only the Jewish high priest was allowed to pronounce the holy name of God (*Yahweh*). He was allowed to say it only once a year – on the Day of Atonement. Some say that the proper pronunciation of the name would be passed on from the high priest to his successor, with the former's last breath. This is why there was confusion for many years about the exact pronunciation of the four letters that state the name of the covenant God of Israel (YHWH). The letters have been pronounced differently over the years. For some time, the letters YHWH were mistakenly pronounced as "Jehovah" instead of "Yahweh" (*Yah-veh*). Adam Clarke wrote in his day (1830): "The Jews never pronounce this name, and so long has it been disused among them that the true pronunciation is now totally lost."

v. Many religiously observant Jewish people also would not write the name of God, because if that paper were destroyed, it might be considered blasphemy or taking the name of the LORD in vain. So, they would write *Adonai* ("Lord") instead of *Yahweh*. Instead of "God," they would write "G-d." They would refer to God with names like "the Name" instead of saying "God."

4. (17-18) The punishment for murder and unlawful killing of animals.

'Whoever kills any man shall surely be put to death. Whoever kills an animal shall make it good, animal for animal.

a. **Whoever kills any man shall surely be put to death**: In the context of giving the penalty for the Egyptian blasphemer, God stated a fundamental principle of His justice – crimes must be punished, but in proportion appropriate to the crime.

b. **Whoever kills an animal shall make it good**: When the animal of anther was killed without permission, restitution was required. This showed the value and dignity of animal life. Yet, the person who wrongly killed an animal was not a murderer and did not have to die for their wrong – only **make it good** with money or another animal. This showed the difference between human life and animal life.

5. (19-22) The right measure of judgment.

'If a man causes disfigurement of his neighbor, as he has done, so shall it be done to him; fracture for fracture, eye for eye, tooth for tooth; as he has caused disfigurement of a man, so shall it be done to him. And whoever kills an animal shall restore it; but whoever kills a man shall be put to death. You shall have the same law for the stranger and for one from your own country; for I *am* the LORD your God.'"

a. **As he has done, so shall it be done to him**: This is the fundamental principle of punishment according to measure. This principle was **the same law for the stranger and for the one from your own country**. God did not give the Israelite an unfair advantage over a foreigner in terms of the law.

b. **Fracture for fracture, eye for eye, tooth for tooth**: Many people have taken **eye for eye, tooth for tooth** as a command; instead, God intended it as a *limit* – so no man or judge would set judgment merely as they pleased.

> i. This law did not mean that the **eye** of an offender would be literally gouged out of his head if he took the **eye** of another man. The Law of Moses had a system of financial restitution in such cases. "For example, if a slave loses an eye, an eye of the one responsible is not to be plucked out but rather the slave is to be given his freedom as compensation for the eye (Exodus 21:26)." (Rooker)

> ii. Human nature is often either much too lenient or far too severe. Here, God both required that crime be punished, and He set appropriate limit to the punishment.

> iii. Jesus rightly condemned the taking of this command regarding law and order in the community and applying it to personal relationships, where love, forgiveness, and going the extra mile are to be the rule, and not equal retribution (Matthew 5:38-42).

6. (23) The execution of the Egyptian blasphemer.

Then Moses spoke to the children of Israel; and they took outside the camp him who had cursed, and stoned him with stones. So the children of Israel did as the LORD commanded Moses.

a. **Then Moses spoke to the children of Israel**: We are not told how Moses felt about this. His job was to be the messenger of God's commands, apart from his own personal feelings and opinions.

b. **They took outside the camp him who had cursed, and stoned him with stones**: This verse is important. It demonstrates to us that the law of God was not given to Israel for interesting facts or mere guidelines; God expected them to obey it. Here, they obeyed even when it was difficult.

> i. "The Jews themselves tell us that their manner of stoning was this: they brought the condemned person without the camp, because his crime had rendered him *unclean*, and whatever was unclean must be put *without the camp*. When they came within four cubits of the place of execution, they stripped the criminal, if a man, leaving him nothing but a cloth about the waist. The place on which he was to be executed was elevated, and the witnesses went up with him to it, and laid their

hands upon him, for the purposes mentioned ver. 14. Then one of the witnesses struck him with a stone upon the loins; if he was not killed with that blow, then the witnesses took up a great stone, as much as two men could lift, and threw it upon his breast. This was the *coup de grace*, and finished the tragedy." (Clarke)

Leviticus 25 – Special Sabbaths and Jubilees

A. The Sabbath Year.

1. (1-2) The land and its Sabbath.

And the LORD spoke to Moses on Mount Sinai, saying, "Speak to the children of Israel, and say to them: 'When you come into the land which I give you, then the land shall keep a sabbath to the LORD.

a. **When you come into the land which I give you**: These laws were given in faith. Israel was still in the wilderness, and not yet in the Promised Land. Additionally, as far as Moses and the people knew, they were only a matter of months from entering in.

   i. God spoke **to Moses on Mount Sinai**. This reminds us that Israel was still camped at **Mount Sinai**, and that Moses received these laws from God as he met with the LORD on the mountain. Israel remained at Mount Sinai from the time of Exodus 19, all through Leviticus, and up to Numbers 10.

b. **The land shall keep a sabbath to the LORD**: We are familiar with the idea of a sabbath of days, where one day out of seven is specially dedicated to God and His rest. This described a Sabbath of years for **the land**, where the land received a rest one year out of seven. This was mentioned before in Exodus 23:11.

c. **Then the land shall keep a sabbath to the LORD**: Obviously, this called Israel to truly trust God. They had to trust God that He would provide enough in the harvest of six years to see them through the seventh year of rest.

   i. In the Feast of Tabernacles on the Sabbath year, the law was to be read to all the people by the priests (Deuteronomy 31:9-13). Each Sabbath year was also to be a time for an extensive Bible seminar for the whole nation.

2. (3-7) How to give the land its Sabbath.

Six years you shall sow your field, and six years you shall prune your vineyard, and gather its fruit; but in the seventh year there shall be a sabbath of solemn rest for the land, a sabbath to the LORD. You shall neither sow your field nor prune your vineyard. What grows of its own accord of your harvest you shall not reap, nor gather the grapes of your untended vine, *for* it is a year of rest for the land. And the sabbath *produce* of the land shall be food for you: for you, your male and female servants, your hired man, and the stranger who dwells with you, for your livestock and the beasts that *are* in your land—all its produce shall be for food.

a. **In the seventh year there shall be a sabbath of solemn rest for the land**: This applied to both grain crops and fruit-bearing plants. Israel was to do this as a radical demonstration that the land belonged to God, not to them.

i. "During the sabbatical year there must be no systematic harvesting of self-seeding crops, or such fruits as figs and grapes. Anything of this nature that the land produces without human aid is the property of all, and people are to obtain food wherever they can find it, just as the Israelites did in their wilderness wanderings." (Harrison)

ii. "In the intertestamental period Alexander the Great and Julius Caesar remitted Israel's taxes during sabbatical years." (Rooker)

b. **And the sabbath produce of the land shall be food for you**: Observing the sabbath year was also a powerful testimony of dependence on God. Israel declared their belief that God would meet their needs. This was truly living by faith, and God wanted His people to live trusting Him.

i. It was wise management of the land. Giving the land some rest every seven years helped restore vital nutrients to the soil that are depleted by constant use.

ii. Matthew Poole gave an interesting additional reason for the sabbath year. He suggested that one of the reasons for the Sabbath year was to put everyone in Israel in the same place as the poor of the land, who had to simply trust that God would provide in unlikely circumstances. This would give them compassion for the poor, who had to live that way *every* year.

iii. Israel's failure to keep this command determined the length of their captivity. Leviticus 26:34 said that if Israel was not obedient, God would make sure the land gets its sabbaths by removing the people to the land of an enemy. This was fulfilled in the Babylonian captivity of Israel (2 Chronicles 36:20-21).

iv. Today, some observant Jewish people find a way around the sabbath year law. On the seventh year, they "sell" their land to a Gentile, work it, and then "buy" it back from the Gentile when the Sabbath year is over. The Gentile makes a little money, and the Jewish person could say, "It wasn't my land on the Sabbath year, so it was all right if I worked it." Others observe this by only cultivating six-sevenths of their land at any one time, and over seven years the entire land has a year of rest.

B. The Year of Jubilee.

1. (8-12) The year of Jubilee to be observed every fiftieth year.

'**And you shall count seven sabbaths of years for yourself, seven times seven years; and the time of the seven sabbaths of years shall be to you forty-nine years. Then you shall cause the trumpet of the Jubilee to sound on the tenth** *day* **of the seventh month; on the Day of Atonement you shall make the trumpet to sound throughout all your land. And you shall consecrate the fiftieth year, and proclaim liberty throughout** *all* **the land to all its inhabitants. It shall be a Jubilee for you; and each of you shall return to his possession, and each of you shall return to his family. That fiftieth year shall be a Jubilee to you; in it you shall neither sow nor reap what grows of its own accord, nor gather** *the grapes* **of your untended vine. For it** *is* **the Jubilee; it shall be holy to you; you shall eat its produce from the field.**

a. **You shall count seven sabbaths of years for yourself, seven times seven years**: The year of **Jubilee** was something like a double sabbath year, in the sense that crops were not planted, and the land was given a rest for two years.

i. "The traditional rendering of the name for this special year is 'Jubilee,' which is ultimately a transliteration of a Hebrew word meaning 'ram's horn.'" (Peter-Contesse)

ii. "Two fallow years in succession would have been a severe test of faith. The Israelites were called upon to trust totally in God and acknowledge in a profound way that he was the provider of the basic necessities of life." (Rooker)

iii. Some take the prophecy of Isaiah 61:1-3 to speak of a Jubilee year. Since Jesus read this passage in a Nazareth synagogue at the beginning of His ministry, some have speculated that Jesus' ministry began in a year of Jubilee – though it was mostly not observed among the Jewish people at that time.

iv. **On the tenth day of the seventh month**: "It is worthy of remark that the jubilee was not proclaimed till the tenth day of the seventh month, *on the very day* when the great *annual atonement* was made for the sins of the people; and does not this prove that the great *liberty* or *redemption* from thraldom, published under the Gospel, could not take place till the great *Atonement*, the sacrifice of the Lord Jesus, had been offered up?" (Clarke)

b. **Proclaim liberty throughout all the land to all its inhabitants**: The wonderful liberty of a Jubilee was joyfully announced through all the land, announcing that all slaves were free. We don't have much of a record of this being observed in the Old Testament; there may be examples in Nehemiah 8 and 10.

i. "Slave laws in Exodus (Exodus 21:2–6) and Deuteronomy (Deuteronomy 15:12–18) provide the option of a slave agreeing to remain with his master after six years of enslavement; in the Jubilee even that slave is set free." (Rooker)

ii. "In the year of jubilee, moreover, the slave was to be liberated, thus reminding men that they could have no absolute and final property in any human being." (Morgan)

iii. The founding fathers of the United States were aware of the principle of the year of Jubilee and the freedom associated with it. On the Liberty Bell they inscribed the phrase from verse 10: **proclaim liberty throughout all the land**.

c. **Each of you shall return to his possession, and each of you shall return to his family**: When the trumpet sounded on the Day of Atonement to proclaim a Jubilee, it meant more than the land receiving an extra year of rest. It was also a liberation of sorts, which the following verses will explain. Land was to return to the family it was originally given to, and people (including slaves) were expected to return home.

i. "The context indicates that what is involved here is property that has had to be sold during difficult times. The former owner was allowed during this special year to retake possession of his land." (Peter-Contesse)

2. (13-17) In the year of Jubilee, the land went back to its original family.

'In this Year of Jubilee, each of you shall return to his possession. And if you sell anything to your neighbor or buy from your neighbor's hand, you shall not oppress one another. According to the number of years

after the Jubilee you shall buy from your neighbor, and according to the number of years of crops he shall sell to you. According to the multitude of years you shall increase its price, and according to the fewer number of years you shall diminish its price; for he sells to you *according* to the number *of the years* of the crops. Therefore you shall not oppress one another, but you shall fear your God; for I *am* the LORD your God.

a. **In this Year of Jubilee, each of you shall return to his possession**: When Israel came into the Promised Land, the land was allotted according to tribes and families. These initial tracts of land would be the permanent possession of those families, and therefore land in Israel could never be permanently sold; it could only be leased, and the amount of the lease would be based on **the number of years** which were left until the **Jubilee**.

i. In Joshua chapters 13 through 21, the Promised Land was divided among the tribes of Israel. Each tribe received an area within the land, and each clan or large family unit of the tribes received their portion within that land. These were the assignments returned to each Year of Jubilee. What God gave to a clan or large family unit in Joshua 13-21 was to be theirs forever.

ii. This meant that no family would be forever without land. Every fifty years, every family would have the opportunity to start again.

iii. **Each of you shall return to his possession**: Believers are citizens of heaven (Philippians 3:20). The day will come when we will hear the blast of a trumpet (1 Thessalonians 4:16-17) and come to our true and eternal home.

b. **Therefore you shall not oppress one another**: Though this was extremely charitable and helpful to the families in Israel, this was not a socialist system, because only land was re-distributed. Most effectively, this helped protect against the existence of a permanent underclass in Israel.

i. We don't know for a fact that the Year of Jubilee was ever actually observed. Jeremiah 34:8-15 describes an attempt to implement some of the principles of the Jubilee. "Just how widely the concept of the jubilee year was observed through the history of the Israelites is difficult to state for lack of direct evidence." (Harrison)

ii. Yet to whatever degree it was observed, this system was a blessing to Israel in the ancient world. It meant no clan or large family unit was forever poor; every fifty years there was a "reset" in the economy of Israel with debts canceled, servants liberated, and the return of land. However, this worked for a society based on agriculture, and agriculture on the scale possible in pre-modern times. It also worked for a society that did not have dramatic population growth over the centuries.

iii. The economy of Israel under God's law, including the law of Jubilee, found a middle course between unrestrained capitalism and the oppression of a state-controlled economy. "The jubilee was a wonderful institution, and was of very great service to the *religion, freedom,* and *independence* of the Jewish people." (Clarke)

iv. "Debts were to be remitted, slaves emancipated, and so the mountains of wealth and the valleys of poverty were to be somewhat levelled, and the nation carried back to its original framework of a simple agricultural community of small owners, each 'sitting under his own vine and fig-tree.'" (Maclaren)

v. Today, some of the *principles* of the Year of Jubilee would be a blessing for modern society, such as a system of the cancellation of debts every fifty years. However, since God did not assign land for modern people across the globe as He did for Israel in Joshua 13-21, we can't take every principle of a Jubilee and apply it to the modern world.

3. (18-22) God's provision for the Sabbath year.

'So you shall observe My statutes and keep My judgments, and perform them; and you will dwell in the land in safety. Then the land will yield its fruit, and you will eat your fill, and dwell there in safety. 'And if you say, "What shall we eat in the seventh year, since we shall not sow nor gather in our produce?" Then I will command My blessing on you in the sixth year, and it will bring forth produce enough for three years. And you shall sow in the eighth year, and eat old produce until the ninth year; until its produce comes in, you shall eat *of* the old *harvest.*

a. **So you shall observe My statutes and keep My judgments, and perform them; and you will dwell in the land in safety**: God promised that if Israel obeyed Him, He would provide so much on the sixth year, that they would not only be supplied for the seventh year when they gave the land rest, but they would also be eating the produce of the sixth year some **three years** later.

b. **Then I will command My blessing on you in the sixth year**: If Israel trusted God to provide as He promised in the sixth year – to provide enough for three years in the sixth year – God promised to **command** a blessing upon them. The promise was so sure that God said He would **command** it.

i. If we obey God – even when it doesn't make sense – we can trust He will provide our every need. If we seek first the kingdom of God, and

His righteousness, all those practical things will be provided (Matthew 6:33).

C. Rules regarding the redemption of property.

1. (23) The fundamental principle.

'The land shall not be sold permanently, for the land *is* Mine; for you *are* strangers and sojourners with Me.

> a. **For the land is Mine**: The whole earth is the LORD's (Psalm 24:1). Yet, God has a special regard for the land of Israel, which He calls His *Holy Land* (Zechariah 2:12). Here God proclaimed that **the land** of Israel is His in a special way, beyond the sense in which all the earth belongs to Him.

>> i. In theory, God's chosen nation and the drama of redemption could have been centered at almost anywhere on the globe. Yet He chose **the land** of Israel as that place. In terms of geography, it is the stage upon which God has centered His plan of the ages.

> b. **The land shall not be sold permanently**: Because the Promised Land belonged to God in a special sense, the land could be leased, but never sold. Every lease would expire in the year of Jubilee. In addition, the lease could be bought out at any time by a *kinsman-redeemer* (Leviticus 25:25).

> c. **For you are strangers and sojourners with Me**: One could say that the Promised Land never truly belonged to Israel. It belonged to God. In this, God reminded Israel that their real home was in heaven with Him, and they were only **strangers** and visitors to this earth. This is true of Christians today (1 Peter 2:11 and Hebrews 11:13).

>> i. To always be **strangers and sojourners** doesn't sound like a blessing. But for God to tell us, "**you are strangers and sojourners with Me**" changes everything. To be **with** God means all things are ours and we have a far better citizenship and homeland.

2. (24-28) The role of the redeeming relative.

And in all the land of your possession you shall grant redemption of the land. 'If one of your brethren becomes poor, and has sold *some* of his possession, and if his redeeming relative comes to redeem it, then he may redeem what his brother sold. Or if the man has no one to redeem it, but he himself becomes able to redeem it, then let him count the years since its sale, and restore the remainder to the man to whom he sold it, that he may return to his possession. But if he is not able to have *it* restored to himself, then what was sold shall remain in the hand of him who bought it until the Year of Jubilee; and in the Jubilee it shall be released, and he shall return to his possession.

a. **In all the land of your possession you shall grant redemption of the land**: This redemption of the land was accomplished through the **redeeming relative** (in Hebrew, *goel*). The *goel* was a designated close relative who had the right (and responsibility) to do three essential things for a clan or family:

- The *goel* would redeem a family member sold into slavery.
- The *goel* would redeem the family's land or inheritance sold outside the family.
- The *goel* would avenge the murder of a member of the family.

i. The book of Ruth describes a redeeming relative transaction. When Naomi returned from Moab, poor and in debt, her nearest redeeming relative was willing to buy back the land for her but stopped short when he found he would also have to marry Ruth and raise up an heir for the property. When this nearest redeeming relative did not fulfill his obligation, Boaz was the next closest redeeming relative, and he fulfilled the responsibility out of love for Ruth (Ruth 3).

ii. The *goel* is also a wonderful picture of Jesus, our **redeeming relative**.

- Jesus redeems us from slavery to sin (Romans 3:24 and 1 Corinthians 6:20).
- Jesus restores our inheritance and more. "What we have lost in the first Adam we have more than regained in the second. For innocence, we have purity; for external fellowship with God, His indwelling; for the delights of an earthly paradise, the fullness of God's blessedness and joy." (Meyer)
- Jesus avenges the soul-murder of His people, defeating the one who came to kill (John 10:10).

iii. The *goel* would redeem slaves or property with money. "We have been redeemed, not with corruptible things, but with the precious blood of Christ. We have been made free by right, and have only to claim and act upon the freedom with which the risen Christ has made us free." (Meyer)

b. **Let him count the years since its sale, and restore the remainder**: When a *goel* (the **redeeming relative**) bought back land on behalf of the family, the price was determined by how many years stood since its sale and until the next Jubilee.

i. "Presumably he would pay back to the buyer the money he received minus the amount the purchaser had earned from the land since the sale. The value of the property would decrease the closer they were to the next Jubilee." (Rooker)

c. **In the Jubilee it shall be released, and he shall return to his possession**: If the **redeeming relative** was unable to buy his brother out of debt before a Jubilee, the land would return to the debtor at the Jubilee year.

3. (29-34) The exception for land in walled cities.

'If a man sells a house in a walled city, then he may redeem it within a whole year after it is sold; *within* **a full year he may redeem it. But if it is not redeemed within the space of a full year, then the house in the walled city shall belong permanently to him who bought it, throughout his generations. It shall not be released in the Jubilee. However the houses of villages which have no wall around them shall be counted as the fields of the country. They may be redeemed, and they shall be released in the Jubilee. Nevertheless the cities of the Levites,** *and* **the houses in the cities of their possession, the Levites may redeem at any time. And if a man purchases a house from the Levites, then the house that was sold in the city of his possession shall be released in the Jubilee; for the houses in the cities of the Levites** *are* **their possession among the children of Israel. But the field of the common-land of their cities may not be sold, for it** *is* **their perpetual possession.**

a. **If a man sells a house in a walled city, then he may redeem it within a whole year after it is sold**: The laws of property as described in previous verses did not apply to urban property (**in a walled city**). The previously described laws applied to rural land where most ancient Israelites lived. For them, the land was more than a place to live; it was a place to earn one's livelihood.

i. "The reason for this distinction apparently lies in the fact that houses within walled cities fell outside the jurisdiction of family property inheritance and were not critical for the economic survival of the family." (Rooker)

b. **The house in the walled city shall belong permanently to him who bought it**: In cities, property was usually only a place to live. Therefore, this property could be bought or sold more freely, without the same restrictions which applied to the original allotments of land given to Israel when they came into the Promised Land.

c. **If a man purchases a house from the Levites, then the house that was sold in the city of his possession shall be released in the Jubilee**: However, there was an exception to the special rules regarding urban real estate. The property of **the Levites** would be theirs forever, redeemable at any time, in a city or in a rural area.

D. Care of the poor.

1. (35-38) Lending to the poor.

'If one of your brethren becomes poor, and falls into poverty among you, then you shall help him, like a stranger or a sojourner, that he may live with you. Take no usury or interest from him; but fear your God, that your brother may live with you. You shall not lend him your money for usury, nor lend him your food at a profit. I *am* the LORD your God, who brought you out of the land of Egypt, to give you the land of Canaan *and* to be your God.

a. **If one of your brethren becomes poor**: These commands specifically prohibit making money from the misfortune of a poor brother. Instead of making profit from the misery of a poor brother, the command was simple: **you shall help him**.

b. **Take no usury or interest from him; but fear your God, that your brother may live with you**: Jesus made a similar command in Luke 6:34, when He asked what credit could it be to us if we give to or help only those whom we know can help us back.

i. "Usury, at present, signifies unlawful interest for money." (Clarke)

ii. "The prophet Ezekiel listed usury as among the most serious crimes, including murder and adultery (Ezekiel 18:11–13; also Ezekiel 22:12). This law prohibiting usury was violated by the postexilic community (Nehemiah 5:1–11)." (Rooker)

iii. In medieval Europe, Christians often refused to loan money at interest because of these Biblical laws against usury. Motivated by hatred of the Jews, Christians often pushed Jewish people into occupations that were thought of as low and inferior – collecting taxes and rents, and moneylending. Christians thought of these occupations as necessary evils and thought to make the Jews bear the evil of the necessities. Yet because of this, Jewish people in medieval Europe dominated many aspects of banking and financial business – which often made them more envied and resented by the Christians of Europe.

c. **I am the LORD your God, who brought you out of the land of Egypt, to give you the land of Canaan**: God's kindness and generosity to Israel were an example of the type of kindness and generosity they were to show to others.

2. (39-46) When a Hebrew becomes a slave because of debt.

'And if *one of* your brethren *who dwells* by you becomes poor, and sells himself to you, you shall not compel him to serve as a slave. As a hired servant *and* a sojourner he shall be with you, *and* shall serve you until the Year of Jubilee. And *then* he shall depart from you; he and his children with him; and shall return to his own family. He shall return to the possession of his fathers. For they *are* My servants, whom I brought out of the land of Egypt; they shall not be sold as slaves. You shall not rule over him with rigor, but you shall fear your God. And as for your male and female slaves whom you may have; from the nations that are around you, from them you may buy male and female slaves. Moreover you may buy the children of the strangers who dwell among you, and their families who are with you, which they beget in your land; and they shall become your property. And you may take them as an inheritance for your children after you, to inherit *them as* a possession; they shall be your permanent slaves. But regarding your brethren, the children of Israel, you shall not rule over one another with rigor.**

a. **You shall not compel him to serve as a slave**: It was normal in the ancient world for someone in life-threatening poverty or unable to pay their debts to become a slave. The law of Moses would not allow an Israelite to do this for one of his **brethren**. He was not to be regarded **as a slave**, but as a **hired servant and a sojourner**.

i. Though it is almost impossible for us to relate to in the modern world, this kind of slavery was necessary and helpful in the ancient world. For most of humanity's history, the poorest people were sometimes confronted with a choice between death by starvation or becoming a slave. In such circumstances, it is hard to call slavery *good*, but it was certainly preferred to the alternative (death).

ii. **A slave**: "The Hebrew word usually translated *slave* designates a 'subordinate,' or someone who is under the authority of a person above him in a hierarchy. It may be used of a cabinet minister serving under a king, of an army officer under his supreme commander, or of a slave serving under his master." (Peter-Contesse)

b. **Shall serve you until the Year of Jubilee**: The Israelite brother who was regarded as a **hired servant and a sojourner** could be released from his obligation when his debt was paid. But every **hired servant** and **sojourner** was released at the **Year of Jubilee**.

i. **For they are My servants**: "The Hebrew word used here is actually 'slave,' as in verse 39, and should be so translated so that the connection between this statement and the previous verses may be clear. The people of Israel had been slaves of the Egyptians, but when they were delivered they became the property of the one who redeemed them, the LORD himself." (Peter-Contesse)

c. **You shall not rule over him with rigor, but you shall fear your God**: God commanded that slaves and workers should not be mistreated. They were not to be worked excessively or to their harm. God cares about working conditions and does not want workers to be mistreated in their labor.

> i. "Labour beyond the person's strength, or labour too long continued, or in unhealthy or uncomfortable places and circumstances, or without sufficient food, etc., is *labour exacted with rigour*, and consequently inhuman; and this law is made, not for the Mosaic dispensation and the Jewish people, but for every dispensation and for every people under heaven." (Clarke)

d. **And as for your male and female slaves whom you may have; from the nations that are around you, from them you may buy male and female slaves**: Foreign slaves from debt or poverty did not have the same rights as Israelites who went into servitude because of debt. They could be held as slaves for life (assuming their debt or obligation was never paid), though they had to be treated humanely (Exodus 20:8-11).

> i. Exodus 21:16 specifically says that kidnapping a man to sell him was a sin, and not allowed in Israel. Later, the prophet Amos rebuked Tyre for their traffic in slaves as a violation of the *covenant of brotherhood* (Amos 1:9-10).

> ii. This is a subtle yet important difference between slavery as it was (and is) commonly practiced and slavery as regulated in the Bible. Most slavery (ancient and modern) was actually a form of *kidnapping* – the taking and imprisoning of a person against their will. As regulated in the Bible (and as practiced in some other ancient cultures), slavery was received *willingly* (usually as payment for debt) or, in the case of war, was an alternative to death. In ancient Israel, people from other cultures were not kidnapped and enslaved (as was the practice in the African slave trade).

3. (47-55) Redeeming a Hebrew slave from a foreigner.

'Now if a sojourner or stranger close to you becomes rich, and *one of* your brethren *who dwells* by him becomes poor, and sells himself to the stranger *or* sojourner close to you, or to a member of the stranger's family, after he is sold he may be redeemed again. One of his brothers may redeem him; or his uncle or his uncle's son may redeem him; or

anyone who is near of kin to him in his family may redeem him; or if he is able he may redeem himself. **Thus he shall reckon with him who bought him: The price of his release shall be according to the number of years, from the year that he was sold to him until the Year of Jubilee;** *it shall be* according to the time of a hired servant for him. **If** *there are* **still many years** *remaining,* **according to them he shall repay the price of his redemption from the money with which he was bought. And if there remain but a few years until the Year of Jubilee, then he shall reckon with him,** *and* **according to his years he shall repay him the price of his redemption. He shall be with him as a yearly hired servant, and he shall not rule with rigor over him in your sight. And if he is not redeemed in these** *years,* **then he shall be released in the Year of Jubilee; he and his children with him. For the children of Israel** *are* **servants to Me; they** *are* **My servants whom I brought out of the land of Egypt: I** *am* **the LORD your God.**

a. **Sells himself to the stranger or sojourner**: This deals with an Israelite man forced to sell himself to a foreigner, who may not respect his rights under God's law.

b. **After he is sold he may be redeemed again**: As in the redemption of land, the kinsman-redeemer was responsible to buy the Hebrew slave out of servitude if he could, and the price was reckoned in relation to the **Year of Jubilee**. If he could not be redeemed earlier, he was to **be released in the Year of Jubilee**.

c. **The children of Israel are servants to Me**: God's care for Israel and their redemption was based on the idea that they were first **servants** to the LORD, their covenant God.

Leviticus 26 – Blessing and Curses

A. Blessings on obedient Israel.

1. (1-2) Do not worship idols.

'You shall not make idols for yourselves; neither a carved image nor a *sacred* pillar shall you rear up for yourselves; nor shall you set up an engraved stone in your land, to bow down to it; for I *am* the LORD your God. You shall keep My Sabbaths and reverence My sanctuary: I *am* the LORD.

a. **You shall not make idols for yourselves**: Leviticus 26 is a remarkable chapter promising blessings to an obedient Israel and curses to a disobedient Israel. Before the blessings and curses are proclaimed, God reminded Israel of the foundational law: that Yahweh, the LORD, covenant God of Israel – that He alone must be worshipped.

b. **Neither a carved image nor a sacred pillar**: The **carved image** usually represented a god. The **sacred pillar** was associated with the immoral worship of the fertility gods.

i. **Idols…a carved image…a sacred pillar…an engraved stone**: "This fourfold description of the making of idols is the most comprehensive concentration of references to image making in the Bible, thus ruling out any type of idol worship." (Rooker)

ii. Peter-Contesse explained each of the terms:

- **Idols**: "The root of the word thus translated really means 'worthless; insufficient; inadequate.'"

- **A carved image**: "This refers to something fashioned into the shape of an object, animal, or a person. It may be made of stone, clay, wood, or metal. According to the context here, the purpose of making such a likeness was to provide an object that could be worshiped."

- **A sacred pillar**: "This probably refers to a long stone that was made to stand up by itself and served as an object of worship."

- **An engraved stone**: "Compare Numbers 33:52. It is uncertain exactly what this refers to. The root meaning of the word has to do with the verb 'to look.'"

c. **You shall keep My Sabbaths and reverence My sanctuary**: Practically speaking, an important part of the way Israel honored God was by observing the **Sabbath** and regarding God's **sanctuary** with **reverence**.

2. (3-8) Blessings on obedient Israel: plentiful harvests, peace, victory in battle.

'If you walk in My statutes and keep My commandments, and perform them, then I will give you rain in its season, the land shall yield its produce, and the trees of the field shall yield their fruit. Your threshing shall last till the time of vintage, and the vintage shall last till the time of sowing; you shall eat your bread to the full, and dwell in your land safely. I will give peace in the land, and you shall lie down, and none will make *you* afraid; I will rid the land of evil beasts, and the sword will not go through your land. You will chase your enemies, and they shall fall by the sword before you. Five of you shall chase a hundred, and a hundred of you shall put ten thousand to flight; your enemies shall fall by the sword before you.

a. **If you walk in My statutes and keep My commandments, and perform them, then I will give you rain in its season**: God was determined to reveal Himself to the world through Israel, either by making them so blessed, the world would know only God could have blessed them so; or by making them so cursed, that *only God* could have cursed them and yet cause them to still survive. The choice was up to Israel.

i. "Leviticus 26 deals with the subject of blessings and cursings, a common feature of ancient Near Eastern treaty covenants." (Rooker)

b. **Five of you shall chase a hundred, and a hundred of you shall put ten thousand to flight**: This clearly speaks of a Divine blessing. These remarkable promises have a supernatural element.

i. The principle behind that particular blessing is remarkable; the ratio of five to one hundred is one routing twenty, but the ratio of one hundred to ten thousand is one routing one hundred.

ii. Gideon's 300 defeated 135,000 Midianites; Jonathan and his armorbearer alone defeated a Philistine army. In 2 Kings 7, God sent the sound of a mighty army to the camp of the Syrians laying siege to the city of Samaria (2 Kings 7:6-7). From that story, you could say that God used four men (lepers!) to defeat a Syrian army of many thousands.

3. (9-13) Blessings on obedient Israel: abundance, the presence of God, freedom.

For I will look on you favorably and make you fruitful, multiply you and confirm My covenant with you. You shall eat the old harvest, and clear out the old because of the new. I will set My tabernacle among you, and My soul shall not abhor you. I will walk among you and be your God, and you shall be My people. I *am* the LORD your God, who brought you out of the land of Egypt, that *you* should not be their slaves; I have broken the bands of your yoke and made you walk upright.

a. **And confirm My covenant with you**: As a literary form, this chapter is similar to ancient treaties between a king and his people; this is God the king, making a covenant with His people, Israel.

i. "In the ancient Near East it was customary for legal treaties to conclude with passages containing blessings upon those who observed the enactments, and curses upon those who did not." (Harrison)

b. **I will set My tabernacle among you, and My soul shall not abhor you. I will walk among you and be your God, and you shall be My people**: The best promises are saved for last: First, that Israel would enjoy a special relationship with God. If not for this, all the material blessings described previously would be empty.

i. When Israel walked after the LORD, these blessings were real; one example of this is when the queen of Sheba came to Solomon and saw a nation so blessed, she knew it had to be of God (1 Kings 10:1-13).

ii. **I will walk among you and be your God, and you shall be My people**: The Apostle Paul quoted this line in 2 Corinthians 6:16 to explain what it means for the church to be God's temple, His dwelling place.

c. **I have broken the bands of your yoke and made you walk upright**: This final blessing speaks of freedom and dignity. This passage almost feels like the New Testament, God proclaims the liberty of His people and then invites them to walk in it.

i. "Thus the text offers the image of a slave bowed by an enormous burden. He suddenly has the weight removed, which expresses the establishment of Israel's special relationship with God." (Rooker)

B. Curses on disobedient Israel.

1. (14-17) Disobedient Israel will be cursed with fear and weakness.

'But if you do not obey Me, and do not observe all these commandments, and if you despise My statutes, or if your soul abhors My judgments, so that you do not perform all My commandments, *but* break My covenant, I also will do this to you: I will even appoint terror over you, wasting disease and fever which shall consume the eyes and cause sorrow of heart. And you shall sow your seed in vain, for your enemies shall eat it. I will set My face against you, and you shall be defeated by your enemies. Those who hate you shall reign over you, and you shall flee when no one pursues you.

a. **If you do not obey Me**: Here begins the section where God promises to curse a disobedient Israel. To fail to **obey** God and to **observe** His commandments is to **despise** His word and to **abhor** His word (**statutes, judgments**). For Israel, it was to **break** the **covenant** they made with Yahweh (Exodus 24:1-8).

i. The section on curses is twice as long as the section on blessings. This speaks to human nature, which is more motivated by the fear of threats than by the promises of blessing.

b. **I will even appoint terror over you**: God promised to bring a sense of **terror** over a disobedient Israel. They would be afflicted with **wasting disease and fever**. Because God would **set** His **face against** them, they would **be defeated** in battle. They would be so confused and afraid that they would **flee when no one pursues**.

2. (18-20) Disobedient Israel will be cursed with poor harvests.

'And after all this, if you do not obey Me, then I will punish you seven times more for your sins. I will break the pride of your power; I will make your heavens like iron and your earth like bronze. And your strength shall be spent in vain; for your land shall not yield its produce, nor shall the trees of the land yield their fruit.

a. **After all this, if you do not obey Me**: This section is arranged to give the sense that God would multiply curse upon curse if Israel continued in stubborn disobedience. He would **punish you seven times more for your sins**.

b. **I will break the pride of your power**: The core problem with chronic, continued disobedience is **pride** in one's own **power**. This pride must be broken.

c. **Your strength shall be spent in vain**: A disobedient and cursed Israel would not know the benefit and fruit of their own work. Their **strength** would bring no reward. They would do all the necessary work for farming, but there would be little **produce** from the land or **fruit** from their trees.

3. (21-22) Disobedient Israel will be cursed by wild beasts.

'Then, if you walk contrary to Me, and are not willing to obey Me, I will bring on you seven times more plagues, according to your sins. I will also send wild beasts among you, which shall rob you of your children, destroy your livestock, and make you few in number; and your highways shall be desolate.

a. **I will bring on you seven times more plagues**: As Israel continued in their disobedience, God would multiply their **plagues** and sorrows – **according** to their multiplied **sins**.

i. "The word translated *plagues* actually refers to 'punishment.'" (Peter-Contesse)

b. **I will also send wild beasts among you**: God promised to send **wild beasts among** His rebellious people. They would cause much destruction, to their families, their **livestock**, and their trade (**your highways shall be desolate**). One record of this happening is found in 2 Kings 17:25.

4. (23-26) Disobedient Israel will be cursed with pestilence and famine.

'And if by these things you are not reformed by Me, but walk contrary to Me, then I also will walk contrary to you, and I will punish you yet seven times for your sins. And I will bring a sword against you that will execute the vengeance of the covenant; when you are gathered together within your cities I will send pestilence among you; and you shall be delivered into the hand of the enemy. When I have cut off your supply of bread, ten women shall bake your bread in one oven, and they shall bring back your bread by weight, and you shall eat and not be satisfied.

a. **If by these things you are not reformed by Me**: If Israel did respond with humility and repentance in response to the curses and calamities already mentioned, God would regard it as being **reformed** by God Himself. If they did not allow these terrible things to reform them, more calamity would come.

b. **I will bring a sword against you...I will send pestilence.... ten women shall bake your bread in one oven**: The God-sent disasters would continue. They would be conquered, afflicted by **pestilence**, and famine. The famine would be so severe that **ten women** could share one oven because there was so little to use to make bread. There would not be enough food to **be satisfied**.

i. **Bread by weight**: "There will be so little that they will have to measure out the small quantities to each recipient. Compare Ezekiel 4:16–17." (Peter-Contesse)

5. (27-35) Disobedient Israel will be cursed by death, desolation, and exile.

'**And after all this, if you do not obey Me, but walk contrary to Me, then I also will walk contrary to you in fury; and I, even I, will chastise you seven times for your sins. You shall eat the flesh of your sons, and you shall eat the flesh of your daughters. I will destroy your high places, cut down your incense altars, and cast your carcasses on the lifeless forms of your idols; and My soul shall abhor you. I will lay your cities waste and bring your sanctuaries to desolation, and I will not smell the fragrance of your sweet aromas. I will bring the land to desolation, and your enemies who dwell in it shall be astonished at it. I will scatter you among the nations and draw out a sword after you; your land shall be desolate and your cities waste. Then the land shall enjoy its sabbaths as long as it lies desolate and you *are* in your enemies' land; then the land shall rest and enjoy its sabbaths. As long as *it* lies desolate it shall rest; for the time it did not rest on your sabbaths when you dwelt in it.**

a. **If you do not obey Me, but walk contrary to Me**: God continued His description of Israel's multiplied wickedness, and His response to punish them.

b. **I will chastise you seven times for your sins**: Significantly, God did not say the He would forsake Israel, only that they will be cursed. Sadly, these curses became the tragic story of Israel's history – defeat, deprivation, exile, desolation, and disease all too often have marked the history of the Jewish people.

i. Rooker noted a symmetry between the blessings and curses in this chapter.

Blessings	Curses
Fertile land (4-5, 10)	Unproductive land (16, 19-20, 26)
Live in safety (5)	Live in foreign nation (33)
Savage beasts removed (6)	Beasts will devour (22)
Sword removed (6)	Sword avenges (25)
Victory over enemies (7)	Defeated by enemies (17, 25)
God's favor (9)	God's disfavor (17)

c. **You shall eat the flesh of your sons**: God promised that famine would be so severe among them that they would resort to eating their **sons** and their **daughters**. This horrific cannibalism was fulfilled in 2 Kings 6:26-29.

i. The Jewish historian Josephus also described cannibalism in Jerusalem when they were under siege by the Romans in A.D. 70. He described how a woman killed and ate her own baby son (*Wars*, 6.3.4).

d. **I will scatter you among the nations**: If they continued in their disobedience, Israel would be conquered and removed from the land, dispersed among the Gentiles. Because they did not obey God's command regarding the sabbath year (Leviticus 25:1-7), God would empty the land so it could **enjoy its sabbaths**.

i. "The term 'scatter' (*zrh*) is borrowed from the agricultural realm, where it describes the winnowing process (Ruth 3:2; Isaiah 30:24; 41:16). The word is often employed in the Old Testament in reference to the exile of people." (Rooker)

6. (36-39) Even in exile, disobedient Israel will be cursed with fear, faintness, and wasting away.

'And as for those of you who are left, I will send faintness into their hearts in the lands of their enemies; the sound of a shaken leaf shall cause them to flee; they shall flee as though fleeing from a sword, and they shall fall when no one pursues. They shall stumble over one another, as it were before a sword, when no one pursues; and you shall have no *power* to stand before your enemies. You shall perish among the nations, and the land of your enemies shall eat you up. And those of you who are left shall waste away in their iniquity in your enemies' lands; also in their fathers' iniquities, which are with them, they shall waste away.

a. **I will send faintness into their hearts in the lands of their enemies**: As Israel continued to disobey, God promised to continue to be against them in the lands where they were scattered. They would be filled with fear so great that **the sound of a shaken leaf** would be to them as the sound of a **sword**. They would even **fall when no one pursues**.

i. "Brave men are not frightened by the sound of battle, but God will cause his people to be so fearful that a mere leaf blowing in the wind will make them run away." (Peter-Contesse)

b. **You shall perish among the nations**: This is not intended to say that the Jewish people would disappear, but that they would become very few, weak, and almost extinct. They would **waste away** under the curse of God.

C. The promise of restoration on repentant Israel.

1. (40-42) Restoration for a humble and repentant Israel.

'*But* if they confess their iniquity and the iniquity of their fathers, with their unfaithfulness in which they were unfaithful to Me, and that they also have walked contrary to Me, and *that* I also have walked contrary to them and have brought them into the land of their enemies; if their uncircumcised hearts are humbled, and they accept their guilt—then I will remember My covenant with Jacob, and My covenant with Isaac and My covenant with Abraham I will remember; I will remember the land.

> a. **If they confess their iniquity and the iniquity of their fathers**: This displays the greatness of God's mercy. Despite how cursed Israel might be, God would always remember, receive, and bless a repentant Israel. This would involve recognition of their sin, of God's righteous discipline (**I also have walked contrary to them**), and understanding they were as bad as the Gentiles (**their uncircumcised hearts**). They would have to be **humbled** to **accept their guilt**.

> > i. **That I also have walked contrary to them**: "They must recognize that their punishment is deserved before restoration and forgiveness can be experienced." (Rooker)

> b. **Then I will remember My covenant with Jacob**: God promised to **remember** the covenant He made with **Abraham**, with **Isaac**, and with **Jacob**. Remembering the covenant, God would be quick to restore and bless repentant Israel. God would also **remember the land** – implying that He would restore it to Israel.

> > i. "It is most instructive in the giving of the law, to observe how the declension and wandering of the people was evidently known to the King, and that notwithstanding this fact, these promises of final restoration were made. Thus, while human responsibility is most solemnly enforced, it is done in such a way as to create the conviction that the love of God will prove itself finally victorious over all human failure." (Morgan)

2. (43-45) The unbreakable nature of God's covenant with Israel.

The land also shall be left empty by them, and will enjoy its sabbaths while it lies desolate without them; they will accept their guilt, because they despised My judgments and because their soul abhorred My statutes. Yet for all that, when they are in the land of their enemies, I will not cast them away, nor shall I abhor them, to utterly destroy them and break My covenant with them; for I *am* the Lord their God. But

for their sake I will remember the covenant of their ancestors, whom I brought out of the land of Egypt in the sight of the nations, that I might be their God: I *am* the LORD.'"

a. **The land also shall be left empty by them**: Even when Israel would be in exile, God would not cast them off. God would remain ready to restore Israel when they turned back to Him.

b. **When they are in the land of their enemies, I will not cast them away, nor shall I abhor them, to utterly destroy them and break My covenant with them**: The mercy and kindness of God are remarkable. He promised that even when Israel was at their worst, God would not **break** His **covenant with them**. God redeemed Israel **out of the land of Egypt**, and He did it **in the sight of the nations**. Yahweh would not give up on His covenant people.

i. "This restoration upon repentance did in fact occur when the Israelites repented and turned to God while in exile in Babylon (Daniel 9:1–19). In fact Leviticus 26:32–45 should be understood as a preview of the history of Israel that includes the experiences of apostasy, exile, and restoration." (Rooker)

ii. "From this place the Jews take great comfort, and assure themselves of deliverance out of their present servitude and misery. And from this, and such other places, St. Paul concludes that the Israelitish nation, though then rejected and ruined, should be gathered again and restored." (Poole)

3. (46) Conclusion to the blessing and curses upon Israel.

These *are* the statutes and judgments and laws which the LORD made between Himself and the children of Israel on Mount Sinai by the hand of Moses.

a. **These are the statutes and judgments and laws**: In a sense, this concludes the book of Leviticus. Chapter 27 seems to be something of an added appendix to the book.

b. **Which the LORD made between Himself and the children of Israel**: This covenant was specifically made between God and Israel (Exodus 24:1-8). Especially when it comes to the matter of these promises of blessings and curses, it is good to ask if the same principles of blessings and curses apply to God's people under the New Covenant.

i. To some, Galatians 6:7 demonstrates that we are under the same principle of blessings and curses: *Do not be deceived, God is not mocked, for whatever a man sows, that he will also reap.* But in context, Paul did not promote a principle of spiritual karma that promised we will always prosper when we do good, or we will always suffer when we act badly. If there were such an absolute principle, it would condemn us all. Instead, the Apostle Paul simply spoke about the management of our resources (see Galatians 6:6-10). Essentially, Paul said that we may fool ourselves by expecting much when we sow little, but we cannot fool God – and the result of our poor sowing will be evident.

ii. Galatians 3:13-14 makes it clear: Jesus received this curse upon Himself as He hung on the cross, fulfilling the Deuteronomy 21:23 promise of a curse to all who are not only executed but have their bodies publicly exposed to shame. Jesus bore the curse so that we (even Gentiles) might bear the blessings of Abraham (the blessings of righteousness and life by faith) – but these blessings only come to those *in Christ Jesus.*

iii. Therefore under the New Covenant we are blessed not because of our obedience, but because we are in Christ Jesus; and there is no more curse for us from God because all the curse was borne by Jesus.

iv. This does not deny the chastening hand of God; but the correction of a loving parent is good and desirable, though not pleasant at the time (Hebrews 12:7-11). Nor does it deny the cause-and-effect nature of sin in our world; sin often carries its own curse, which in some ways is distinct from God's direct curse upon us.

Leviticus 27 – Regarding Things Given to God

A. Consecrating persons to the LORD.

1. (1-2) **When a man consecrates** certain persons to the LORD with a vow.

Now the LORD spoke to Moses, saying, "Speak to the children of Israel, and say to them: 'When a man consecrates by a vow certain persons to the LORD, according to your valuation,

a. **When a man consecrates by a vow certain persons to the LORD:** This chapter deals with things that are given to God **by a vow**. That means they were not required by a command of the law, but the **vow** was a freely promised and given gift to God. In this case, it deals with **persons** that were promised to the LORD in a vow.

i. "A vow is a promise made to God voluntarily and not in obedience to any divine requirement." (Morgan)

ii. For example, a man from the tribe of Judah, in a time of distress, out of gratitude, or out of a sense of calling, might want to consecrate his son to the LORD. He could not give his son to the service of the tabernacle, because he was not a priestly family. So, to consecrate his son, he would follow the procedures in the following verses.

iii. "According to Judges 11:29–40 and 1 Samuel 1:11, it was possible for a person to dedicate another human being to God…. it was expected that the person so dedicated would serve in the sanctuary. But this passage shows that such a person could be set free by the payment of money." (Peter-Contesse)

b. **When a man consecrates by a vow certain persons to the LORD:** The beauty of these commands is that it gave the one making a vow of consecration something definite to *do*. The vow of consecration was therefore far more than mere words, it had a definite action associated with it – and prevented people from making empty vows to God.

i. "It was not a sin to refrain from making a vow (Deuteronomy 23:22), but once a vow was made, it had to be kept (Deuteronomy 23:21–23; Numbers 30:2; Ecclesiastes 5:4–6). Substitutions could be made, however, and it was this possibility of making a substitution that distinguished the vow from the sacrificial offering made on the altar." (Rooker)

2. (3-7) Assigning a valuation for persons consecrated by a vow.

If your valuation is of a male from twenty years old up to sixty years old, then your valuation shall be fifty shekels of silver, according to the shekel of the sanctuary. If it *is* a female, then your valuation shall be thirty shekels; and if from five years old up to twenty years old, then your valuation for a male shall be twenty shekels, and for a female ten shekels; and if from a month old up to five years old, then your valuation for a male shall be five shekels of silver, and for a female your valuation shall be three shekels of silver; and if from sixty years old and above, if *it is* a male, then your valuation shall be fifteen shekels, and for a female ten shekels.

a. **If your valuation is of a male from twenty years old up to sixty years old**: Persons were assigned a value according to their age and general usefulness to society; especially in an agricultural society, there was a definite sense in which a man between 20 and 50 was more "valuable" than a child one month to five years old.

Age	Male	Female
0-4	5 shekels	3 shekels
5-19	20 shekels	10 shekels
20-59	50 shekels	30 shekels
60 and over	15 shekels	10 shekels

b. **Fifty shekels of silver.... thirty shekels...twenty shekels**: The valuation was made mostly in terms of an estimation of the physical labor value of the person. The normal 25-year-old man could do more labor on behalf of the tabernacle than a five-year-old boy.

i. "The prices (values) of the individuals should be understood as representing either the wage of a worker (which was a shekel a month in the biblical period) or the relative worth of the value of the person's services in the tabernacle. If the services included heavy manual labor in working with sacrificial animals or in transporting the tabernacle, it is easy to see why young men would be given higher value." (Rooker)

3. (8) Provision for the poor in consecration by a vow.

'But if he is too poor to pay your valuation, then he shall present himself before the priest, and the priest shall set a value for him; according to the ability of him who vowed, the priest shall value him.

a. **If he is too poor to pay your valuation**: Importantly, no one was prohibited from fulfilling a vow of consecration because they did not have enough money; if they were poor, the priests would be flexible with the valuation.

i. *Everyone* can give their life to the LORD; there are none who are too small, or too insignificant, or too useless. God wants to use each and every one.

b. **According to the ability of him who vowed, the priest shall value him**: When God accepted a substitute of money for the actual thing **vowed**, the priest was to take into account the financial **ability** of the one who made the vow. God did not only want the rich to vow things to Him; we wanted to make this special devotion and consecration within the reach of everyone.

i. "Reader, hast thou ever dedicated thyself, or any part of thy property, to the service of thy Maker? If so, hast thou paid thy vows? Or hast thou *altered* thy *purpose*, or *changed* thy *offering?*" (Clarke)

B. Redeeming property consecrated to God by a vow.

1. (9-13) Redeeming animals.

'If *it is* an animal that men may bring as an offering to the LORD, all that *anyone* gives to the LORD shall be holy. He shall not substitute it or exchange it, good for bad or bad for good; and if he at all exchanges animal for animal, then both it and the one exchanged for it shall be holy. If *it is* an unclean animal which they do not offer as a sacrifice to the LORD, then he shall present the animal before the priest; and the priest shall set a value for it, whether it is good or bad; as you, the priest, value it, so it shall be. But if he *wants* at all *to* redeem it, then he must add one-fifth to your valuation.

a. **If it is an animal that men may bring as an offering to the LORD**: If an animal was clean (fit for sacrifice), and you wanted to redeem it from the vow of consecration to the LORD (perhaps because the animal was especially useful), you could exchange it for another animal – as long as that animal was also clean, and equally suitable for sacrifice.

b. **If it is an unclean animal**: If an animal was unclean (unfit for sacrifice), it could still be vowed to the LORD and then redeemed; but the priest would set a value on the animal, and one would add one-fifth to that value (20%) and give the total to the tabernacle treasury.

> i. Again, if one simply wanted to give their unclean animal (a donkey, for example) to the LORD, he could give it to a priest, who would use it or sell it, giving the money to the tabernacle treasury; but if they desired to keep the animal, while still consecrating it with a vow to the LORD, they had to pay the price of the animal plus 20%. You could give your donkey and use him too, but it would cost you the value of the donkey plus 20%.

2. (14-15) Redeeming houses.

'And when a man dedicates his house *to be* holy to the LORD, then the priest shall set a value for it, whether it is good or bad; as the priest values it, so it shall stand. If he who dedicated it *wants to* redeem his house, then he must add one-fifth of the money of your valuation to it, and it shall be his.

> a. **When a man dedicates his house to be holy to the LORD**: With a house, as in the case with an unclean animal, if a man wanted to consecrate by a vow the house to the LORD, while still using it, the priest would set a value on the house.

> b. **He must add one-fifth**: After the value of the home was estimated, an additional 20% was added. That total was given to the tabernacle treasury and the vow was considered fulfilled.

3. (16-21) Redeeming land that belongs to the family by allotment.

'If a man dedicates to the LORD *part* of a field of his possession, then your valuation shall be according to the seed for it. A homer of barley seed *shall be valued* at fifty shekels of silver. If he dedicates his field from the Year of Jubilee, according to your valuation it shall stand. But if he dedicates his field after the Jubilee, then the priest shall reckon to him the money due according to the years that remain till the Year of Jubilee, and it shall be deducted from your valuation. And if he who dedicates the field ever wishes to redeem it, then he must add one-fifth of the money of your valuation to it, and it shall belong to him. But if he does not want to redeem the field, or if he has sold the field to another man, it shall not be redeemed anymore; but the field, when it is released in the Jubilee, shall be holy to the LORD, as a devoted field; it shall be the possession of the priest.

> a. **If a man dedicates to LORD part of a field of his possession**: This deals with land that belonged to the buyer's family or clan according to the division of land that would later happen in Joshua 13-21.

b. **If he dedicates his field**: For land, its value was based on its potential production, as well as the number of years until the **Year of Jubilee**.

4. (22-25) Redeeming land that does not belong to the family by allotment.

'And if a man dedicates to the Lord a field which he has bought, which is not the field of his possession, then the priest shall reckon to him the worth of your valuation, up to the Year of Jubilee, and he shall give your valuation on that day *as* a holy *offering* to the Lord. In the Year of Jubilee the field shall return to him from whom it was bought, to the one who *owned* the land as a possession. And all your valuations shall be according to the shekel of the sanctuary: twenty gerahs to the shekel.

a. **If a man dedicates to the Lord a field which he has bought, which is not the field of his possession**: This deals with land that did not belong to the buyer's family or clan according to the division of land that would later happen in Joshua 13-21. In a sense, the land was not truly purchased, only leased until the next **Year of Jubilee**.

b. **The priest shall reckon to him the worth**: The priest made an estimate of the land's value, taking into account the number of years until the next Jubilee. This amount was then given **as a holy offering to the Lord**, and God regarded the land as truly dedicated unto Him.

i. "*Gerahs*: a unit of weight which was, according to this verse, one twentieth of a shekel. Compare also Exodus 30:13.... the 'gerah' was the smallest unit of measurement in the system used at that time. It was equivalent to about a half a gram." (Peter-Contesse)

5. (26-27) Redemption of the consecration vow for the firstborn.

'But the firstborn of the animals, which should be the Lord's firstborn, no man shall dedicate; whether *it is* an ox or sheep, it *is* the Lord's. And if *it is* an unclean animal, then he shall redeem *it* according to your valuation, and shall add one-fifth to it; or if it is not redeemed, then it shall be sold according to your valuation.

a. **But the firstborn of the animals, which should be the Lord's firstborn, no man shall dedicate**: Since the firstborn already belonged to God (Exodus 13:2), it was not allowed to give it to the Lord in a vow. If the **firstborn** animal was a clean animal, it had to be sacrificed.

b. **It shall be sold according to your valuation**: However, an unclean **firstborn** animal could either be sold or **redeemed** (bought back) from the Lord.

6. (28-29) One cannot redeem things or persons **devoted** to the Lord.

'Nevertheless no devoted *offering* that a man may devote to the LORD of all that he has, *both* man and beast, or the field of his possession, shall be sold or redeemed; every devoted *offering is* most holy to the LORD. No person under the ban, who may become doomed to destruction among men, shall be redeemed, *but* shall surely be put to death.

a. **Every devoted offering is most holy to the LORD**: To **devote** something to the LORD was a further step than consecration by a vow; it often had the meaning of destroying the item (or executing the person) so that it could not be used by anyone else, and all of its value was given to God. Therefore if something was already declared a **devoted offering**, it could not be given in a vow. It already belonged to God and was **most holy to the LORD**.

i. Joshua 6:17, among other passages, translates this word **devoted** with the word *accursed* – because that thing devoted to God would be destroyed, being used for no other purpose.

b. **Nevertheless no devoted offering that a man may devote to the LORD of all that he has**: For these reasons, an item **devoted** to God could not be redeemed for a price. It already belonged to the LORD and had to be given to Him.

i. "**No devoted thing,** i.e. nothing which is absolutely devoted to God, with a curse upon themselves or others if they disposed not of it according to their vow; as the Hebrew word implies." (Poole)

c. **No person under the ban, who may become doomed to destruction among men, shall be redeemed, but shall surely be put to death**: In this sense also, one could not escape execution by being "bought back" from the LORD. They had to face their fate or penalty.

i. An example of this is found in 1 Samuel 15 where King Saul was commanded to bring God's judgment against the Amalekites. They were **devoted** and **doomed to destruction**. Saul failed to do this and greatly displeased the LORD.

ii. "The law mentioned in these two verses has been appealed to by the enemies of Divine revelation as a proof, that under the Mosaic dispensation *human sacrifices* were offered to God; but this can never be conceded. Had there been such a law, it certainly would have been more explicitly revealed, and not left in the compass of a few words only, where the meaning is very difficult to be ascertained; and the words themselves differently translated by most interpreters." (Clarke)

7. (30-33) The payment of tithes.

And all the tithe of the land, *whether* of the seed of the land *or* of the fruit of the tree, *is* the LORD's. It *is* holy to the LORD. If a man wants at all to

redeem *any* **of his tithes, he shall add one-fifth to it. And concerning the tithe of the herd or the flock, of whatever passes under the rod, the tenth one shall be holy to the LORD. He shall not inquire whether it is good or bad, nor shall he exchange it; and if he exchanges it at all, then both it and the one exchanged for it shall be holy; it shall not be redeemed.'"**

a. **And all the tithe of the land**: In this context, **the tithe** simply means "the tenth" or "ten percent." Israel gave ten percent of their flocks, of their grain, and of their fruit to God. This **tithe**, the ten percent, was sacred and separated unto God (**It is holy to the LORD**).

i. "The word 'tithe' (*ma aser*) is related to the number 'ten' (*eser*) and thus refers to a tenth. The concept of a tithe was not a new one for the Israelites, since we observe the practice before the giving of the Law (Genesis 14:20; 28:20-22). Thus what we have in Leviticus 27 is a systematization of an earlier practice." (Rooker)

ii. Ancient Israel observed at least two tithes. Here in Leviticus 27:30-33 is the general tithe, which also seems to be described in Deuteronomy 14:22-27. Deuteronomy 14:28-29 describes a second tithe paid every three years and given to the Levite and to the poor. Some believe Leviticus 27:30-33 and Deuteronomy 14:22-27 describe two different required tithes, but there is no compelling reason to think they are different.

iii. While the New Testament does not command or emphasize tithing, it presents giving as a duty for God's people and does not speak negatively of tithing. Jesus approved of the careful tithing of the religious leaders of His day (Luke 11:42) while rebuking them for what they left undone. Melchizedek was praised when he gave Abraham a tithe of all (Hebrews 7:4-10). The New Testament does give many principles for the giving of believers under the New Covenant.

- Giving is commanded and is not an option (1 Corinthians 16:1-2).

- Giving is to be *regular*, *planned*, and *proportional*. It should never be *manipulated* (1 Corinthians 16:2).

- True giving comes as we first give ourselves to the Lord, then we will give our financial resources as we should (2 Corinthians 8:5).

- Giving cannot be commanded of any individual believer at a particular moment, not even by an apostle (2 Corinthians 8:8).

- Giving is a valid test of the sincerity of our love for God and others (2 Corinthians 8:8).

- Giving should be seen as *investing* money, not as *spending* money (2 Corinthians 9:6).

- Giving should be *not grudging or of necessity* (2 Corinthians 9:7).

- *God loves a cheerful giver* (2 Corinthians 9:7).

- Giving must always include giving to the ministries that directly feed us spiritually (1 Corinthians 9:7-13).

iv. Because the New Testament emphasis is on *giving* more than *tithing*, there is no one answer to the question, "How much am I supposed to give?" Many people go back to the Old Testament law of the tithe. Since giving is to be proportional (1 Corinthians 16:2), we should be giving *some* percentage – and ten percent is a good benchmark – a starting place! We should have the attitude of some early Christians, who essentially said: "We're not under the tithe – we can give *more!*" Giving and financial management are *spiritual* issues, not only financial issues (Luke 16:11).

b. **If a man wants at all to redeem any of his tithes, he shall add one-fifth to it**: Tithes could also be redeemed or "bought back" from the LORD. For example, instead of tithing good seed from his field, a farmer could pay the value of the seed plus 20%.

i. **Whatever passes under the rod**: "According to Jewish commentators, this expression is an allusion to the way in which animals were selected for the tithe. The animals were counted as they passed single file under the staff of the herdsman. Every tenth animal was marked with a red colored stick, to show that it had been chosen for the tithe." (Peter-Contesse)

8. (34) Conclusion: **These are the commandments**.

These *are* the commandments which the LORD commanded Moses for the children of Israel on Mount Sinai.

a. **These are the commandments**: These were not mere traditions and customs, though men began to attach traditions and customs to these commandments; these were – and are – the commandments (not suggestions) of the LORD.

b. **Which the LORD commanded Moses for the children of Israel on Mount Sinai**: As we have seen before in Leviticus, the phrase **before the LORD** occurs more than 60 times – more than any other book in the Bible. What happens in Leviticus happens **before the LORD**, and every point of obedience it calls us to illustrates – either by a specific command or in a precious picture – how to walk **before the LORD**.

i. "READER, thou hast now gone through the whole of this most interesting book; a book whose subject is too little regarded by Christians in general. Here thou mayest discover the rigid requisitions of Divine justice, the sinfulness of sin, the exceeding breadth of the commandment, and the end of all human perfection.... By this law then is the *knowledge*, but not the *cure* of sin.... We see then that Christ was the END of the law for *righteousness* (for *justification*) to everyone that believeth." (Clarke)

Bibliography

Clarke, Adam *The Old Testament with A Commentary and Critical Notes, Volume I* (New York: Eaton & Mains, 1831)

Coates, C.A. *An Outline of the Book of Leviticus* (Kingston-on-Thames, Stow Hill Bible and Tract Depot, 1922)

Cole, R. Alan *Exodus, An Introduction and Commentary* (London: Inter-Varsity Press, 1973)

Harris, R. Laird "Leviticus" *The Expositor's Bible Commentary Volume 2* (Grand Rapids, Michigan: Zondervan, 1990)

Harrison, R.K. *Leviticus – An Introduction and Commentary* (Leicester, England, Inter-Varsity Press, 1980)

Jukes, Andrew *The Law of the Offerings* (Old Tappan, New Jersey: Revell 1980)

Kaiser, Walter C. Jr. "Exodus" *The Expositor's Bible Commentary Volume 2* (Grand Rapids, Michigan: Zondervan, 1990)

Maclaren, Alexander *Expositions of Holy Scripture, Volume 1* (Grand Rapids, Michigan: Baker Book House, 1984)

McMillen, S.I. *None of These Diseases* (Old Tappan, New Jersey: Fleming H. Revell Company, 1968)

Meyer, F.B. *Our Daily Homily* (Westwood, New Jersey: Revell, 1966)

Morgan, G. Campbell *An Exposition of the Whole Bible* (Old Tappan, New Jersey: Revell, 1959)

Morgan, G. Campbell *Searchlights from the Word* (New York, Revell: 1936)

Peter-Contesse, Rene and Ellington, John *A Handbook on Leviticus* (New York: The United Bible Societies, 1990)

Poole, Matthew *A Commentary on the Holy Bible, Volume 1 (London, Banner of Truth Trust, 1968)*

Rooker, Mark F. *The New American Commentary – Leviticus* (Nashville, Tennessee: Broadman & Holman Publishers, 2000)

Spurgeon, Charles Haddon *The New Park Street Pulpit, Volumes 1-6 and The Metropolitan Tabernacle Pulpit, Volumes 7-63* (Pasadena, Texas: Pilgrim Publications, 1990)

Taylor, William M. *The Miracles of Our Saviour Expounded and Illustrated* (New York: A.C. Armstrong & Son, 1890)

Trapp, John *A Commentary on the Old and New Testaments,*

As the years pass, I love the work of studying, learning, and teaching the Bible more than ever. I'm so grateful that God is faithful to meet me in His word.

Once again, I am tremendously grateful to Alison Turner for her proofreading and editorial suggestions, especially with a challenging manuscript. Alison, thank you so much!

Thanks to Brian Procedo for the cover design and the graphics work.

Most especially, thanks to my wife Inga-Lill. She is my loved and valued partner in life and in service to God and His people.

David Guzik

David Guzik's Bible commentary is regularly used and trusted by many thousands who want to know the Bible better. Pastors, teachers, class leaders, and everyday Christians find his commentary helpful for their own understanding and explanation of the Bible. David and his wife Inga-Lill live in Santa Barbara, California.

You can email David at
david@enduringword.com

For more resources by David Guzik,
go to www.enduringword.com